Orvis K. [illegible]

Cresco Junior College

Class of '29.

Riverside College Classics

ON HEROES, HERO-WORSHIP,

AND

THE HEROIC IN HISTORY

BY

THOMAS CARLYLE

EDITED FOR STUDY

BY

JOHN CHESTER ADAMS, Ph.D.

ASSISTANT PROFESSOR OF ENGLISH IN YALE UNIVERSITY

HOUGHTON MIFFLIN COMPANY

BOSTON · NEW YORK · CHICAGO · DALLAS
SAN FRANCISCO
The Riverside Press Cambridge

PR
4426
.A1
1907a

824
C28
DA

14020

COPYRIGHT 1907 BY HOUGHTON, MIFFLIN AND COMPANY

ALL RIGHTS RESERVED

The Riverside Press
CAMBRIDGE · MASSACHUSETTS
PRINTED IN THE U.S.A

PREFATORY NOTE

THIS edition of " Heroes and Hero-Worship " is intended for the beginner, not the experienced Carlylean.
It is important, therefore, that he should have all the
time available to study Carlyle's thought and style,
and be relieved of the need of hunting over dictionaries and encyclopedias for mere information. An attempt has been made in the footnotes to supply such
mechanical apparatus as would be useful to a student
of the last years in the High School or of Freshman
or Sophomore year in college in gaining a verbal
understanding of the text. The " Additional Notes "
contain suggestions for his more deliberate and careful study of Carlyle's teaching. The editor has not
felt any obligation to stand over the author with a rod
of correction for the occasional petty slips of his memory or the imperfect scholarship of his generation;
for the value of the book consists primarily in its
power to stimulate mind and heart and soul, rather
than in the amount of historical or other knowledge
that one may gather from it.

The text is that of the Library Edition of Carlyle's
works, London, 1869–71, of which the People's Edition, the only later one issued during Carlyle's life,
was a cheap reprint.

CONTENTS

CONTENTS

LIST OF ILLUSTRATIONS

INTRODUCTION

I

LIFE OF CARLYLE

In a small country village in southwestern Scotland, toward the latter part of the eighteenth century, there grew up five brothers, who by their character and occupation earned the title of the "five fighting masons," — "a curious sample o' folks, pithy, bitter-speaking bodies, and awful fighters." The second of these concerns us here, James Carlyle, a steady, abstemious, self-reliant, hard-working, thorough-working, devout-minded man, living in a house built by his own hands. A stone bridge of his building was regarded with pride by his famous son as a more honorable work than any of his own books. When James Carlyle died in 1832, his son Thomas, unable to return home to see his burial, found consolation in writing down "Reminiscences" of him: "In several respects I consider my father as one of the most interesting men I have known, . . . of perhaps the very largest natural endowment of any it has been my lot to converse with. None of you will ever forget that bold glowing style of his, flowing free from his untutored soul, full of metaphors (though he knew not what a metaphor was), with all manner of potent words. Nothing did I ever hear him undertake to render visible which did not become almost ocularly so. Emphatic I have heard him beyond all men. . . . His words were like sharp arrows that smote into the very heart. . . . Let me write my books as he built his houses, and walk as blamelessly through this shadow world. . . . We all had to complain that we durst not freely love him. . . . Till late years I was ever more or less awed and chilled by him."

His wife was of a more tender, approachable nature. She it was that taught Tom at an early age to read, though her own equipment did not enable her to go far with him. When he grew up she learned to write that she might keep better in touch with him in his absence. To her in later years he wrote constantly of his doings and thinkings. She encouraged him by her confidence in his powers, and studied his books with loving pride in his accomplishment. And as long as she lived it was one of his chiefest joys to return from the society of the distinguished literary world to the talk of her "with whom alone my heart played freely," as they smoked their pipes together by the hearth in simple peasant fashion.

Of James Carlyle and Margaret Aitken, his wife, Thomas was the eldest child, born December 4, 1795, in the village of Ecclefechan in Dumfriesshire. His education began early in the home. To the reading taught him by his mother, the father added a scanty supply of arithmetic. At the age of five he began to attend school. At seven he was pronounced " complete in English,"— in some ways almost a foreign tongue to the Annandale peasant boy. Two years later he added further to his knowledge, if not to his happiness, by being sent to the Annan Grammar School six miles away, to be prepared for the University. How Carlyle fared there is reflected in " Sartor Resartus " [1] in the account of Teufelsdröckh's experiences at the Hinterschlag Gymnasium : " My Teachers were hide-bound Pedants, without knowledge of man's nature, or of boy's ; or of aught save their lexicons and quarterly account-books. Innumerable dead Vocables (no dead Language, for they themselves knew no Language) they crammed into us, and called it fostering the growth of mind. . . . The Professors knew syntax enough ; and of the human soul thus much : that it had a faculty called Memory, and could be acted-on through the muscular integument by the appliance of birch-rods."

In November, 1809, Carlyle walked the eighty and odd miles across the country to Edinburgh University. His career there was not distinguished, except perhaps inwardly, by a more than usually strenuous conflict of irrepressible personality with institutional conventions. " Had you, anywhere in Crim Tartary," says Teufelsdröckh,[2] " walled-in a square enclosure ; furnished it with a small, ill-chosen Library ; and then turned loose into it eleven-hundred Christian striplings, to tumble about as they listed, from three to seven years : certain persons, under the title of Professors, being stationed at the gates, to declare aloud that it was a University, and exact considerable admission-fees, — you had, not indeed in mechanical structure, yet in spirit and result, some imperfect resemblance of our High Seminary." " What I have found the Uni-

[1] II, iii.　　　　[2] *Ibid.*

versity did for me, was that it taught me to read in
various languages and various sciences, so that I could
go into the books that treated of these things, and try
anything I wanted to make myself master of gradually,
as I found it suit me."[1] He was more than ordinarily
proficient in mathematics, but the University gave
him little Latin and less Greek. For two years after
his departure (in 1814), without a degree, he was
mathematical tutor at Annan, and the following two
years at Kirkcaldy. The teaching had been undertaken as a temporary means of support until he
should be ready for ordination as a minister of the
Kirk of Scotland, the goal of his parents' ambition
for him. But theological uncertainties caused him to
feel the impossibility of ever preaching from a pulpit,
— though preacher he was to the end of his days.
The change was a bitter disappointment to his father
and mother and a bitter grief to himself for their
sakes.

Convinced that " it were better to perish than to
continue school-mastering," in 1818 he returned to Edinburgh to attend law lectures. The law soon showed
itself no more satisfactory than other professions ; and
while he supported himself by teaching private pupils
and writing articles, distinguished by no trace of indi-
viduality of thought or style, for the " Edinburgh Ency-
clopedia," he dragged through the three most wretched
years of his life. His frugal and irregular living in
university days, in an attempt to spare as much as possible the family supply of oatmeal, had rendered him
a victim to unutterable torments of dyspepsia: " A

[1] Inaugural Address, *On the Choice of Books.*

rat was gnawing at the pit of my stomach." To this
continual agony was added "eating of the heart, mis-
givings as to whether there shall be presently anything
else to eat, disappointment of the nearest and dear-
est as to the hoped-for entrance on the ministry, and
steadily-growing disappointment of self — above all,
wanderings through mazes of doubt, perpetual questionings unanswered." A pretty complete list of woes!
Carlyle had been brought up in the strict Scotch Calvinistic faith and practice ; the practice he held to always, the faith was struggling for existence. His wide
reading and thinking had opened to him visions of
truth far wider than were possible to the Ecclefechan
stone-mason and his wife. He felt himself drifting
toward materialism, — a belief, or " no-belief," which
he had been taught to consider tenable only by one
possessed of the Devil, and of which he continued to
the end to hold essentially the same opinion. It was
the completest upheaval of his inmost nature, and he
suffered as a man suffers only when the deepest feelings of his heart are torn up by the roots. How, in
June, 1821, he won the decisive battle of the campaign
against the " Everlasting No " is told in the chapter
so entitled in " Sartor Resartus." His great helper in the
struggle was Goethe, to whom he wrote, " It can never
be forgotten that to you I owe the all-precious knowledge and experience that Reverence is still possible :
that instead of conjecturing and denying, I can again
believe and know." Financial aid came to him succes-
sively by his appointment as a tutor in a wealthy family, and by the success of his " Life of Schiller " and his
translation of " Wilhelm Meister ; " but the dyspepsia

clung closer than a brother for the rest of his life,
though relenting a little after his eightieth year.

In June, 1821, Carlyle had met Miss Jane Baillie
Welsh (born 1801). Her father was a successful physician of the town of Haddington. He alone, and not
always he, could control the merry, mocking, keen-
witted, and sometimes sharp-tongued maid with raven
locks and sparkling black eyes. He died in 1819.
Her mother was of the sort excellently qualified for
spoiling such a daughter. From the first there was no
doubt of Jane Welsh's unusual intellectual gifts. At
the age of ten her admiration for the heroes of ancient
Rome — she had been reading Vergil — led her to
abjure her dolls, which were surrendered to the flames in
humble imitation of Dido of Carthage. Her literary
tastes and aspirations formed a strong bond of sympathy
between her and Carlyle in the beginnings of their
acquaintance. In spite of his peasant awkwardness of
person and manners her quick penetration discovered
the promise of his genius. Their letters were at first
of things literary ; then the personal note began to be
heard. Their courtship — " a sore fight : but he won it,"
as Carlyle says of Knox's life — was marked by many
advances and retrogressions, declarations and recanta-
tions, and has been represented in many different lights.
Professor Norton is the present guardian of their letters, and has told how they impress him, in the Ap-
pendix to his edition of the " Early Letters of Thomas
Carlyle," vol. i. They were married in October,
1826.

Carlyle's character as a husband has been one of the
battle-grounds of literature. If we were to take at full

value everything which Mrs. Carlyle said about their married life to her friends, or wrote in her letters and journal, and everything that Carlyle wrote in his grief-stricken, remorseful " Reminiscences " after her death, we could hardly avoid the conclusion that he was a veritable ogre, and that she led one of the most wretched lives recorded in books. During most of their married life she suffered from varying degrees of ill health, — sometimes being so unstrung nervously as to be hardly herself, and hardly responsible for her bitter words. Under such conditions trifles easily became tragedies in her judgment, and her husband had too much of the same tendency to be able to restore the balance. At times both seemed, as Hume said of Rousseau, to have been " born without a skin." Carlyle's entire absorption in his work and consequent thoughtless neglect of his wife's comfort when a book was in process of creation, as well as his occasional violent bursts of temper while under the exhausting strain of steady writing, were matters which doubtless every one will agree with Mrs. Carlyle in wishing otherwise. And no doubt one also wishes that her talent for enduring much hardness had been mated with a better talent for consuming her own smoke, and a softer tact in bringing her husband's real tenderness to the surface. But after the worst has been told, as it has been most abundantly, it is still visible to the discriminating eye that the love between them was far too deep and strong for any temporary irritations and misunderstandings to extinguish. "Oh! if I could but see her once more," he wrote, in his loneliness after her death, " were it but for five minutes, to let her know that I always loved her through all that! She never did know it, never!" But I believe she did know it, nevertheless.

After living a year and a half just out of Edinburgh, Carlyle writing for the reviews, they gave up the financial struggle and retired to a farm far out in the country at Craigenputtock, "Hill of Hawks," belonging to the Welshes. It was not an ideal spot for a vivacious and high-spirited society belle, but Mrs. Carlyle's life was not, as some would persuade us, one of unrelieved gloom and unthanked drudgery; her nature had other sides, and she was above all things desirous, now and all her life, with unflinching loyalty, of doing whatever would promote Carlyle's effectiveness in his literary work. Here, with a brief sojourn in London and another in Edinburgh, he battled on for six years, with Jane Welsh's help, writing numerous miscellaneous essays (including "Burns") and "Sartor Resartus," — of all his books the most completely expressive of the author, and containing the germ of almost all his later teachings. The manuscript of "Sartor" was at first refused by all the publishers — by some more abruptly than by others; it was finally published serially in "Frazer's Magazine," 1833–4, and provoked a storm of ridicule and disgust. Mrs. Carlyle pronounced it "a work of genius, dear;" but Emerson, in America, and one Father O'Shea, of Cork, seemed to be the only "Public" that essentially disagreed with the reviewer who pronounced it "a heap of clotted nonsense." Not long before Carlyle's death thirty thousand copies of a cheap edition were sold in a few weeks.

Meanwhile Carlyle, seeing that Craigenputtock was in various respects ill suited to his needs as a literary

man, determined to burn his ships and seek his fortune in London. He himself went on ahead to engage
a house, and in June, 1834, they settled at No. 5 (now
24) Cheyne Row, Chelsea, their home for the rest of
their lives. Poverty still dogged his heels. "It is now
some three-and-twenty months," he writes, in February,
1835, "since I have earned one penny by the craft of
literature. . . . I have been ready to work, I am abler
than ever to work, . . . yet so it stands." By about
the end of the month the first volume of the "French
Revolution" was finished. It represented five months
of the most exacting labor, besides a great deal of
earlier reading and thinking. The manuscript, having been lent to Carlyle's friend Mill, was carelessly
exposed to the ravages of a serving-maid, and, " except
four or five bits of leaves, irrevocably annihilated."
" Well, Mill, poor fellow, is terribly cut up," were
Carlyle's first words to his wife, when Mill left their
house after reporting the calamity; " we must endeavor to hide from him how very serious this business is to us." He braced himself manfully for the
effort of re-writing, and the entire work was published
early in 1837, winning immediate and enthusiastic
recognition. "Everybody," said Thackeray, who reviewed it for "The Times," "is astonished at every
other body's being pleased with this wonderful performance." But Carlyle always felt, contrary to Mrs.
Carlyle's opinion, that the re-written first volume was
inferior to the original. The same year saw Carlyle's
first appearance on the platform in a successful course
of lectures on "German Literature," — followed in
successive years by other courses, ending with "Heroes

1834
1795

and Hero-Worship," 1840. The lean years were over, and his "place and subsistence" were thenceforth assured.

Carlyle had read much on Cromwell before treating him in "Heroes," and was already hard at work on the book which was to finish the work of vindication begun in the lecture, when he turned aside for a few weeks, in the first months of 1843, to write "Past and Present." "Oliver Cromwell's Letters and Speeches" appeared in 1845, and established a new reputation for Carlyle as an original historian. His deep scorn and distrust of contemporary political and economic methods were expressed in the denunciatory "Latter-Day Pamphlets" of 1850. "He wrote in his study, alone with his anger, his grief, and his biliousness." But the atmosphere was clear and serene in his "Life of Sterling," 1851.

The Carlyles entered "the valley of the shadow of Frederick" the next year, Carlyle making a trip to Germany to collect materials, though the first volumes did not appear until 1858. As time went on the book became an increasingly intolerable burden to him: "A task that I cannot do," he wrote to Emerson, "that generally seems to me not worth doing, and yet that must be done. No job approaching to it in ugliness was ever cut out for me; nor had I any motive to go on, except the sad negative one, Shall we be beaten in our old days?" The final volumes appeared in 1865. For vivid realistic picturing and story, and for completeness and accuracy of detail, "The History of Frederick II, commonly called the Great" is one of the greatest of historical works.

In 1865 the students of Edinburgh University elected Carlyle Lord Rector, and the following April he fulfilled the sole duty of that honorary office in the delivery of the most famous of all Lord-Rectorial addresses, " On the Choice of Books." It was heard with tremendous enthusiasm, the students thronging about him at the close with hearts deeply moved. " A perfect triumph," Professor Tyndall telegraphed to Mrs. Carlyle. Her pride and delight in her husband's success were unbounded. While all the land was still reëchoing praise of the address there came to him, in the North, a telegram announcing Mrs. Carlyle's death. She had died suddenly, of heart failure, while riding in Hyde Park. The next day Carlyle received her last letter, full of affectionate anticipation of his return. On her tomb at Haddington are inscribed the following words, written by Carlyle : " In her bright existence she had more sorrows than are common, but also a soft invincibility, a capacity of discernment, and a noble loyalty of heart that are rare. For forty years she was the true and loving helpmate of her husband, and by act and word unweariedly fowarded him as none else could in all of worthy that he did or attempted. She died at London, 21st April, 1866, suddenly snatched from him, and the light of his life is as if gone out."

During the remaining years of his life Carlyle produced a few essays, but no great work. His latest writings were dictated, for the palsy of his hand prevented his writing himself. Honors showered in on him from his own country and from abroad. He was persuaded to accept the Prussian *Ordre pour le Mérite* ; and was offered the Grand Cross of the Bath, which he declined. He died on the 4th of February, 1881, and was buried, according to his own request, beside the graves of his own kin in the Ecclefechan kirkyard, though offer was made, as he had foreseen it might be, of a place in Westminster Abbey.

Carlyle's was far too great and too complex a nature to be disposed of in a few paragraphs of an Introduction, but the main traits were clearly marked. To the reader of " Heroes " one fundamental characteristic of its author is evident on every page, — his uncompromising love of truth. Whether or not his judgments in specific cases were right or wrong, it is clear to even the most unsympathetic that they were delivered earnestly by one of the most genuinely sincere of men. From the begining to the end he waged ceaseless war with all forms of shams and conventionalities, — " simulacra " and " formulas." His intensity was like that of his Hero-poet, Dante. He demanded of others the same sterling honesty of purpose which was exemplified in himself ; and his indignation, provoked by any sort of injustice or hypocrisy, uttered itself in blasting denunciation or ridicule, according to his mood. But in conversation his keen sense of humor often got the better of his indignation, and " he would dissolve his fiercest objurgations and tumults of wrath," says Professor Masson, " in some sudden phantasy of the sheerly absurd, and a burst of uproarious laughter."

" A man who does not know rigor, cannot pity either," writes Carlyle in his characterization of Dante. Of Carlyle's quick sympathy and generosity

the stories are innumerable, — toward his family first
of all and always, to old friends of Ecclefechan days,
to London street beggars, and to charitable and
philanthropic causes of all sorts, to which in the later
years of prosperity he gave bountifully and usually
anonymously. " His only expensive luxury was char-
ity." " All the bitterness is love with the point re-
versed," was Mrs. Browning's interpretation of his
occasional seeming harshness. Similar is Harriet
Martineau's comment : " His excess of sympathy has
been, I believe, the master-pain of his life, . . . and
the savageness which has come to be a main characteristic . . . is, in my opinion, a mere expression of
his intolerable sympathy with suffering." " I believe,"
wrote Leigh Hunt, who lived near him in Chelsea,
" that what Mr. Carlyle loves better than all his fault-
finding, with all its eloquence, is the face of any human
creature that looks suffering and loving and sincere."
The emphasis that Carlyle lays upon these qualities in
several of his Heroes reflects their presence in himself.

A third trait of character revealed in " Heroes " is
his deep religiousness. Carlyle's creed was not Christian, if " Christian " implies belief in the miraculous
elements of the New Testament story ; and no form of
church organization or creed won more than tolerance
from him. But as deep and unshakable as a man's
could be, was his belief in the reality of an unseen,
spiritual universe, — infinite, eternal, mysterious, yet
touching the world of men intimately at all points.
To his faith there was no dividing line between the
natural and the supernatural : all was miraculous.
That communion of the spirit of man with the " In-

finite Unnamable " was possible, was his conviction.
" Can a man's soul, to this hour, get guidance by any
other method than intrinsically by that same, — devout prostration of the earnest struggling soul before
the Highest, the Giver of all Light ; be such *prayer*
a spoken, articulate, or be it a voiceless, inarticulate
one ? There is no other method." [1]

Carlyle had the defects of his qualities. The intensity of his hatred of semblances and untruths
occasionally lacked the sense of proportion, and led
him to spend his energies in attack on insignificant
evils. He thought sometimes that he had " roused a
lion," when he had only " started a hare." And his
own opinions were held with so much earnestness that
he was at times deaf to valid arguments on the other
side of the question.

If he was sensitively pitiful of the pains and hard-
ships of others, he was also sometimes over-impressed
with the sense of his own distresses, some of which,
in truth, were not light. Against the petty irritations
of daily life, — interruptions of his work-time, defects
of cooking, or excess of miscellaneous neighborhood
noises, — he was defenceless by temperament, dyspepsia, and sleeplessness. But one remembers the story of
Mill and the burned manuscript, and forbears to cast
a stone. " Not how much chaff is in you ; but whether
you have any wheat." [2]

As time enables us to judge more justly of this,
the most remarkable personality in the literary world
of the last century, we see in him increasingly much
to admire, much to love, and much less to pardon.

[1] *Heroes*, p. 303.   [2] *Heroes*, p. 86.

II

THE FOUR COURSES OF LECTURES, AND THE PUBLICATION OF HEROES AND HERO-WORSHIP

About the time that the Carlyles settled in London, Emerson had suggested to Carlyle that he should come to America to lecture; but the project was not carried out, though Emerson made most alluring estimates of the profit and recognition to be gained by such a trip, and the possibility was debated in their letters for a number of years. However, at the suggestion of Miss Martineau and several other friends, it was decided to make the experiment of lecturing in London, they undertaking the responsibility of all business arrangements. The subject of the course was "German Literature," a subject on which Carlyle was supremely qualified to speak. Nevertheless he was alarmed at the prospect; for he had never but once before addressed an audience — at a dinner at Dumfries, when he had said a few words — and he was determined to speak, not read. He "felt as if . . . the natural speech for (him) would be this: 'Good Christians, it has become entirely impossible for me to talk to you about German or any other literature or terrestrial thing; one request only I have to make, that you would be kind enough to cover me under a tub for the next six weeks and to go your ways with all my blessing.'" "Fool creatures come hither for diversion" were likely to be his opening words, Mrs. Carlyle suggested. "The audience . . . was very humane to me," he wrote to his brother

turn

John at the end of the course. "They seemed indeed to be not a little astonished at the wild Annandale voice which occasionally grew high and earnest. . . . I hardly ever in my life had such a moment as that of the commencement. . . . I was wasted and fretted to a thread. My tongue, let me drink as I would, continued dry as charcoal. The people were there; I was obliged to tumble in and start." To this Mrs. Carlyle added a P. S.: "I do not find that my husband has given you any adequate notion of the success of his lectures; but you will make large allowance for the known modesty of the man. Nothing that he has ever tried seems to me to have carried such conviction to the public heart that he is a real man of genius, and worth being kept alive at a moderate rate." The course was given in May, 1837, and netted one hundred and thirty-five pounds.

A second course, on "The History of Literature," followed, the next year, with still greater harvest of fame and funds. Even the lecturer could not blind himself to its success. He wrote to his mother: "The lectures went on better and better, and grew at last, or threatened to grow, quite a flaming affair. I had people *greeting* [weeping] yesterday. . . . My audience was supposed to be the best, for rank, beauty, and intelligence, ever collected in London." And to Emerson: "The superfine people listened to the rough utterance with patience, with favour, increasing to the last."

At one of the lectures of this year Mrs. Carlyle tells of Carlyle's being seized with sudden panic, which nevertheless he suppressed: "He was imputing the profound attention with which the audience listened, to an

·awful sympathising expectation on their part of a mo-
mentary break-down, when all at once they broke into
loud plaudits, and he thought they must all have gone
clean out of their wits ! " But the " loud plaudits" were
after all not greatly to his taste, and certainly paid him
ill for the agonies of lecturing. " If dire famine drive
me," he declared, " I must even lecture, but not otherwise."

In 1839, the third course, on " The Revolutions of
Modern Europe," attracted a still larger, still more distinguished audience. The inward tumult and torment
of the lecturer, hardly diminished by growing familiarity with his task, appeared in a new guise. " Unless he
can get *hardened* in this trade," wrote Mrs. Carlyle,
" he certainly ought to discontinue it ; for no gain or
éclat that it can yield is compensation enough for the
martyrdom it is to himself, and through him to me.
. . . In defect of the usual measure of agitation *before-
hand*, he has taken to the new and curious crotchet
of being ready to hang himself *after*, in the idea that
he has made a ' horrible pluister [mess] of it,' . . .
and he remains, under applause that would turn the
head of most Lecturers, haunted by the pale ghost of
last day's Lecture ' shaking its gory locks at him ' till
next day's arrive to take its place and torment him in
its turn." " In short, I felt, after it was over, like a
man that had been robbing henroosts," is the lecturer's
picturesque confession. But, after all, he admitted
that in the last lecture of the course he gave " very
considerably the nearest approach to a good lecture
they ever got out of me, carried the whole business
glowing after me, and ended half an hour beyond my

time with universal decisive applause sufficient for the situation."

The best was yet to be. In February, 1840, Carlyle was beginning to plan for the coming season's lectures, and to "have even, or seem to have, some *primordium* of a subject" in view. Once in motion the plan developed rapidly. The course was definitely outlined some time before the 1st of April, when he bespoke Emerson's pity for his "frightful outlook with a Course of Lectures to give ' On Heroes and Hero-Worship,' — from Odin to Robert Burns!" The "hardening" that Mrs. Carlyle desired for him was yet a great way off : " My lectures come on this day two weeks. O heaven! I cannot ' speak ;' I can only gasp and writhe and stutter, a spectacle to gods and fashionables, being forced to it by want of money." He wrote out these lectures more carefully than the preceding ones, but delivered them, as before, without notes.[1] At the first lecture the "room was considerably fuller than even before — the bonniest and brawest of people," wrote Carlyle to his mother; and the company was still larger at the later lectures. The second lecture was, even to the lecturer, a manifest success : " The people seemed greatly astonished and greatly pleased. I vomited forth on them like wild Annandale grapeshot." But we hear soon that " Jane says, and indeed I rather think it is true, that these [fourth and fifth] lectures are among the best I ever gave." Finally, " I got through the last lecture yesterday in very tolerable style, seemingly much to the

[1] See a hitherto unpublished letter in MacMechan's *Heroes and Hero-Worship* (Ginn & Co.), p. xxvii.

satisfaction of all parties ; and the people all expressed in a great variety of ways much very genuine-looking friendliness for me. . . . I will not be in haste to throw myself into such a tumble again." To his brother John he reported that "the lecturing business went off with sufficient *éclat*. The course was generally judged, and I rather join therein myself, to be the bad *best* I have yet given. . . . In a word, we got right handsomely through." Carlyle's next appearance as a lecturer was not until 1866, before the Edinburgh students. Though he began to feel, as he wrote to Emerson a month and more later, that he might in the end learn to speak, and was still grateful to " the beautiful people " that " listened with boundless tolerance, eager attention," nevertheless he writes to a friend, " It is my most ardent hope that this exhibition may be my last of such ; that Necessity with her bayonet at my back, may never again drive me up thither." By the spring of the next year Necessity's bayonet was permanently unfixed, and the " mixture of prophecy and play-actorism," as he dubbed it, renounced at the height of his success, was never undertaken again.

Of Carlyle's personal appearance at this time, and the way it impressed his audience, we have plentiful description. His figure was tall, wiry, and gaunt, his erect carriage showing no sign as yet of the stoop of the later years ; his hair was heavy, dark, and wavy, over a face, smooth-shaven, whose rugged features revealed the sturdy strength of the Scotch peasant character. The eyes were gray-blue, large and clear and

piercing, deep-set under a craggy brow. The complexion was ruddy. He had none of the arts of the practised orator, — at least at the start. He spoke with a
strong Scotch accent, vehemently, " the Annandale
voice gollying at them," determination to say only
the things known for certain sounding forth in every
tone of it. "Yellow as a guinea, with downcast eyes,
broken speech at the beginning, and fingers which
nervously picked at the desk before him, he could not
for a moment be supposed to enjoy his own effort,"
is the impression recorded by Harriet Martineau, the
prime mover of the whole project. That the experience of lecturing had not been profitless to him was
evidenced at the opening lecture of the second course.
Mrs. Carlyle attended and " took one glimpse at him
(just one) when he came on the stage, — and to be sure
he was as white as a pocket-handkerchief, but he made
no gasping and spluttering, as I found him doing last
year at the *fourth* lecture. By and by, . . . he had re-
covered all that ' bonny red in his cheeks ; ' . . . and
having a very fine light from above shining down on
him he really looked a surprisingly beautiful man.
. . . He delivered it very gracefully ; that is to say,
without any air of thinking about his delivery, which
is the best grace of any." One final glimpse of him,
almost at the end of the last course, is vouchsafed
us through the eyes of the gifted young Quakeress,
Caroline Fox : " The audience . . . was very thoughtful and earnest in appearance ; it had come to hear
the Hero portrayed in the form of the Man of Letters. Carlyle soon appeared, and looked as if he felt
a well-dressed London crowd scarcely the arena for

him to figure in as a popular lecturer. He is a tall, robust-looking man ; rugged simplicity and indomitable strength are in his face, and such a glow of genius in it — not always smouldering there, but flashing from his beautiful grey eyes, from the remoteness of their deep setting under that massive brow. His manner is very quiet, but he speaks like one tremendously convinced of what he utters, and who had much — very much in him that was quite unutterable, quite unfit to be uttered to the uninitiated ear ; and when the Englishman's sense of beauty or truth exhibited itself in vociferous cheers, he would impatiently, almost contemptuously, wave his hand, as if that were not the sort of homage Truth demanded. He began in a rather low nervous voice, with a broad Scotch accent, but it soon grew firm, and shrank not abashed from its great task."

While the lectures were still in progress, Carlyle had already thought of printing them as a book ; and rewriting them for publication (" with Emendations and Additions," say the early title-pages) was the task he laid upon himself to accomplish before taking a trip to Scotland. Two were finished in June ; " My fourth lecture was finished three days ago," he could write to his mother, the first of August ; " a week hence I will attack my two remaining lectures and dash them off speedily." He was well tired of his task before it was finished. " The whole business seems to me wearisome triviality, yet toilsome to produce, which I would like to throw into the fire." To find a publisher was the next step, but publishers were discouragingly unresponsive. As late as the 9th of December, "My Hero-Lectures lie still in Manuscript," Emerson is told. "Fraser offers no amount of cash adequate to be an outward motive." But in February, 1841, he has "bargained with Fraser," he writes to his mother, and the lectures "are now at press. . . . He would give me only £75, the dog."

Emerson had made arrangements for the publication of the book in America, but Appleton anticipated him with a pirated edition in April. At the end of that month, Emerson writes, "The New York newspapers print the book in chapters, and you circulate for six cents per newspaper at the corners of all streets in New York and Boston; gaining in fame what you lose in coin." Of editions since on both sides of the water the number is incalculable.

III

CARLYLE'S STYLE IN HEROES AND HERO-WORSHIP

The book thus given to the world occupies in literary form and style a middle ground between the half extempore lecture and the finished essay, being more carefully wrought than the former, but in a manner consciously more informal, less literary, than the latter. "The style of them requires to be low-pitched, as like talk as possible," Carlyle wrote to his brother while preparing the book for the press. Nevertheless it exhibits many of the characteristics of the typical "Carlylese," the strength which is more often the might of the full mountain torrent than the quiet power of the wide river. In "Heroes" the unex-

pected turns and transitions are more noticeable even
than in Carlyle's usual style, and the mention in his
gracious apologetic farewell of "these abrupt utterances thrown-out isolated" is not without justification.
The sudden breaks and changes of construction, the
dismembered sentences, the unusual (or at least un-
literary) idiomatic expressions, are "as like talk as
possible;" while the accent and intonation of the lecturer's voice become almost audible with the aid of
unusually plentiful italics, capitals, dashes, and ex-
clamation points. As he wrote, it seems as if he must
have imagined himself once again actually speaking
to his audience.

Although talk, even when as carefully prepared as
these lectures were, can never without affectation dis-
play as much literary ornament as befits the more
deliberate and accomplished forms of writing, yet the
style of "Heroes" is notable, if in a less degree than
that of Carlyle's other books, for its wealth of illustration, allusion, and quotation, the abundant fruit of
his voracious reading and retentive memory. In a
similar way the diction of "Heroes," more simple
than that of "Sartor Resartus" or "The French Revolution," is nevertheless conspicuous for its rich variety, — the vocabulary employed in Carlyle's works all
together being, by accession of borrowed, coined, and
new-compounded words, more extensive than that of
any other English writer save Shakspeare.

One of the most characteristic marks of Carlyle's
literary handiwork is his love of concrete image or picturesque illustration, even when dealing with abstract
or undefined material. Out of this arises incidentally

the oft employed device of pluralizing proper nouns, the "Dantes" and "Luthers" of the old Norse race, the "Goethes" and "Shakspeares" of the modern world, summing up in a word the substance of pages of conjecture or comment. Conversely, such an image as that of the whole of human existence, "the infinite conjugation of the verb *To do*," figured concretely in the Tree Igdrasil, wins at once his enthusiastic acceptance.

If he pictures abstract ideas, so much the more do his words, like his father's, render "almost ocularly visible" the external aspects of nature or "the human face divine," — as witness, in "Heroes," the descriptions of Iceland and Arabia, and the portraits of Dante and Luther. Emerson, in a letter to Carlyle, speaks of "those thirsty eyes, those portrait-eating, portrait-painting eyes of thine." It is a fact worthy of note that one of the most persuasive expounders of the mystical transcendental philosophy, whose favorite quotation was Prospero's famous words in "The Tempest," "We are such stuff as dreams are made on," should be conspicuous above most other writers for the realism and concreteness of his style.

Sincerity and strength made a more forcible appeal to Carlyle than grace and delicacy, as his style plainly indicates. He is Thor, thundering at false semblance of every sort, gripping the hammer of his prose style "till the knuckles grow white," illuminating his subject with lightning flashes of insight, rather than Apollo, beautiful, radiant, casting a gently increasing light, quelling serpents with carefully aimed arrows. "A certain homely truthfulness and rustic strength, a

great rude sincerity, discloses itself here," as Carlyle
himself said of Thor's religion as compared with
Apollo's. So much the more, by contrast, the occasional sudden glory of beauty or tenderness," like bright
metal on a sullen ground," surprises and delights.
Carlyle had no talent for versifying, nor had he patience to obey the rules of metrical composition, though
some of his verse translations are well done ; but the
rhythm of his prose rises spontaneously at times into
Miltonic harmonies, and with other gifts of the poet
he was richly endowed. " There are," says Mr. Augustine Birrell,[1] in one of the best short appreciations of
Carlyle ever written, " passages in ' Sartor Resartus '
and the ' French Revolution ' which have long appeared
to me to be the sublimest poetry of the century ; and
it was therefore with great pleasure that I found Mr.
Justice Stephen . . . introducing a quotation from
the eighth chapter of the third book of ' Sartor Resartus ' with the remark that ' it is perhaps the most memorable utterance of the greatest poet of the age.' "

One quality of the true Carlylese, and that nearly
if not quite the most pervasive, the play of a somewhat grotesque sense of humor, is almost entirely miss-
ing from " Heroes." There is just a touch of it in the
" reservoir of Dukes " at Leipzig,[2] and in one or two
other passages ; but one may imagine that the travail
of soul that accompanied the preparation of the lectures, as well as the scorn of cheap methods of winning applause, might have discouraged its customary
activity. And after all, the Carlylean humor was never
of the platform type.

[1] *Obiter Dicta, First Series,* pp. 44. 45.   [2] Page 196.

IV

CARLYLE'S TEACHINGS IN HEROES AND HERO-WORSHIP

 The main thesis of the book is that " Universal History is at bottom the History of the Great Men who have worked here; " or, stating the same idea from a different point of view, that " in all times and places the Hero has been worshipped. It will ever be so . . . we all of us reverence and must ever reverence Great Men." This doctrine, like most of Carlyle's, had been already clearly propounded in " Sartor Resartus." In the chapter entitled " The Centre of Indifference " he writes : " Great Men are the inspired (speaking and acting) Texts of that divine BOOK OF REVELATIONS, whereof a Chapter is completed from epoch to epoch, and by some named HISTORY ; to which inspired Texts your numerous talented men, and your innumerable untalented men, are the better or worse exegetic commentaries, and wagonload of too-stupid, heretical or orthodox, weekly Sermons. For my study, the inspired Texts themselves ! " And again, later in the book, in " Organic Filaments : " " Meanwhile, observe with joy, so cunningly has Nature ordered it, that whatsoever man ought to obey he cannot but obey. Before no faintest revelation of the Godlike did he ever stand irreverent ; least of all, when the Godlike showed itself revealed in his fellow-man. Thus is there a true religious Loyalty forever rooted in his heart ; nay, in all ages, even in ours, it manifests itself as a more or less orthodox *Hero-worship*. In which fact, that Hero-worship exists, has existed, and will forever exist, universally among Mankind, mayest thou discern the corner-stone of living-rock, whereon all Polities for the remotest time may stand secure."

The varieties of Heroes are, of course, as many as the varieties of human activity; in the present book Carlyle chose to recognize six classes because he was to give a course of six lectures. But one of the basal ideas of Carlyle's hero-doctrine is that all heroes are of essentially the same stuff : "The Hero can be Poet, Prophet, King, Priest, or what you will, according to the kind of world he finds himself born into." "True, there are aptitudes of Nature," he grants, but into what form of activity the God-given hero-stuff shall be finally molded by circumstances is "an inexplicably complex controversial-calculation between the world and him ! " Carlyle gives many names to the heroic quality which " we have no good name for : " sincerity, originality, intellect, genius, inspiration, insight, — they have all at bottom the idea of the ability to see through the deceitful "shows of things " into the true heart of things, the power to distinguish between the essential and the superficial. "The flame-image of Reality glares-in " upon the hero ; and, obedient to the irresistible power of that vision, he orders his life in accord with eternal truth. Such is the " sincerity " upon which, with ever intensified emphasis, Carlyle insists.

The stress thus laid upon "the seeing eye," the power to penetrate through appearances, is associated with a fundamental conception in Carlyle's philosophy, often expressed in the following pages, that what is perceived in the material world is rather what the senses have the power of perceiving than what really exists. " The world of Nature, for every man, is the Phantasy of Himself." How much more, then, do the more subjective aspects of spiritual truth demand a clear inner vision !

The immediate practical aim of the individual lectures was, by the application of the theory in specific cases, to establish a right — in several instances, a new — interpretation of the character, and a right valuation of the influence, of certain great men of the past ; among whom Mahomet, Knox, Boswell, Burns, and Cromwell owe mainly to Carlyle the recognition that the present age accords them. Thus the book becomes " a gallery of biographical portraiture, which no student of the men depicted by it can neglect."

In the weariness of re-writing the lectures, Carlyle had condemned them as having " nothing *new*, nothing that to me is not *old*." The charge is true, in a sense, of the moral teaching of all of his books after " Sartor Resartus." The gospel that he felt called to preach consisted of a few fundamental principles which he proclaimed repeatedly with unflagging earnestness. That higher than happiness is blessedness, the blessedness of knowing and doing one's work ; that surrender of self, " trusting imperturbably in the appointment and *choice* of the upper Powers," is not only a duty but a necessity ; that " a man lives by believing something," and that without belief no genuine, fruitful acting is possible, but only " dexterous Similitude of Acting ;" that the nature of duty is infinite : " Would in this world is a mere zero to Should;" that right and might are in the long run identical; that the ideal government for any people is a government of the ablest man or men, a hero-archy; and that the business of government is not *laisser faire*, to let things take care of themselves, but to be the guardian and guide of the less heroic — the principle of state interference being a fundamental point of Carlyle's political teaching: these were the truths that he strove without ceasing to impress upon his age and generation. To the persevering reader of Carlyle they become as familiar actors on the scene, having their exits and their entrances, and each one in its time playing its part in many different books.

Of "Heroes" in particular the moral appeal is comprehended in the words with which Carlyle closes his discussion of the function of the Hero-Priest :[1] "If Hero mean *sincere man*, why may not every one of us be a Hero? A world all sincere, a believing world: the like has been; the like will be again, — cannot help being. That were the right sort of Worshippers for Heroes: never could the truly Better be so reverenced as where all were True and Good!"

"It is a *goustrous* determined speaking out of the truth about several things," was Carlyle's final comment on the book. "The people will be no worse for it at present. The astonishment of many of them is likely to be considerable." "Heroes and Hero-Worship" no longer astonishes; for Carlyle's teaching has become an essential, indistinguishable element in the thought of the present age: even as he says in the opening lec-

[1] *Heroes*, p. 178.

ture, " Every true Thinker to this hour is a kind of Odin, teaches men *his* way of thought, spreads a shadow of his own likeness over sections of the History of the World." To us the book stands as the impassioned utterance of a great modern prophet, a powerful inspiration to nobler thinking and feeling and doing, a scripture in which we may rightly think we have " flame-images " of eternal truths.

ON HEROES, HERO-WORSHIP,

AND THE

HEROIC IN HISTORY

LECTURE I

THE HERO AS DIVINITY. ODIN. PAGANISM: SCANDINAVIAN MYTHOLOGY

[Tuesday, 5th May 1840.]

WE have undertaken to discourse here for a little on Great Men, their manner of appearance in our world's business, how they have shaped themselves in the world's history, what ideas men formed of them, what work they did; — on Heroes, namely, and on their reception and performance; what I call Hero-worship and the Heroic in human affairs. Too evidently this is a large topic; deserving quite other treatment than we can expect to give it at present. A large topic; indeed, an illimitable one; wide as Universal History itself. For, as I take it, Universal History, the history of what man has accomplished in this world, is at bottom the History of the Great Men who have worked here. They were the leaders of men, these great ones; the modellers, patterns, and in a wide sense creators, of whatsoever the general mass of men contrived to do or to attain; all things that we see standing accomplished in the world are properly the outer material result, the practical realisation and embodiment, of Thoughts that dwelt in the Great Men sent into the world : the soul of the whole world's history, it may justly be considered, were the history of these. Too clearly it is a topic we shall do no justice to in this place !

One comfort is, that Great Men, taken up in any way, are profitable company. We cannot look, however imperfectly, upon a great man, without gaining something by him. He is the living light-fountain, which it is good and pleasant to be near. The light which enlightens, which has enlightened the darkness of the world ; and this not as a kindled lamp only, but rather as a natural luminary shining by the gift of Heaven ; a flowing light-fountain, as I say, of native original insight, of manhood and heroic nobleness ; — in whose radiance all souls feel that it is well with them. On any terms whatsoever, you will not grudge to wander in such neighbourhood for a while. These Six classes of Heroes, chosen out of widely-distant countries and epochs, and in mere external figure differing altogether, ought, if we look faithfully at them, to illustrate several things for us. Could we see *them* well, we should get some glimpses into the very marrow of the world's history. How happy, could I but, in any measure, in such times as these, make manifest to you the meanings of Heroism ; the divine relation (for I may well call it such) which in all times unites a Great Man to other men ; and thus, as it were, not exhaust my subject, but so much as break ground on it ! At all events, I must make the attempt.

It is well said, in every sense, that a man's religion is the chief fact with regard to him. A man's, or a nation of men's. By religion I do not mean here the church-creed which he professes, the articles of faith which he will sign and, in words or otherwise, assert; not this wholly, in many cases not this at all. We see men of all kinds of professed creeds attain to almost all degrees of worth or worthlessness under each or any of them. This is not what I call religion, this profession and assertion; which is often only a profession and assertion from the outworks of the man, from the mere argumentative region of him, if even so deep as that. But the thing a man does practically believe (and this is often enough *without* asserting it even to himself, much less to others); the thing a man does practically lay to heart, and know for certain, concerning his vital relations to this mysterious Universe, and his duty and destiny there, that is in all cases the primary thing for him, and creatively determines all the rest. That is his *religion;* or, it may be, his mere scepticism and *no-religion:* the manner it is in which he feels himself to be spiritually related to the Unseen World or No-World; and I say, if you tell me what that is, you tell me to a very great extent what the man is, what the kind of things he will do is. Of a man or of a nation we inquire, therefore, first of all, What religion they had? Was it Heathenism, — plurality of gods, mere sensuous representation of this Mystery of Life, and for chief recognised element therein Physical Force? Was it Christianism; faith in an Invisible, not as real only, but as the only reality; Time, through every meanest moment of it, resting on Eternity; Pagan empire of Force displaced by a nobler supremacy, that of Holiness? Was it Scepticism, uncertainty and inquiry whether there was an Unseen World, any

Mystery of Life except a mad one; — doubt as to all this, or perhaps unbelief and flat denial? Answering of this question is giving us the soul of the history of the man or nation. The thoughts they had were the parents of the actions they did; their feelings were parents of their thoughts: it was the unseen and spiritual in them that determined the outward and actual; — their religion, as I say, was the great fact about them. In these Discourses, limited as we are, it will be good to direct our survey chiefly to that religious phasis of the matter. That once known well, all is known. We have chosen as the first Hero in our series, Odin the central figure of Scandinavian Paganism; an emblem to us of a most extensive province of things. Let us look for a little at the Hero as Divinity, the oldest primary form of Heroism.

Surely it seems a very strange-looking thing this Paganism; almost inconceivable to us in these days. A bewildering, inextricable jungle of delusions, confusions, falsehoods, and absurdities, covering the whole field of Life! A thing that fills us with astonishment, almost, if it were possible, with incredulity, — for truly it is not easy to understand that sane men could ever calmly, with their eyes open, believe and live by such a set of doctrines. That men should have worshipped their poor fellow-man as a God, and not him only, but stocks and stones, and all manner of animate and inanimate objects; and fashioned for themselves such a distracted chaos of hallucinations by way of Theory of the Universe: all this looks like an incredible fable. Nevertheless, it is a clear fact that they did it. Such hideous inextricable jungle of misworships, misbeliefs, men, made as we are, did actually hold by, and live at home in. This is strange. Yes, we may pause in sorrow and silence over the depths of darkness that are in man; if we rejoice in the heights of purer vision he has attained to. Such things were and are in man; in all men; in us too.

Some speculators have a short way of accounting for the Pagan religion: mere quackery, priestcraft, and dupery, say they; no sane man ever did believe it, — merely contrived to persuade other men, not worthy of the name of sane, to believe it! It will be often our duty to protest against this sort of hypothesis about men's doings and history; and I here, on the very threshold, protest against it in reference to Paganism, and to all other *isms* by which man has ever for a length of time striven to walk in this world. They have all had a truth in them, or men would not have taken them up. Quackery and dupery do abound; in religions, above all in the more advanced decaying stages of religions, they have fearfully abounded; but quackery was never the originating influence in such things; it was not the health and life of such things, but their disease, the sure precursor of their being about to die! Let us never forget this. It seems to me a most mournful hypothesis, that of quackery giving birth to any faith even in savage men. Quackery gives birth to nothing; gives death to all things. We shall not see into the true heart of anything, if we look merely at the quackeries of it; if we do not reject the quackeries altogether; as mere diseases, corruptions, with which our and all men's sole duty is to have done with them, to sweep them out of our thoughts

as out of our practice. Man everywhere is the born
enemy of lies. I find Grand Lamaism[1] itself to have
a kind of truth in it. Read the candid, clear-sighted,
rather sceptical Mr. Turner's *Account of his Embassy*[2] to that country, and see. They have their
belief, these poor Thibet people, that Providence sends
down always an Incarnation of Himself into every
generation. At bottom some belief in a kind of
Pope! At bottom still better, belief that there is a
Greatest Man; that *he* is discoverable; that, once
discovered, we ought to treat him with an obedience
which knows no bounds! This is the truth of Grand
Lamaism; the 'discoverability' is the only error here.
The Thibet priests have methods of their own of dis-
covering what Man is Greatest, fit to be supreme over
them. Bad methods: but are they so much worse
than our methods, — of understanding him to be always
the eldest-born of a certain genealogy? Alas, it is a
difficult thing to find good methods for! — We shall
begin to have a chance of understanding Paganism,
when we first admit that to its followers it was, at one
time, earnestly true. Let us consider it very certain

[1] *Lamaism* is a form of Buddhism. Buddha is supposed to be
incarnate in the grand lamas, the priest-gods, of whom the
Dalai Lama at Lhassa is the most important. On the death of a
grand lama, the spirit passes to another incarnation, either telling
before death or indicating afterward by a sign in what young
child it is to be found.

[2] Captain Samuel Turner, *An Account of an Embassy to the
Court of the Teshoo Lama in Tibet*, etc. London, 1806. See especially Part II, chaps. viii and ix. He describes (pp. 333–335) his
official visit to an eighteen months' old lama who received him
with great dignity and decorum, and every evidence of understanding, though not yet old enough to talk.

that men did believe in Paganism; men with open eyes, sound senses, men made altogether like ourselves; that we, had we been there, should have believed in it. Ask now, What Paganism could have been?

Another theory, somewhat more respectable, attributes such things to Allegory. It was a play of poetic minds, say these theorists; a shadowing-forth, in allegorical fable, in personification and visual form, of what such poetic minds had known and felt of this Universe. Which agrees, add they, with a primary law of human nature, still everywhere observably at work, though in less important things. That what a man feels intensely, he struggles to speak-out of him, to see represented before him in visual shape, and as if with a kind of life and historical reality in it. Now doubtless there is such a law, and it is one of the deepest in human nature; neither need we doubt that it did operate fundamentally in this business. The hypothesis which ascribes Paganism wholly or mostly to this agency, I call a little more respectable; but I cannot yet call it the true hypothesis. Think, would *we* believe, and take with us as our life-guidance, an allegory, a poetic sport? Not sport but earnest is what we should require. It is a most earnest thing to be alive in this world; to die is not sport for a man. Man's life never was a sport to him; it was a stern reality, altogether a serious matter to be alive!

I find, therefore, that though these Allegory theorists are on the way towards truth in this matter, they have not reached it either. Pagan Religion is indeed an Allegory, a Symbol of what men felt and knew about the Universe; and all Religions are Sym-

bols of that, altering always as that alters : but it seems
to me a radical perversion, and even *in*version, of the
business, to put that forward as the origin and moving cause, when it was rather the result and termina-
tion. To get beautiful allegories, a perfect poetic symbol, was not the want of men ; but to know what they
were to believe about this Universe, what course they
were to steer in it ; what, in this mysterious Life of
theirs, they had to hope and to fear, to do and to forbear doing. The *Pilgrim's Progress* is an Allegory,
and a beautiful, just and serious one : but consider
whether Bunyan's [1] Allegory could have *preceded* the
Faith it symbolises ! The Faith had to be already
there, standing believed by everybody ; — of which the
Allegory could *then* become a shadow ; and, with all
its seriousness, we may say a *sportful* shadow, a mere
play of the Fancy, in comparison with that awful Fact
and scientific certainty which it poetically strives to
emblem. The Allegory is the product of the certainty,
not the producer of it ; not in Bunyan's nor in any
other case. For Paganism, therefore, we have still to
inquire, Whence came that scientific certainty, the
parent of such a bewildered heap of allegories, errors
and confusions ? How was it, what was it ?

Surely it were a foolish attempt to pretend ' explaining,' in this place, or in any place, such a phenomenon as that far-distant distracted cloudy imbroglio [2] of
Paganism, — more like a cloudfield than a distant
continent of firm land and facts ! It is no longer a

---

[1] *John Bunyan :* 1628-1688, *Pilgrim's Progress*, First Part,
1678 ; Second Part, 1684.

[2] Entanglement.

reality, yet it was one. We ought to understand that this seeming cloudfield was once a reality; that not poetic allegory, least of all that dupery and deception was the origin of it. Men, I say, never did believe idle songs, never risked their soul's life on allegories: men in all times, especially in early earnest times, have had an instinct for detecting quacks, for detesting quacks. Let us try if, leaving out both the quack theory and the allegory one, and listening with affectionate attention to that far-off confused rumour of the Pagan ages, we cannot ascertain so much as this at least, That there was a kind of fact at the heart of them; that they too were not mendacious and distracted, but in their own poor way true and sane!

You remember that fancy [1] of Plato's, of a man who had grown to maturity in some dark distance, and was brought on a sudden into the upper air to see the sun rise. What would his wonder be, his rapt astonishment at the sight we daily witness with indifference! With the free open sense of a child, yet with the ripe faculty of a man, his whole heart would be kindled by that sight, he would discern it well to be Godlike, his soul would fall down in worship before it. Now, just such a childlike greatness was in the primitive nations. The first Pagan Thinker among rude men, the first man that began to think, was precisely this child-man of Plato's. Simple, open as a child, yet with the depth and strength of a man. Nature had as yet no name to

[1] " Behold ! human beings living in an underground den." Plato's *Republic*, beginning of Bk. vii. See Jowett's translation (N. Y. 1892), iii, 214–217.

him; he had not yet united under a name the infinite
variety of sights, sounds, shapes and motions, which
we now collectively name Universe, Nature, or the
like, — and so with a name dismiss it from us. To
the wild deep-hearted man all was yet new, not veiled
under names or formulas; it stood naked, flashing-in
on him there, beautiful, awful, unspeakable. Nature
was to this man, what to the Thinker and Prophet it
for ever is, *preter*natural. This green flowery rock-
built earth, the trees, the mountains, rivers, many-
sounding seas; — that great deep sea of azure that
swims overhead; the winds sweeping through it; the
black cloud fashioning itself together, now pouring
out fire, now hail and rain; what *is* it? Ay, what?
At bottom we do not yet know; we can never know
at all. It is not by our superior insight that we escape
the difficulty; it is by our superior levity, our inatten-
tion, our *want* of insight. It is by *not* thinking that
we cease to wonder at it. Hardened round us, encas-
ing wholly every notion we form, is a wrappage of
traditions, hearsays, mere *words*. We call that fire
of the black thunder-cloud ' electricity,' and lecture
learnedly about it, and grind the like of it out of
glass and silk: but *what* is it? What made it? Whence
comes it? Whither goes it? Science has done much
for us; but it is a poor science that would hide from us
the great deep sacred infinitude of Nescience, whither
we can never penetrate, on which all science swims as a
mere superficial film. This world, after all our science
and sciences, is still a miracle; wonderful, inscrutable,
magical and more, to whosoever will *think* of it.

That great mystery of TIME, were there no other;

the illimitable, silent, never-resting thing called Time, rolling, rushing on, swift, silent, like an all-embracing ocean-tide, on which we and all the Universe swim like exhalations, like apparitions which *are*, and then *are not:* this is for ever very literally a miracle ; a thing to strike us dumb, — for we have no word to speak about it. This Universe, ah me — what could the wild man know of it; what can we yet know? That it is a Force, and thousandfold Complexity of Forces; a Force which is *not we*. That is all; it is not we, it is altogether different from *us*. Force, Force, everywhere Force; we ourselves a mysterious Force in the centre of that. ' There is not a leaf rotting on the highway but has Force in it: how else could it rot?' Nay surely, to the Atheistic Thinker, if such a one were possible, it must be a miracle too, this huge illimitable whirlwind of Force, which envelops us here; never-resting whirlwind, high as Immensity, old as Eternity. What is it? God's creation, the religious people answer; it is the Almighty God's ! Atheistic science babbles poorly of it, with scientific nomenclatures, experiments and what-not, as if it were a poor dead thing, to be bottled-up in Leyden jars and sold over counters : but the natural sense of man, in all times, if he will honestly apply his sense, proclaims it to be a living thing, — ah, an unspeakable, godlike thing; towards which the best attitude for us, after never so much science, is awe, devout prostration and humility of soul ; worship if not in words, then in silence.

But now I remark further : What in such a time as ours it requires a Prophet or Poet to teach us, namely, the stripping-off of those poor undevout wrappages, nomenclatures and scientific hearsays, — this, the ancient earnest soul, as yet unencumbered with these things, did for itself. The world, which is now divine only to the gifted, was then divine to whosoever would turn his eye upon it. He stood bare before it face to face. ' All was Godlike or God : ' — Jean Paul [1] still finds it so ; the giant Jean Paul, who has power to escape out of hearsays : but there then were no hearsays. Canopus [2] shining-down over the desert, with its blue diamond brightness (that wild blue spirit-like brightness, far brighter than we ever witness here), would pierce into the heart of the wild Ishmaelitish [3] man, whom it was guiding through the solitary waste there. To his wild heart, with all feelings in it, with no *speech* for any feeling, it might seem a little eye, that Canopus, glancing-out on him from the great deep Eternity ; revealing the inner Splendour to him. Cannot we understand how these men *worshipped* Canopus ; became what we call Sabeans [4] worshipping the stars ? Such is to me the secret of all forms of Paganism. Worship is transcendent

---

[1] *Jean Paul Friedrich Richter* (1763–1825), the greatest humorist in modern German literature. His rather barbarous and chaotic style and his idealism powerfully influenced Carlyle, who wrote two essays on him, and quotes him constantly. The quotation here is from Carlyle's translation of Richter's *Quintus Fixlein*, end.

[2] A bright star in *Argo*, in the Southern Hemisphere, invisible in most of North America.

[3] See p. 68, n. 3.

[4] From *Saba*, the host of heaven. They worshipped the sun, moon, fixed stars, and planets, which they believed to be the bodily appearances of celestial spirits. See p. 67, top.

wonder ; wonder for which there is now no limit or
measure ; that is worship. To these primeval men,
all things and everything they saw exist beside them
were an emblem of the Godlike, of some God.

And look what perennial fibre of truth was in that.
To us also, through every star, through every blade of
grass, is not a God made visible, if we will open our
minds and eyes ? We do not worship in that way now :
but is it not reckoned still a merit, proof of what we
call a ' poetic nature,' that we recognise how every
object has a divine beauty in it ; how every object
still verily is ' a window through which we may look
into Infinitude itself ' ? He that can discern the love-
liness of things, we call him Poet, Painter, Man of
Genius, gifted, lovable. These poor Sabeans did even
what he does, — in their own fashion. That they did
it, in what fashion soever, was a merit : better than
what the entirely stupid man did, what the horse and
camel did, — namely, nothing !

But now if all things whatsoever that we look upon
are emblems to us of the Highest God, I add that
more so than any of them is man such an emblem.
You have heard of St. Chrysostom's [1] celebrated saying
in reference to the Shekinah,[2] or Ark of Testimony,
visible Revelation of God, among the Hebrews : " The
true Shekinah is Man ! " Yes, it is even so : this is
no vain phrase ; it is veritably so. The essence of our

---

[1] *Chrysostom*, " Golden-mouthed " (347–407), preacher-orator
of the early Greek Church. Archbishop of Constantinople from
398.

[2] The symbol of the Divine Presence in shape of a cloud or
light over the Jewish Ark of the Covenant. See Exodus xxv,
10 ff. ; Numbers vii, 89 ; ix, 15 ff.

being, the mystery in us that calls itself " I," — ah, what words have we for such things? — is a breath of Heaven; the Highest Being reveals himself in man. This body, these faculties, this life of ours, is it not all as a vesture for that Unnamed? 'There is but one Temple in the Universe,' says the devout Novalis,[1] 'and that is the Body of Man. Nothing is holier than that high form. Bending before men is a reverence done to this Revelation in the Flesh. We touch Heaven when we lay our hand on a human body!' This sounds much like a mere flourish of rhetoric; but it is not so. If well meditated, it will turn out to be a scientific fact; the expression, in such words as can be had, of the actual truth of the thing. *We* are the miracle of miracles, — the great inscrutable mystery of God. We cannot understand it, we know not how to speak of it; but we may feel and know, if we like, that it is verily so.

Well; these truths were once more readily felt than now. The young generations of the world, who had in them the freshness of young children, and yet the depth of earnest men, who did not think they had finished-off all things in Heaven and Earth by merely giving them scientific names, but had to gaze direct at them there, with awe and wonder : they felt better what of divinity is in man and Nature ; — they, without being mad, could *worship* Nature, and man more

---

[1] The pseudonym of Friedrich Leopold von Hardenberg (1772–1801), German poet and mystic. See Carlyle's essay on him. In the quotation, Novalis adapts from 1 Cor. iii : " Know ye not that ye are the temple of God, and that the Spirit of God dwelleth in you ? If any man defile the temple of God, him shall God destroy; for the temple of God is holy, which temple ye are."

than anything else in Nature. Worship, that is, as I said above, admire without limit: this, in the full use of their faculties, with all sincerity of heart, they could do. I consider Hero-worship to be the grand modifying element in that ancient system of thought. What I called the perplexed jungle of Paganism sprang, we may say, out of many roots : every admiration, adoration of a star or natural object, was a root or fibre of a root; but Hero-worship is the deepest root of all; the tap-root, from which in a great degree all the rest were nourished and grown.

And now if worship even of a star had some meaning in it, how much more might that of a Hero! Worship of a Hero is transcendent admiration of a Great Man. I say great men are still admirable! I say there is, at the bottom, nothing else admirable! No nobler feeling than this of admiration for one higher than himself dwells in the breast of man. It is to this hour, and at all hours, the vivifying influence in man's life. Religion I find stand upon it; not Paganism only, but far higher and truer religions, — all religion hitherto known. Hero-worship, heartfelt prostrate admiration, submission, burning, boundless, for a noblest godlike Form of Man, — is not that the germ of Christianity itself? The greatest of all Heroes is One — whom we do not name here! Let sacred silence meditate that sacred matter ; you will find it the ultimate perfection of a principle extant throughout man's whole history on earth.

Or coming into lower, less *un*speakable provinces, is not all Loyalty akin to religious Faith also? Faith is loyalty to some inspired Teacher, some spiritual Hero.

And what therefore is loyalty proper, the life-breath of
all society, but an effluence of Hero-worship, submissive admiration for the truly great? Society is founded
on Hero-worship. All dignities of rank, on which human association rests, are what we may call a *Hero*-
archy (Government of Heroes), — or a Hierarchy, for
it is 'sacred' enough withal! The Duke means *Dux*,
Leader; King is *Kön-ning*, *Kan-ning*, Man that *knows*
or *cans.*[1] Society everywhere is some representation,
not *in*supportably inaccurate, of a graduated Worship
of Heroes; — reverence and obedience done to men
really great and wise. Not *in*supportably inaccurate,
I say! They are all as bank-notes, these social dignitaries, all representing gold; — and several of them,
alas, always are *forged* notes. We can do with some
forged false notes; with a good many even; but not
with all, or the most of them forged! No: there have
to come revolutions then; cries of Democracy, Liberty
and Equality, and I know not what: — the notes being
all false, and no gold to be had for *them*, people take
to crying in their despair that there is no gold, that
there never was any! — 'Gold,' Hero-worship, *is* nevertheless, as it was always and everywhere, and cannot
cease till man himself ceases.

I am well aware that in these days Hero-worship, the
thing I call Hero-worship, professes to have gone out,
and finally ceased. This, for reasons which it will be
worth while some time to inquire into, is an age that
as it were denies the existence of great men; denies the

---

[1] King is really O. E. *cyning* (*cynn* + patronymic *ing*) or *cyng*
= scion of the (noble) kin, or son (or descendant) of one of (noble) birth.

desirableness of great men. Show our critics a great
man, a Luther for example, they begin to what they
call 'account' for him ; not to worship him, but take
the dimensions of him, — and bring him out to be a
little kind of man ! He was the ' creature of the Time,'
they say ; the Time called him forth, the Time did
everything, he nothing — but what we the little critic
could have done too ! This seems to me but melancholy
work. The Time call forth ? Alas, we have known
Times *call* loudly enough for their great man ; but not
find him when they called ! He was not there ; Providence had not sent him ; the Time, *calling* its loudest,
had to go down to confusion and wreck because he
would not come when called.

For if we will think of it, no Time need have gone
to ruin, could it have *found* a man great enough, a
man wise and good enough : wisdom to discern truly
what the Time wanted, valour to lead it on the right
road thither ; these are the salvation of any Time.
But I liken common languid Times, with their unbelief, distress, perplexity, with their languid doubting
characters and embarrassed circumstances, impotently
crumbling down into ever worse distress towards final
ruin ; — all this I liken to dry dead fuel, waiting for
the lightning out of Heaven that shall kindle it. The
great man, with his free force direct out of God's own
hand, is the lightning. His word is the wise healing
word which all can believe in. All blazes round him
now, when he has once struck on it, into fire like his
own. The dry mouldering sticks are thought to have
called him forth. They did want him greatly ; but as
to calling him forth — ! — Those are critics of small

vision, I think, who cry : " See, is it not the sticks that made the fire ? " No sadder proof can be given by a man of his own littleness than disbelief in great men. There is no sadder symptom of a generation than such general blindness to the spiritual lightning, with faith only in the heap of barren dead fuel. It is the last consummation of unbelief. In all epochs of the world's history, we shall find the Great Man to have been the indispensable saviour of his epoch; — the lightning, without which the fuel never would have burnt. The History of the World, I said already, was the Biography of Great Men.

Such small critics do what they can to promote unbelief and universal spiritual paralysis : but happily they cannot always completely succeed. In all times it is possible for a man to arise great enough to feel that they and their doctrines are chimeras [1] and cobwebs. And what is notable, in no time whatever can they entirely eradicate out of living men's hearts a certain altogether peculiar reverence for Great Men ; genuine admiration, loyalty, adoration, however dim and perverted it may be. Hero-worship endures forever while man endures. Boswell venerates his Johnson, right truly even in the Eighteenth century. The unbelieving French believe in their Voltaire ; [2] and burst-out

[1] A fire-breathing monster of Greek mythology, with a lion's head, a goat's body, and a serpent's tail, or sometimes represented as having the heads of these three animals. A favorite term of Carlyle's for an imposing-looking inanity or unreality.

[2] Witty satirist, poet and dramatist, and miscellaneous prose-writer (1694–1778). Most of the matters alluded to in the rest of the paragraph are narrated in Carlyle's *Essay on Voltaire*.

round him into very curious Hero-worship, in that last act of his life when they ' stifle him under roses.' It has always seemed to me extremely curious this of Voltair Truly, if Christianity be the highest instance of Hero-worship, then we may find here in Voltaireism one of the lowest! He whose life was that of a kind of Antichrist, does again on this side exhibit a curious contrast. No people ever were so little prone to admire at all as those French of Voltaire. *Persiflage* [1] was the character of their whole mind ; adoration had nowhere a place in it. Yet see! The old man of Ferney [2] comes up to Paris ; an old, tottering, infirm man of eighty-four years. They feel that he too is a kind of Hero ; that he has spent his life in opposing error and injustice, delivering Calases,[3] unmasking hypocrites in high places ; — in short that *he* too, though in a strange way, has fought like a valiant man. They feel withal that, if *persiflage* be the great thing, there never was such a *persifleur*. He is the realised ideal of every one of them ; the thing they are all wanting to be ; of all Frenchmen the most French. *He* is properly their god, — such god as they are fit for. Accordingly all persons, from the Queen Antoinette to the Douanier [4] at the Porte St. Denis, do they not worship him? People of quality disguise themselves as tavern-waiters. The Maître de Poste, with a broad oath, orders his

[1] Flippant banter, or quizzing.

[2] In eastern France near Geneva, home of Voltaire from 1758.

[3] Jean Calas, victim of religious hatred, was executed unjustly (1762) for murder. His widow fled to Switzerland, and won the sympathy of Voltaire, who vindicated the reputation of the family.

[4] Custom-house officer.

Postillion, "*Va bon train;*[1] thou art driving M. de
Voltaire." At Paris his carriage is 'the nucleus of
a comet, whose train fills whole streets.' The ladies
pluck a hair or two from his fur, to keep it as a sacred
relic. There was nothing highest, beautifulest, noblest
in all France, that did not feel this man to be higher,
beautifuler, nobler.

Yes, from Norse Odin to English Samuel Johnson,
from the divine Founder of Christianity to the withered Pontiff of Encyclopedism,[2] in all times and
places, the Hero has been worshipped. It will ever be
so. We all love great men; love, venerate and bow
down submissive before great men : nay can we honestly bow down to anything else? Ah, does not every
true man feel that he is himself made higher by doing
reverence to what is really above him? No nobler or
more blessed feeling dwells in man's heart. And to
me it is very cheering to consider that no sceptical
logic, or general triviality, insincerity and aridity of
any Time and its influences can destroy this noble in-
born loyalty and worship that is in man. In times of
unbelief, which soon have to become times of revolution, much down-rushing, sorrowful decay and ruin
is visible to everybody. For myself, in these days, I
seem to see in this indestructibility of Hero-worship
the everlasting adamant lower than which the confused wreck of revolutionary things cannot fall. The
confused wreck of things crumbling and even crashing

[1] Go fast.
[2] Voltaire contributed to the *Encyclopédie* of Diderot and
others, which was made the vehicle of radical and materialistic
philosophical views.

and tumbling all round us in these revolutionary ages, will get down so far; *no* farther. It is an eternal corner-stone, from which they can begin to build themselves up again. That man, in some sense or other, worships Heroes; that we all of us reverence and must ever reverence Great Men : this is, to me, the living rock amid all rushings-down whatsoever; — the one fixed point in modern revolutionary history, otherwise as if bottomless and shoreless.

So much of truth, only under an ancient obsolete vesture, but the spirit of it still true, do I find in the Paganism of old nations. Nature is still divine, the revelation of the workings of God; the Hero is still worshipable : this, under poor cramped incipient forms, is what all Pagan religions have struggled, as they could, to set forth. I think Scandinavian Paganism, to us here, is more interesting than any other. It is, for one thing, the latest; it continued in these regions of Europe till the eleventh century : eight-hundred years ago the Norwegians were still worshippers of Odin. It is interesting also as the creed of our fathers; the men whose blood still runs in our veins, whom doubtless we still resemble in so many ways. Strange : they did believe that, while we believe so differently. Let us look a little at this poor Norse creed, for many reasons. We have tolerable means to do it ; for there is another point of interest in these Scandinavian mythologies : that they have been preserved so well.

In that strange island Iceland, — burst-up, the geologists say, by fire from the bottom of the sea; a

wild land of barrenness and lava; swallowed many
months of every year in black tempests, yet with a
wild gleaming beauty in summer-time; towering up
there, stern and grim, in the North Ocean; with its
snow jokuls,[1] roaring geysers, sulphur-pools and horrid
volcanic chasms, like the waste chaotic battle-field of
Frost and Fire; — where of all places we least looked
for Literature or written memorials, the record of
these things was written down. On the seaboard of
this wild land is a rim of grassy country, where cattle
can subsist, and men by means of them and of what
the sea yields; and it seems they were poetic men
these, men who had deep thoughts in them, and uttered
musically their thoughts. Much would be lost, had
Iceland not been burst-up from the sea, not been discovered by the Northmen! The old Norse Poets were
many of them natives of Iceland.

Sæmund, one of the early Christian Priests there,
who perhaps had a lingering fondness for Paganism,
collected certain of their old Pagan songs, just about
becoming obsolete then, — Poems or Chants of a
mythic, prophetic, mostly all of a religious character:
that is what Norse critics call the *Elder* or Poetic
Edda.[2] *Edda*, a word of uncertain etymology, is
thought to signify *Ancestress*. Snorro Sturleson,[3] an

[1] Glaciers.

[2] Misnamed "*Sæmund's Edda*," by its discoverer in Iceland,
1643. The collection was made by an unknown Icelander after
the death of Sæmund (1056–1133), the priest and scholar. The
name Edda (Art of Poetry) does not properly belong to this
book, though it does to Snorro's.

[3] A poet, historian, and grammarian (1178–1241). He com-
piled the *Younger Edda* as a manual of mythology and rules of
poetry for the use of young verse-makers.

Iceland gentleman, an extremely notable personage, educated by this Sæmund's grandson, took in hand next, near a century afterwards, to put together, among several other books he wrote, a kind of Prose Synopsis of the whole Mythology; elucidated by new fragments of traditionary verse. A work constructed really with great ingenuity, native talent, what one might call unconscious art; altogether a perspicuous clear work, pleasant reading still: this is the *Younger* or Prose *Edda*. By these and the numerous other *Sagas*, mostly Icelandic, with the commentaries, Icelandic or not, which go on zealously in the North to this day, it is possible to gain some direct insight even yet; and see that old Norse system of Belief, as it were, face to face. Let us forget that it is erroneous Religion; let us look at it as old Thought, and try if we cannot sympathise with it somewhat.

The primary characteristic of this old Northland Mythology I find to be Impersonation of the visible workings of Nature. Earnest simple recognition of the workings of Physical Nature, as a thing wholly miraculous, stupendous and divine. What we now lecture of as Science, they wondered at, and fell down in awe before, as Religion. The dark hostile Powers of Nature they figure to themselves as '*Jötuns*,' [1] Giants, huge shaggy beings of a demonic character. Frost, Fire, Sea-tempest; these are Jötuns. The friendly Powers again, as Summer-heat, the Sun, are Gods. The empire of this Universe is divided between these two; they dwell apart, in perennial internecine feud. The Gods dwell above in Asgard, the Garden

[1] Pron. Yötun (ö = u in fur).

of the Asen, or Divinities; Jötunheim, a distant dark
chaotic land, is the home of the Jötuns.

Curious all this; and not idle or inane, if we will
look at the foundation of it! The power of *Fire*, or
Flame, for instance, which we designate by some trivial chemical name, thereby hiding from ourselves the
essential character of wonder that dwells in it as
in all things, is with these old Northmen, Loke,[1] a
most swift subtle *Demon*, of the brood of the Jötuns.
The savages of the Ladrones [2] Islands too (say some
Spanish voyagers) thought Fire, which they never
had seen before, was a devil or god, that bit you
sharply when you touched it, and that lived upon dry
wood. From us too no Chemistry, if it had not Stupidity to help it, would hide that Flame is a wonder.
What *is* Flame?—*Frost* the old Norse Seer discerns
to be a monstrous hoary Jötun, the Giant *Thrym*,
Hrym; or *Rime*, the old word now nearly obsolete
here, but still used in Scotland to signify hoar-frost.
Rime was not then as now a dead chemical thing,
but a living Jötun or Devil; the monstrous Jötun
Rime drove home his Horses at night, sat 'combing
their manes,'—which Horses were *Hail-Clouds*, or
fleet *Frost-Winds*. His Cows—No, not his, but a
kinsman's, the Giant Hymir's Cows are *Icebergs:*
this Hymir 'looks at the rocks' with his devil-eye,
and they *split* in the glance of it.

Thunder was not then mere Electricity, vitreous
or resinous; it was the God Donner (Thunder) or

[1] The devil, *par excellence*, of the Norse mythology. See later
notes. He was adopted by the gods, and became the foster-bro-
ther of Odin.   [2] In the Pacific, discovered by Magellan, 1521.

Thor,[1] — God also of beneficent Summer-heat. The
thunder was his wrath; the gathering of the black
clouds is the drawing-down of Thor's angry brows;
the fire-bolt bursting out of Heaven is the all-rending
Hammer flung from the hand of Thor: he urges his
loud chariot over the mountain-tops, — that is the
peal; wrathful he 'blows in his red beard,' — that
is the rustling stormblast before the thunder begin.
Balder[2] again, the White God, the beautiful, the just
and benignant (whom the early Christian Missionaries found to resemble Christ), is the Sun, — beautifulest of visible things; wondrous too, and divine
still, after all our Astronomies and Almanacs! But
perhaps the notablest god we hear tell-of is one of
whom Grimm the German Etymologist finds trace:
the God *Wünsch*, or Wish. The God *Wish;* who
could give us all that we *wished!* Is not this the sincerest and yet rudest voice of the spirit of man? The
rudest ideal that man ever formed; which still shows
itself in the latest forms of our spiritual culture.
Higher considerations have to teach us that the God
Wish is not the true God.

Of the other Gods or Jötuns I will mention only
for etymology's sake, that Sea-tempest is the Jötun
Aegir, a very dangerous Jötun; — and now to this
day, on our river Trent, as I learn, the Nottingham
bargemen, when the River is in a certain flooded state
(a kind of backwater, or eddying swirl it has, very
dangerous to them), call it *Eager;*[3] they cry out,

[1] The son of Odin. Thursday = Thor's day.
[2] See p. 48, n. 1.
[3] The etymology of eager (tidal wave) is uncertain; it is not

" Have a care, there is the *Eager* coming ! " Curious ;
that word surviving, like the peak of a submerged
world ! The *oldest* Nottingham bargemen had believed
in the God Aegir. Indeed our English blood too in
good part is Danish, Norse ; or rather, at bottom,
Danish and Norse and Saxon have no distinction, except a superficial one, — as of Heathen and Christian,
or the like. But all over our Island we are mingled
largely with Danes proper, — from the incessant in-
vasions there were : and this, of course, in a greater
proportion along the east coast ; and greatest of all,
as I find, in the North Country. From the Humber
upwards, all over Scotland, the Speech of the common people is still in a singular degree Icelandic ; its
Germanism has still a peculiar Norse tinge. They too
are ' Normans,' Northmen, — if that be any great
beauty ! —

Of the chief god, Odin, we shall speak by and by.
Mark at present so much ; what the essence of Scandinavian and indeed of all Paganism is : a recognition
of the forces of Nature as godlike, stupendous, personal Agencies, — as Gods and Demons. Not inconceivable to us. It is the infant Thought of man opening itself, with awe and wonder, on this ever-stupendous
Universe. To me there is in the Norse System something very genuine, very great and manlike. A broad
simplicity, rusticity, so very different from the light
gracefulness of the old Greek Paganism, distinguishes
this Scandinavian System. It is Thought ; the genuine
Thought of deep, rude, earnest minds, fairly opened

from the name of the sea god. See *New Eng. Dict.* Aegir is the
wealthiest of the giants.

to the things about them ; a face-to-face and heart-to-heart inspection of the things, — the first characteristic of all good Thought in all times. Not graceful lightness, half-sport, as in the Greek Paganism ; a certain homely truthfulness and rustic strength, a great rude sincerity, discloses itself here. It is strange, after our beautiful Apollo statues and clear smiling mythuses, to come down upon the Norse Gods ' brewing ale ' to hold their feast with Aegir, the Sea-Jötun ; sending out Thor to get the caldron for them in the Jötun country ; Thor, after many adventures, clapping the Pot on his head, like a huge hat, and walking off with it, — quite lost in it, the ears of the Pot reaching down to his heels ! A kind of vacant hugeness, large awkward gianthood, characterises that Norse System ; enormous force, as yet altogether untutored, stalking helpless with large uncertain strides. Consider only their primary mythus of the Creation. The Gods, having got the Giant Ymer slain, a Giant made by ' warm wind,' and much confused work, out of the conflict of Frost and Fire, — determined on constructing a world with him. His blood made the Sea ; his flesh was the Land, the Rocks his bones ; of his eyebrows they formed Asgard their Gods'-dwelling ; his skull was the great blue vault of Immensity, and the brains of it became the Clouds. What a Hyper-Brobdingnagian [1] business ! Untamed Thought, great, giantlike, enormous ; — to be tamed in due time into the compact greatness, not

[1] Alluding to the land of Brobdingnag, peopled by giants, in *Gulliver's Travels* (1726), by Jonathan Swift (1667–1745). During Gulliver's stay in Brobdingnag he was cared for by Glumdalclitch, his "little nurse," a child of nine years, "not above forty feet high, being little for her age."

giantlike, but godlike and stronger than gianthood, of
the Shakspeares, the Goethes! — Spiritually as well
as bodily these men are our progenitors.

I like, too, that representation they have of the
Tree Igdrasil. All Life is figured by them as a Tree.
Igdrasil, the Ash-tree of Existence, has its roots deep-
down in the kingdoms of Hela or Death; its trunk
reaches up heaven-high, spreads its boughs over the
whole Universe: it is the Tree of Existence. At the
foot of it, in the Death-kingdom, sit three *Nornas*,
Fates, — the Past, Present, Future; watering its roots
from the Sacred Well.[1] Its 'boughs,' with their bud-
dings and disleafings, — events, things suffered, things
done, catastrophes, — stretch through all lands and
times. Is not every leaf of it a biography, every fibre
there an act or word? Its boughs are Histories of Nations. The rustle of it is the noise of Human Existence,
onwards from of old. It grows there, the breath of
Human Passion rustling through it; — or stormtost,
the stormwind howling through it like the voice of all
the gods. It is Igdrasil, the Tree of Existence. It is
the past, the present, and the future; what was done,
what is doing, what will be done; 'the infinite conjugation of the verb *To do*.' Considering how human things circulate, each inextricably in communion
with all, — how the word I speak to you today is borrowed, not from Ulfila[2] the Mœsogoth only, but from

---

[1] The fountain of wisdom, presided over by Mimer, the wisest
of the giants. In the dawn of time Odin pawned one of his eyes
for a drink from this well.

[2] Born *c*. 310 ; Bishop of the Goths (341), for whom he translated the Bible into Gothic ; removed (348) to Mœsia, south of
the Danube ; died *c*. 380.

all men since the first man began to speak, — I find no
similitude so true as this of a Tree. Beautiful; altogether beautiful and great. The ' *Machine* of the Universe,' [1] — alas, do but think of that in contrast !

Well, it is strange enough this old Norse view of
Nature ; different enough from what we believe of Nature. Whence it specially came, one would not like to
be compelled to say very minutely ! One thing we may
say : It came from the thoughts of Norse men ; —
from the thought, above all, of the *first* Norse man who
had an original power of thinking. The First Norse
' man of genius,' as we should call him ! Innumerable
men had passed by, across this Universe, with a dumb
vague wonder, such as the very animals may feel ; or
with a painful, fruitlessly inquiring wonder, such as
men only feel ; — till the great Thinker came, the *ori-*
ginal man, the Seer ; whose shaped spoken Thought
awakes the slumbering capability of all into Thought.
It is ever the way with the Thinker, the spiritual Hero.
What he says, all men were not far from saying, were
longing to say. The Thoughts of all start up, as from
painful enchanted sleep, round his Thought ; answering to it, Yes, even so ! Joyful to men as the dawning of day from night ; — *is* it not, indeed, the awakening for them from no-being into being, from death
into life ? We still honour such a man ; call him Poet,
Genius, and so forth : but to these wild men he was
a very magician, a worker of miraculous unexpected
blessing for them ; a Prophet, a God ! — Thought once
awakened does not again slumber ; unfolds itself into

[1] See pp. 104, 238.

a System of Thought; grows, in man after man, generation after generation, — till its full stature is reached, and *such* System of Thought can grow no farther, but must give place to another.

For the Norse people, the Man now named Odin, and Chief Norse God, we fancy, was such a man. A Teacher, and Captain of soul and of body; a Hero, of worth *im*measurable; admiration for whom, transcending the known bounds, became adoration.[1] Has he not the power of articulate Thinking; and many other powers, as yet miraculous? So, with boundless gratitude, would the rude Norse heart feel. Has he not solved for them the sphinx-enigma of this Universe; given assurance to them of their own destiny there? By him they know now what they have to do here, what to look for hereafter. Existence has become articulate, melodious by him; he first has made Life alive! — We may call this Odin, the origin of Norse Mythology: Odin, or whatever name the First Norse Thinker bore while he was a man among men. His view of the Universe once promulgated, a like view starts into being in all minds; grows, keeps ever growing, while it continues credible there. In all minds it lay written, but invisibly, as in sympathetic ink; at his word it starts into visibility in all. Nay, in every epoch of the world, the great event, parent of all others, is it not the arrival of a Thinker in the world? —

One other thing we must not forget; it will explain, a little, the confusion of these Norse Eddas. They are not one coherent System of Thought: but properly the

[1] See p. 12, end.

summation of several successive systems. All this of
the old Norse Belief which is flung-out for us, in one
level of distance in the Edda, like a picture painted
on the same canvas, does not at all stand so in the
reality. It stands rather at all manner of distances
and depths, of successive generations since the Belief
first began. All Scandinavian thinkers, since the first
of them, contributed to that Scandinavian System of
Thought; in ever-new elaboration and addition, it is
the combined work of them all. What history it had,
how it changed from shape to shape, by one thinker's
contribution after another, till it got to the full final
shape we see it under in the *Edda*, no man will now
ever know : *its* Councils of Trebisond,[1] Councils of
Trent,[2] Athanasiuses,[3] Dantes, Luthers, are sunk without echo in the dark night! Only that it had such a
history we can all know. Wheresoever a thinker appeared, there in the thing he thought-of was a contribution, accession, a change or revolution made. Alas,
the grandest 'revolution' of all, the one made by the
man Odin himself, is not this too sunk for us like the
rest! Of Odin what history? Strange rather to reflect that he *had* a history! That this Odin, in his

[1] On southeast coast of the Black Sea, the Trapesus of Xeno-
phon's Ten Thousand. History does not record any Council of
Trebisond.

[2] The nineteenth Ecumenical (General) Council of the Church,
held at Trent, in the Austrian Tyrol, 1545–1563. It settled some
important matters of theological doctrine and church reform.
See p. 172, n. 1.

[3] One of the most celebrated Greek Fathers of the Church
(*c.* 296–373), Bishop of Alexandria. In constant conflict with
various factions in the Church, he was deposed and restored several times.

wild Norse vesture, with his wild beard and eyes, his
rude Norse speech and ways, was a man like us; with
our sorrows, joys, with our limbs, features; — intrinsically all one as we: and did such a work! But the
work, much of it, has perished; the worker, all to the
name. "*Wednes*day" men will say tomorrow; Odin's
day! Of Odin there exists no history; no document
of it; no guess about it worth repeating.

Snorro indeed, in the quietest manner, almost in a
brief business style, writes down in his *Heimskringla*,[1]
how Odin was a heroic Prince, in the Black-Sea region, with Twelve Peers, and a great people straitened
for room. How he led these *Asen*,[2] (Asiatics) of his
out of Asia; settled them in the North parts of Europe,
by warlike conquest; invented Letters, Poetry and so
forth, — and came by and by to be worshipped as Chief
God by these Scandinavians, his Twelve Peers made
into Twelve Sons of his own, Gods like himself: Snorro
has no doubt of this. Saxo Grammaticus,[3] a very curious Northman of that same century, is still more unhes-
itating; scruples not to find out a historical fact in
every individual mythus, and writes it down as a terrestrial event in Denmark or elsewhere. Torfæus,[4] learned
and cautious, some centuries later, assigns by calcu-

---

[1] Snorro's Saga or Story of the Kings of Norway to 1177,
called *Heimskringla*, from its opening words.

[2] See pp. 23, 24.

[3] Died soon after 1200. He wrote a Danish History, *Gesta
Danorum*, to the year 1186. The first eight books present the
stories of Norse divinities as of kings and heroes of antiquity.
See p. 50.

[4] Born in Iceland, 1636. A scholarly antiquary, historian, and
collector of the saga manuscripts. Died 1719.

lation a *date* for it: Odin, he says, came into Europe
about the Year 70 before Christ. Of all which, as
grounded on mere uncertainties, found to be untenable
now, I need say nothing. Far, very far beyond the
Year 70! Odin's date, adventures, whole terrestrial
history, figure and environment are sunk from us for
ever into unknown thousands of years.

Nay Grimm,[1] the German Antiquary, goes so far as
to deny that any man Odin ever existed. He proves
it by etymology. The word *Wuotan*, which is the original form of *Odin*, a word spread, as name of their
chief Divinity, over all the Teutonic Nations everywhere; this word, which connects itself, according to
Grimm, with the Latin *vadere*, with the English *wade*
and suchlike, — means primarily *Movement*, Source
of Movement, Power; and is the fit name of the highest god, not of any man. The word signifies Divinity,
he says, among the old Saxon, German and all Teutonic Nations; the adjectives formed from it all signify
divine, supreme, or something pertaining to the chief
god. Like enough! We must bow to Grimm in matters etymological. Let us consider it fixed that *Wuotan* means *Wading*, force of *Movement*. And now
still, what hinders it from being the name of a Heroic
Man and *Mover*, as well as of a god? As for the adjectives, and words formed from it, — did not the
Spaniards in their universal admiration for Lope,[2] get

[1] Jakob Grimm (1785–1863), one of the Grimm brothers of
fairy-tale fame. Carlyle cites here from his *Teutonic Mythology*
(1882), i, 131.

[2] Lope de Vega (1562–1635), Spanish dramatist, author of
about eighteen hundred plays, besides poems, romances, and
shorter dramatic pieces.

into the habit of saying 'a Lope flower,' 'a Lope *dama*,'
if the flower or woman were of surpassing beauty?
Had this lasted, *Lope* would have grown, in Spain, to
be an adjective signifying *godlike* also. Indeed, Adam
Smith,[1] in his *Essay on Language*, surmises that all
adjectives whatsoever were formed precisely in that
way: some very green thing, chiefly notable for its
greenness, got the appellative name *Green*, and then
the next thing remarkable for that quality, a tree for
instance, was named the *green* tree, — as we still say
'the *steam* coach,' 'four-horse coach,' or the like. All
primary adjectives, according to Smith, were formed
in this way; were at first substantives and things.
We cannot annihilate a man for etymologies like that!
Surely there was a First Teacher and Captain; surely
there must have been an Odin, palpable to the sense
at one time; no adjective, but a real Hero of flesh
and blood! The voice of all tradition, history or echo
of history, agrees with all that thought will teach one
about it, to assure us of this.

How the man Odin came to be considered a *god*,
the chief god? — that surely is a question which nobody would wish to dogmatise upon. I have said,
his people knew no *limits* to their admiration of
him; they had as yet no scale to measure admiration
by. Fancy your own generous heart's-love of some
greatest man expanding till it *transcended* all bounds,
till it filled and overflowed the whole field of your
thought! Or what if this man Odin, — since a great
deep soul, with the afflatus and mysterious tide of

[1] Scotch economist and philosopher (1723–1790), best known
by his *Wealth of Nations* (1776).

vision and impulse rushing on him he knows not
whence, is ever an enigma, a kind of terror and
wonder to himself, — should have felt that perhaps *he*
was divine; that *he* was some effluence of the ' Wuotan,' ' *Movement*,' Supreme Power and Divinity, of
whom to his rapt vision all Nature was the awful
Flame-image ; that some effluence of *Wuotan* dwelt
here in him ! He was not necessarily false ; he was
but mistaken, speaking the truest he knew. A great
soul, any sincere soul, knows not *what* he is, — alter-
nates between the highest height and the lowest
depth ; can, of all things, the least measure — Himself ! What others take him for, and what he guesses
that he may be ; these two items strangely act on one
another, help to determine one another. With all
men reverently admiring him ; with his own wild soul
full of noble ardours and affections, of whirlwind
chaotic darkness and glorious new light ; a divine
Universe bursting all into godlike beauty round him,
and no man to whom the like ever had befallen, what
could he think himself to be ? " Wuotan ? " All
men answered, " Wuotan ! " —

And then consider what mere Time will do in such
cases ; how if a man was great while living, he be
comes tenfold greater when dead. What an enormous
camera-obscura [1] magnifier is Tradition ! How a thing
grows in the human Memory, in the human Imagina-

---

[1] " Dark chamber," whether a room or a box, into which a small
opening, usually provided with a lens, admits light, which
strikes upon a screen opposite, forming an image of the external objects in range of the opening. The picture formed on the
ground glass of an ordinary photographic camera is a *camera-
obscura* image.

tion, when love, worship, and all that lies in the human Heart is there to encourage it. And in the darkness, in the entire ignorance; without date or document, no book, no Arundel-marble;[1] only here and there some dumb monumental cairn. Why, in thirty or forty years, were there no books, any great man would grow *mythic*, the contemporaries who had seen him, being once all dead. And in three-hundred years, and in three-thousand years—!— To attempt *theorising* on such matters would profit little: they are matters which refuse to be *theoremed* and dia-gramed; which Logic ought to know that she *cannot* speak of. Enough for us to discern, far in the utter-most distance, some gleam as of a small real light shin-ing in the centre of that enormous camera-obscura image; to discern that the centre of it all was not a madness and nothing, but a sanity and something.

This light, kindled in the great dark vortex of the Norse Mind, dark but living, waiting only for light; this is to me the centre of the whole. How such light will then shine out, and with wondrous thousandfold expansion spread itself, in forms and colours, depends not on *it*, so much as on the National Mind recipient of it. The colours and forms of your light will be those of the *cut-glass* it has to shine through. — Curious to think how, for every man, any the truest fact is mod-elled by the nature of the man! I said, The earnest man, speaking to his brother men, must always have

[1] The Earl of Arundel and Surrey (1586–1646) made the collection of marbles called by his name, afterward presented to Oxford University, of which the most noted is the *Parian Chronicle*, a chronology of the chief events of Greek history from 1582 to 264 B. C.

stated what seemed to him a *fact*, a real Appearance
of Nature. But the way in which such Appearance or
fact shaped itself, — what sort of *fact* it became for
him, — was and is modified by his own laws of thinking ; deep, subtle, but universal, ever-operating laws.
The world of Nature, for every man, is the Fantasy of
Himself ; this world is the multiplex 'Image of his own
Dream.' Who knows to what unnameable subtleties
of spiritual law all these Pagan Fables owe their
shape ! The number *Twelve*, divisiblest of all, which
could be halved, quartered, parted into three, into six,
the most remarkable number, — this was enough to
determine the *Signs of the Zodiac*, the number of
Odin's *Sons*, and innumerable other Twelves. Any
vague rumour of number had a tendency to settle itself
into Twelve. So with regard to every other matter.
And quite unconsciously too, — with no notion of
building-up 'Allegories'! But the fresh clear glance
of those First Ages would be prompt in discerning the
secret relations of things, and wholly open to obey
these. Schiller [1] finds in the *Cestus* [2] *of Venus* an everlasting æsthetic truth as to the nature of all Beauty ;
curious : — but he is careful not to insinuate that the
old Greek Mythists had any notion of lecturing about
the 'Philosophy of Criticism'! — — On the whole,
we must leave those boundless regions. Cannot we
conceive that Odin was a reality ? Error indeed,
error enough : but sheer falsehood, idle fables, allegory
aforethought, — we will not believe that our Fathers
believed in these.

[1] German poet and dramatist (1759–1805); friend of Goethe.
[2] Girdle, embroidered with various enticements to love.

Odin's *Runes* are a significant feature of him.
Runes, and the miracles of 'magic' he worked by
them, make a great feature in tradition. Runes are
the Scandinavian Alphabet; suppose Odin to have
been the inventor of Letters, as well as 'magic,' among
that people! It is the greatest invention man has ever
made, this of marking-down the unseen thought that
is in him by written characters. It is a kind of second
speech, almost as miraculous as the first. You remember the astonishment and incredulity of Atahualpa [2]
the Peruvian King ; how he made the Spanish Soldier
who was guarding him scratch *Dios* on his thumb-nail,
that he might try the next soldier with it, to ascertain
whether such a miracle was possible. If Odin brought
Letters among his people, he might work magic enough!

Writing by Runes has some air of being original
among the Norsemen : not a Phœnician [3] Alphabet,
but a native Scandinavian one. Snorro tells us farther
that Odin invented Poetry ; the music of human
speech, as well as that miraculous runic marking of it.
Transport yourselves into the early childhood of nations ; the first beautiful morning-light of our Europe,
when all yet lay in fresh young radiance as of a great

---

[1] The earliest Germanic letters. O. E. *rūn* = secret, mystery.
The runic alphabet was called "futhark," from the first six letters.
ᚡ ᚾ ᚦ ᚠ ᚱ ᚲ. The *Elder Edda* tells that Odin hung nine whole
f u th a r k   nights on the wind-rocked tree Igdrasil, and
sacrificed himself to himself. While hanging there he discovered
the runes.

[2] Treacherously executed by Pizarro, 1533.

[3] The alphabet of the Phœnicians, ancient inhabitants of the
eastern coast of the Mediterranean, dates from as far back as
1000 B. C. It is the ancestor of the Greek, Roman, and modern
European alphabets.

sunrise, and our Europe was first beginning to think,
to be ! Wonder, hope ; infinite radiance of hope and
wonder, as of a young child's thoughts, in the hearts
of these strong men ! Strong sons of Nature ; and here
was not only a wild Captain and Fighter ; discerning
with his wild flashing eyes what to do, with his wild
lion-heart daring and doing it ; but a Poet too, all that
we mean by a Poet, Prophet, great devout Thinker
and Inventor, — as the truly Great Man ever is. A
Hero is a Hero at all points ; in the soul and thought
of him first of all. This Odin, in his rude semi-articulate way, had a word to speak. A great heart laid
open to take in this great Universe, and man's Life
here, and utter a great word about it. A Hero, as I
say, in his own rude manner ; a wise, gifted, noblehearted man. And now, if we still admire such a man
beyond all others, what must these wild Norse
souls, first awakened into thinking, have made of
him! To them, as yet without names for it, he was
noble and noblest ; Hero, Prophet, God ; *Wuotan*, the
greatest of all. Thought is Thought, however it speak
or spell itself. Intrinsically, I conjecture, this Odin
must have been of the same sort of stuff as the greatest kind of men. A great thought in the wild deep
heart of him! The rough words he articulated, are
they not the rudimental roots of those English words
we still use ? He worked so, in that obscure element.
But he was as a *light* kindled in it ; a light of Intellect, rude Nobleness of heart, the only kind of lights
we have yet ; a Hero, as I say : and he had to shine
there, and make his obscure element a little lighter,
— as is still the task of us all.

We will fancy him to be the Type Norseman ; the finest Teuton whom that race had yet produced. The rude Norse heart burst-up into *boundless* admiration round him ; into adoration. He is as a root of so many great things ; the fruit of him is found growing, from deep thousands of years, over the whole field of Teutonic Life. Our own Wednesday, as I said, is it not still Odin's Day ? Wednesbury, Wansborough, Wanstead, Wandsworth : Odin grew into England too, these are still leaves from that root ! He was the Chief God to all the Teutonic People ; their Pattern Norseman ; — in such way did *they* admire their Pattern Norseman ; that was the fortune he had in the world.

Thus if the man Odin himself have vanished utterly, there is this huge Shadow of him which still projects itself over the whole History of his People. For this Odin once admitted to be God, we can understand well that the whole Scandinavian Scheme of Nature or dim No-scheme, whatever it might before have been, would now begin to develop itself altogether differently, and grow thenceforth in a new manner. What this Odin saw into, and taught with his runes and his rhymes, the whole Teutonic People laid to heart and carried forward. His way of thought became their way of thought : — such, under new conditions, is the history of every great thinker still. In gigantic confused lineaments, like some enormous camera-obscura shadow thrown upward from the dead deeps of the Past, and covering the whole Northern Heaven, is not that Scandinavian Mythology in some sort the Portraiture of this man Odin ? The gigantic image of *his* natural face, legible or not legible there, expanded and confused in that manner ! Ah, Thought, I say, is always Thought. No great man lives in vain. The History of the world is but the Biography of great men.

To me there is something very touching in this primeval figure of Heroism ; in such artless, helpless, but hearty entire reception of a Hero by his fellow-men. Never so helpless in shape, it is the noblest of feelings, and a feeling in some shape or other perennial as man himself. If I could show in any measure, what I feel deeply for a long time now, That it is the vital element of manhood, the soul of man's history here in our world, — it would be the chief use of this discoursing at present. We do not now call our great men Gods, nor admire *without* limit ; ah no, *with* limit enough ! But if we have no great men, or do not admire at all, — that were a still worse case.

This poor Scandinavian Hero-worship, that whole Norse way of looking at the Universe, and adjusting oneself there, has an indestructible merit for us. A rude childlike way of recognising the divineness of Nature, the divineness of Man ; most rude, yet heartfelt, robust, giantlike ; betokening what a giant of a man this child would yet grow to ! — It was a truth, and is none. Is it not as the half-dumb stifled voice of the long-buried generations of our own Fathers, calling out of the depths of ages to us, in whose veins their blood still runs : " This then, this is what *we* made of the world : this is all the image and notion we could form to ourselves of this great mystery of a Life and Universe. Despise it not. You are raised high above it, to large free scope of vision; but you too are not yet at the top. No, your notion too, so much enlarged, is but a partial, imperfect one; that matter is a thing no man will ever, in time or out of time, comprehend; after thousands of years of ever-new expansion, man will find himself but struggling to comprehend again a part of it: the thing is larger than man, not to be comprehended by him; an Infinite thing!"

The essence of the Scandinavian, as indeed of all Pagan Mythologies, we found to be recognition of the divineness of Nature; sincere communion of man with the mysterious invisible Powers visibly seen at work in the world round him. This, I should say, is more sincerely done in the Scandinavian than in any Mythology I know. Sincerity is the great characteristic of it. Superior sincerity (far superior) consoles us for the total want of old Grecian grace. Sincerity, I think, is better than grace. I feel that these old Northmen were looking into Nature with open eye and soul: most earnest, honest; childlike, and yet manlike; with a great-hearted simplicity and depth and freshness, in a true, loving, admiring, unfearing way. A right valiant, true old race of men. Such recognition of Nature one finds to be the chief element of Paganism: recognition of Man, and his Moral Duty, though this too is not wanting, comes to be the chief element only in purer forms of religion. Here, indeed, is a great distinction and epoch in Human Beliefs; a great landmark in the religious development of Mankind. Man first puts himself in relation with Nature and her Powers, wonders and worships over those; not till a later epoch does he

discern that all Power is Moral, that the grand point
is the distinction for him of Good and Evil, of *Thou
shalt* and *Thou shalt not.*

With regard to all these fabulous delineations in
the *Edda*, I will remark, moreover, as indeed was
already hinted, that most probably they must have
been of much newer date; most probably, even from
the first, were comparatively idle for the old Norsemen, and as it were a kind of Poetic sport. Allegory
and Poetic Delineation, as I said above, cannot be religious Faith; the Faith itself must first be there, then
Allegory enough will gather round it, as the fit body
round its soul. The Norse Faith, I can well suppose,
like other Faiths, was most active while it lay mainly
in the silent state, and had not yet much to say about
itself, still less to sing.

Among those shadowy *Edda* matters, amid all that
fantastic congeries of assertions, and traditions, in their
musical Mythologies, the main practical belief a man
could have was probably not much more than this: of
the *Valkyrs*[1] and the *Hall of Odin;* of an inflexible
Destiny; and that the one thing needful for a man
was *to be brave.* The *Valkyrs* are Choosers of the
Slain; a Destiny inexorable, which it is useless trying
to bend or soften, has appointed who is to be slain;
this was a fundamental point for the Norse believer;
— as indeed it is for all earnest men everywhere, for
a Mahomet, a Luther, for a Napoleon too. It lies at

[1] These wildly beautiful maidens weave the web of battle.
They ride through the air, clad in brilliant armor. As the name
("Choosers of the Slain") implies, they carry the brave war-
riors, slain in battle, to their reward in Valhalla, the Hall of the
Slain. See add. note to p. 47, n. 1.

the basis this for every such man ; it is the woof out
of which his whole system of thought is woven. The
Valkyrs ; and then that these *Choosers* lead the brave
to a heavenly *Hall of Odin ;* only the base and slavish
being thrust elsewhither, into the realms of Hela the
Death-goddess : I take this to have been the soul of the
whole Norse Belief. They understood in their heart
that it was indispensable to be brave ; that Odin would
have no favor for them, but despise and thrust them out,
if they were not brave. Consider too whether there is
not something in this ! It is an everlasting duty, valid
in our day as in that, the duty of being brave. *Valor*
is still *value*. The first duty for a man is still that of
subduing *Fear*. We must get rid of Fear ; we cannot
act at all till then. A man's acts are slavish, not true
but specious ; his very thoughts are false, he thinks
too as a slave and coward, till he have got Fear under
his feet. Odin's creed, if we disentangle the real kernel of it, is true to this hour. A man shall and must
be valiant ; he must march forward, and quit himself
like a man, — trusting imperturbably in the appointment and *choice* of the upper Powers ; and, on the
whole, not fear at all. Now and always, the completeness of his victory over Fear will determine how much
of a man he is.

It is doubtless very savage that kind of valour of
the old Northmen. Snorro tells us they thought it a
shame and misery not to die in battle ; and if natural
death seemed to be coming on, they would cut wounds
in their flesh, that Odin might receive them as warriors
slain. Old kings, about to die, had their body laid
into a ship ; the ship sent forth, with sails set and

slow fire burning it; that, once out at sea, it might blaze-up in flame, and in such manner bury worthily the old hero, at once in the sky and in the ocean! Wild bloody valour; yet valour of its kind; better, I say, than none. In the old Sea-kings, too, what an indomitable rugged energy! Silent, with closed lips, as I fancy them, unconscious that they were specially brave; defying the wild ocean with its monsters, and all men and things; — progenitors of our own Blakes and Nelsons! No Homer sang these Norse Sea-kings; but Agamemnon's was a small audacity, and of small fruit in the world, to some of them; — to Hrolf's of Normandy, for instance! Hrolf, or Rollo [1] Duke of Normandy, the wild Sea-king, has a share in governing England at this hour.

Nor was it altogether nothing, even that wild sea-roving and battling, through so many generations. It needed to be ascertained which was the *strongest* kind of men; who were to be ruler over whom. Among the Northland Sovereigns, too, I find some who got the title *Wood-cutter;* Forest-felling Kings. Much lies in that. I suppose at bottom many of them were forest-fellers as well as fighters, though the Skalds talk mainly of the latter, — misleading certain critics not a little; for no nation of men could ever live by fighting alone; there could not produce enough come out of that! I suppose the right good fighter was oftenest also the right good forest-feller, — the right good improver, discerner, doer and worker in every kind; for true valour, different enough from ferocity, is the basis of all. A more legitimate kind of valour that;

[1] First Duke of Normandy (? 860–? 930).

showing itself against the untamed Forests and dark
brute Powers of Nature, to conquer Nature for us.
In the same direction have not we their descendants
since carried it far? May such valour last for ever
with us!

That the man Odin, speaking with a Hero's voice
and heart, as with an impressiveness out of Heaven,
told his People the infinite importance of Valour, how
man thereby became a god; and that his People, feeling a response to it in their own hearts, believed this
message of his, and thought it a message out of Heaven, and him a Divinity for telling it them: this seems
to me the primary seed-grain of the Norse Religion,
from which all manner of mythologies, symbolic practices, speculations, allegories, songs and sagas would
naturally grow. Grow, — how strangely! I called it
a small light shining and shaping in the huge vortex
of Norse darkness. Yet the darkness itself was *alive;*
consider that. It was the eager inarticulate uninstructed
Mind of the whole Norse People, longing only to become articulate, to go on articulating ever farther! The
living doctrine grows, grows; — like a Banyan-tree;
the first *seed* is the essential thing: any branch strikes
itself down into the earth, becomes a new root; and so,
in endless complexity, we have a whole wood, a whole
jungle, one seed the parent of it all. Was not the
whole Norse Religion, accordingly, in some sense, what
we called 'the enormous shadow of this man's likeness'? Critics trace some affinity in some Norse mythuses, of the Creation and suchlike, with those of the
Hindoos. The Cow Adumbla,[1] 'licking the rime from

---

[1] Interpreted as representing Chaos.

the rocks,' has a kind of Hindoo look. A Hindoo Cow, transported into frosty countries. Probably enough; indeed we may say undoubtedly, these things will have a kindred with the remotest lands, with the earliest times. Thought does not die, but only is changed. The first man that began to think in this Planet of ours, he was the beginner of all. And then the second man, and the third man ; —nay, every true Thinker to this hour is a kind of Odin, teaches men *his* way of thought, spreads a shadow of his own likeness over sections of the History of the World.

Of the distinctive poetic character or merit of this Norse Mythology I have not room to speak ; nor does it concern us much. Some wild Prophecies we have, as the *Völuspa* in the *Elder Edda;* of a rapt, earnest, sibylline sort. But they were comparatively an idle adjunct of the matter, men who as it were but toyed with the matter, these later Skalds ; and it is *their* songs chiefly that survive. In later centuries, I suppose, they would go on singing, poetically symbolising, as our modern Painters paint, when it was no longer from the innermost heart, or not from the heart at all. This is everywhere to be well kept in mind.

Gray's fragments of Norse Lore,[1] at any rate, will give one no notion of it ; — any more than Pope will of Homer. It is no square-built gloomy palace of black ashlar marble, shrouded in awe and horror, as Gray gives it us: no ; rough as the North rocks, as

---

[1] *The Fatal Sisters* and *The Descent of Odin*, free renderings of Norse Odes, by Thomas Gray (1716–1771), the author of the *Elegy Written in a Country Churchyard*. See add. note.

the Iceland deserts, it is; with a heartiness, homeliness, even a tint of good humour and robust mirth in
the middle of these fearful things. The strong old
Norse heart did not go upon theatrical sublimities;
they had not time to tremble. I like much their robust simplicity; their veracity, directness of conception. Thor 'draws down his brows' in a veritable
Norse rage; 'grasps his hammer till the *knuckles
grow white.*' Beautiful traits of pity too, an honest
pity. Balder [1] 'the white God' dies; the beautiful,
benignant; he is the Sungod. They try all Nature
for a remedy; but he is dead. Frigga, his mother,
sends Hermoder [2] to seek or see him: nine days and
nine nights he rides through gloomy deep valleys, a
labyrinth of gloom; arrives at the Bridge with its
gold roof: the Keeper says, " Yes, Balder did pass
here; but the Kingdom of the Dead is down yonder,
far towards the North." Hermoder rides on; leaps
Hell-gate, Hela's gate; does see Balder, and speak
with him; Balder cannot be delivered. Inexorable!
Hela will not, for Odin or any God, give him up. The
beautiful and gentle has to remain there. His Wife
had volunteered to go with him, to die with him. They
shall for ever remain there. He sends his ring to

---

[1] The second son of Odin and Frigga. His mother obtained
an oath from all things except the mistletoe, which was overlooked as harmless, not to hurt Balder. Loke persuaded Balder's
blind brother to cast a sprig of mistletoe at Balder, which killed
him. Hela promised to let Balder return if all the world of beings and things would mourn for him. But one giant-hag, afterwards discovered to be Loke in disguise, refused. See Matthew
Arnold's *Balder Dead*.

[2] The swift messenger, servant of Odin.

Odin ; Nanna his wife sends her *thimble* to Frigga, as a remembrance. — Ah me ! —

For indeed Valour is the fountain of Pity too ; — of Truth, and all that is great and good in man. The robust homely vigour of the Norse heart attaches one much, in these delineations. Is it not a trait of right honest strength, says Uhland,[1] who has written a fine *Essay* on Thor, that the old Norse heart finds its friend in the Thunder-god ? That it is not frightened away by his thunder ; but finds that Summer-heat, the beautiful noble summer, must and will have thunder withal ! The Norse heart *loves* this Thor and his hammer-bolt ; sports with him. Thor is Summer-heat ; the god of Peaceable Industry as well as Thunder. He is the Peasant's friend ; his true henchman and attendant is Thialfi, *Manual Labour*. Thor himself engages in all manner of rough manual work, scorns no business for its plebeianism ; is ever and anon travelling to the country of the Jötuns, harrying those chaotic Frost-monsters, subduing them, at least straitening and damaging them. There is a great broad humour in some of these things.

Thor, as we saw above, goes to Jötun-land, to seek Hymir's Caldron, that the Gods may brew beer. Hymir the huge Giant enters, his grey beard all full of hoar-frost ; splits pillars with the very glance of his eye ; Thor, after much rough tumult, snatches the Pot, claps it on his head ; the ' handles of it reach down to his heels.' The Norse Skald has a kind of loving sport with Thor. This is the Hymir whose cattle, the critics

[1] Lyric poet, essayist, and scholar (1787–1862) ; Essay *Ueber den Mythus von Thor*, 1836.

have discovered, are Icebergs. Huge untutored Brobdingnag genius, — needing only to be tamed-down; into
Shakspeares, Dantes, Goethes! It is all gone now, that
old Norse work, — Thor the Thunder-god changed
into Jack the Giant-killer: but the mind that made it
is here yet. How strangely things grow, and die, and
do not die! There are twigs of that great world-tree of
Norse Belief still curiously traceable. This poor Jack
of the Nursery, with his miraculous shoes of swiftness,
coat of darkness, sword of sharpness, he is one. *Hynde
Etin*, and still more decisively *Red Etin of Ireland*,
in the Scottish Ballads, these are both derived from
Norseland; *Etin*[1] is evidently a *Jötun*. Nay, Shakspeare's *Hamlet* is a twig too of this same world-tree;
there seems no doubt of that. Hamlet, *Amleth*, I find,
is really a mythic personage; and his Tragedy, of the
poisoned Father, poisoned asleep by drops in his ear,
and the rest, is a Norse mythus! Old Saxo, as his
wont was, made it a Danish history; Shakspeare, out
of Saxo, made it what we see. That is a twig of the
world-tree that has *grown*, I think; — by nature or
accident that one has grown!

In fact, these old Norse songs have a *truth* in them,
an inward perennial truth and greatness, — as, indeed,
all must have that can very long preserve itself by
tradition alone. It is a greatness not of mere body
and gigantic bulk, but a rude greatness of soul. There
is a sublime uncomplaining melancholy traceable in
these old hearts. A great free glance into the very
deeps of thought. They seem to have seen, these brave

[1] Or *eten* = giant, dropped out of use in English speech in the
seventeenth century. See *New Eng. Dict.*

old Northmen, what Meditation has taught all men in all ages, That this world is after all but a show, — a phenomenon or appearance, no real thing. All deep souls see into that, — the Hindoo Mythologist, the German Philosopher, — the Shakspeare, the earnest Thinker, wherever he may be : —

' We are such stuff as Dreams are made of ! '[1]

One of Thor's expeditions, to Utgard (the *Outer* Garden, central seat of Jötun-land), is remarkable in this respect. Thialfi was with him, and Loke. After various adventures, they entered upon Giant-land; wandered over plains, wild uncultivated places, among stones and trees. At nightfall they noticed a house; and as the door, which indeed formed one whole side of the house, was open, they entered. It was a simple habitation; one large hall, altogether empty. They stayed there. Suddenly in the dead of the night loud noises alarmed them. Thor grasped his hammer; stood in the door, prepared for fight. His companions within ran hither and thither in their terror, seeking some outlet in that rude hall; they found a little closet at last, and took refuge there. Neither had Thor any battle : for, lo, in the morning it turned-out that the noise had been only the *snoring* of a certain enormous but peaceable Giant, the Giant Skrymir, who lay peaceably sleeping near by ; and this that they took for a house was merely his *Glove*, thrown aside there ; the door was the Glove-wrist ; the little closet they had fled into was the Thumb ! Such a glove ; — I remark too that it had not fingers as ours have, but only a thumb, and the rest undivided : a most ancient, rustic glove !

[1] Carlyle's favorite quotation. See p. 156.

Skrymir now carried their portmanteau all day; Thor, however, had his own suspicions, did not like the ways of Skrymir; determined at night to put an end to him as he slept. Raising his hammer, he struck down into the Giant's face a right thunderbolt blow, of force to rend rocks. The Giant merely awoke; rubbed his cheek, and said, Did a leaf fall? Again Thor struck, so soon as Skrymir again slept; a better blow than before; but the Giant only murmured, Was that a grain of sand? Thor's third stroke was with both his hands (the 'knuckles white,' I suppose), and seemed to dint deep into Skrymir's visage; but he merely checked his snore, and remarked, There must be sparrows roosting in this tree, I think; what is that they have dropt?— At the gate of Utgard, a place so high that you had to 'strain your neck bending back to see the top of it,' Skrymir went his ways. Thor and his companions were admitted; invited to share in the games going on. To Thor, for his part, they handed a Drinking-horn; it was a common feat, they told him, to drink this dry at one draught. Long and fiercely, three times over, Thor drank; but made hardly any impression. He was a weak child, they told him: could he lift that Cat he saw there? Small as the feat seemed, Thor with his whole godlike strength could not; he bent-up the creature's back, could not raise its feet off the ground, could at the utmost raise one foot. Why, you are no man, said the Utgard people; there is an Old Woman that will wrestle you! Thor, heartily ashamed, seized this haggard Old Woman; but could not throw her.

And now, on their quitting Utgard, the chief Jötun,

escorting them politely a little way, said to Thor :
" You are beaten then : — yet be not so much ashamed ;
there was deception of appearance in it. That Horn
you tried to drink was the *Sea;* you did make it ebb ;
but who can drink that, the bottomless ! The Cat you
would have lifted, — why, that is the *Midgard-snake,*[1]
the Great World-serpent, which, tail in mouth, girds
and keeps-up the whole created world ; had you torn
that up, the world must have rushed to ruin ! As for
the Old Woman, she was *Time*, Old Age, Duration :
with her what can wrestle ? No man nor no god with
her ; gods or men, she prevails over all ! And then
those three strokes you struck,— look at these *three
valleys;* your three strokes made these ! " Thor looked
at his attendant Jötun : it was Skrymir; — it was, say
Norse critics, the old chaotic rocky *Earth* in person,
and that glove-*house* was some Earth-cavern ! But
Skrymir had vanished ; Utgard with its skyhigh gates,
when Thor grasped his hammer to smite them, had
gone to air ; only the Giant's voice was heard mocking : " Better come no more to Jötunheim ! " —

This is of the allegoric period, as we see, and half
play, not of the prophetic and entirely devout : but as
a mythus is there not real antique Norse gold in it ?
More true metal, rough from the Mimer-stithy,[2] than
in many a famed Greek Mythus *shaped* far better ! A
great broad Brobdingnag grin of true humour is in
this Skrymir ; mirth resting on earnestness and sadness, as the rainbow on black tempest : only a right
valiant heart is capable of that. It is the grim humour

[1] According to the *Prose Edda*, one of the offspring of Loke.
[2] Forged by old Norse wisdom. See p. 28, n. 1.

of our own Ben Jonson,[1] rare old Ben; runs in the
blood of us, I fancy; for one catches tones of it,
under a still other shape, out of the American Back-
woods.

That is also a very striking conception that of the
Ragnarök,[2] Consummation, or *Twilight of the Gods*.
It is in the *Völuspa* Song; seemingly a very old, prophetic idea. The Gods and Jötuns, the divine Powers
and the chaotic brute ones, after long contest and
partial victory by the former, meet at last in universal world-embracing wrestle and duel; World-serpent
against Thor, strength against strength; mutually
extinctive; and ruin, 'twilight,' sinking into darkness,
swallows the created Universe. The old Universe with
its Gods is sunk; but it is not final death: there is to
be a new Heaven and a new Earth; a higher supreme
God,[3] and Justice to reign among men. Curious: this
law of mutation, which also is a law written in man's
inmost thought, had been deciphered by these old earnest Thinkers in their rude style; and how, though all
dies, and even gods die, yet all death is but a phœnix [4]

[1] The most famous of the dramatists contemporary with
Shakespeare (1574–1637). "O rare Ben Johnson" (*sic*) is inscribed on his tombstone in Westminster Abbey.

[2] After the death of Balder the gods are on the losing side.
Loke puts off all pretence of virtue, and becomes the leader of
the hosts of Hela in the final battle. Thor slays the World-serpent, but is suffocated by the fumes of its poison.

[3] The gods of the old mythology were not morally without spot;
in knowledge they were surpassed by the giants, who antedated
them. After the Ragnarök the gods that arose were to be sin-
less.

[4] The Phœnix myth appears in Eastern mythology in various
forms. According to the most familiar version, alluded to here, the

fire-death, and new-birth into the Greater and the Better! It is the fundamental Law of Being for a creature made of Time, living in this Place of Hope. All earnest men have seen into it; may still see into it.

And now, connected with this, let us glance at the *last* mythus of the appearance of Thor; and end there. I fancy it to be the latest in date of all these fables; a sorrowing protest against the advance of Christianity, — set forth reproachfully by some Conservative Pagan. King Olaf [1] has been harshly blamed for his over-zeal in introducing Christianity; surely I should have blamed him far more for an under-zeal in that! He paid dear enough for it; he died by the revolt of his Pagan people, in battle, in the year 1033, at Stickelstad, near that Drontheim, where the chief Cathedral of the North has now stood for many centuries, dedicated gratefully to his memory as *Saint* Olaf. The mythus about Thor is to this effect. King Olaf, the Christian Reform King, is sailing with fit escort along the shore of Norway, from haven to haven; dispensing justice, or doing other royal work: on leaving a certain haven, it is found that a stranger, of grave eyes and aspect, red beard, of stately robust figure, has stept in.

Phœnix, upon growing five or six centuries old, builds itself a funeral pyre, and from its ashes arises a new Phœnix: hence its frequent use as a symbol of immortality. Only one of the kind is in existence at a time.

[1] King Olaf, the Saint (*c.* 995–1033; King, 1015–1028), is confused here with the earlier Olaf Trygvason (964–1000; King from 995), about whom the story is told in the original. Both Olafs employed strenuous methods in behalf of Christianity in Norway.

The courtiers address him ; his answers surprise by
their pertinency and depth : at length he is brought
to the King. The stranger's conversation here is not
less remarkable, as they sail along the beautiful shore ;
but after some time, he addresses King Olaf thus :
" Yes, King Olaf, it is all beautiful, with the sun
shining on it there ; green, fruitful, a right fair home
for you ; and many a sore day had Thor, many a wild
fight with the rock Jötuns, before he could make it so.
And now you seem minded to put away Thor. King
Olaf, have a care ! " said the stranger, drawing-down
his brows ; — and when they looked again, he was
nowhere to be found. — This is the last appearance of
Thor on the stage of this world !

Do we not see well enough how the Fable might
arise, without unveracity on the part of any one ? It
is the way most Gods have come to appear among
men : thus, if in Pindar's [1] time ' Neptune [2] was seen
once at the Nemean Games,' what was this Neptune
too but a ' stranger of noble grave aspect,' — *fit* to be
' seen ' ! There is something pathetic, tragic for me
in this last voice of Paganism. Thor is vanished, the
whole Norse world has vanished ; and will not return
ever again. In like fashion to that, pass away the highest things. All things that have been in this world,
all things that are or will be in it, have to vanish : we
have our sad farewell to give them.

[1] Greek poet (B. C. 522 to soon after 450).
[2] The Latin equivalent for the Greek sea god Poseidon, who
was honored especially in the games held on the Corinthian
Isthmus, where he was frequently seen. He had no special connection with the Nemean Games, another of the great national
festivals of Greece, held at Argolis in the Peloponnesus.

That Norse Religion, a rude but earnest, sternly impressive *Consecration of Valour* (so we may define it), sufficed for these old valiant Northmen. Conse-cration of Valour is not a *bad* thing! We will take it for good, so far as it goes. Neither is there no use in *knowing* something about this old Paganism of our Fathers. Unconsciously, and combined with higher things, it is in *us* yet, that old Faith withal! To know it consciously, brings us into closer and clearer rela-tion with the Past, — with our own possessions in the Past. For the whole Past, as I keep repeating, is the possession of the Present; the Past had always some-thing *true*, and is a precious possession. In a different time, in a different place, it is always some other *side* of our common Human Nature that has been develop-ing itself. The actual True is the *sum* of all these; not any of them by itself constitutes what of Human Nature is hitherto developed. Better to know them all than misknow them. " To which of these Three Religions do you specially adhere?" inquires Meister of his Teacher. "To all the Three!" answers the other: "To all the Three; for they by their union first constitute the True Religion." [1]

[1] The "Three" who preside over sacred things in the Utopian community visited by Meister have just previously explained to him the three religions regarded among them, depending upon reverence for (1) what is above us, (2) what is around us, (3) what is beneath us, — which they call the Ethnic, the Philosophi-cal, and the Christian. The "Three" give the answer quoted. (Carlyle's translation of Goethe's *Wilhelm Meister*, Centenary Ed., II, pp. 267, 268.)

LECTURE II

[Friday, 8th May 1840.]

FROM the first rude times of Paganism among the
Scandinavians in the North, we advance to a very different epoch of religion, among a very different people:
Mahometanism among the Arabs. A great change;
what a change and progress is indicated here, in the
universal condition and thoughts of men!

The Hero is not now regarded as a God among his
fellow-men; but as one God-inspired, as a Prophet. It
is the second phasis of Hero-worship: the first or oldest, we may say, has passed away without return; in
the history of the world there will not again be any
man, never so great, whom his fellow-men will take for
a god. Nay we might rationally ask, Did any set of human beings ever really think the man they *saw* there
standing beside them a god, the maker of this world?
Perhaps not: it was usually some man they remembered, or *had* seen. But neither can this any more be.
The Great Man is not recognized henceforth as a god
any more.

It was a rude gross error, that of counting the
Great Man a god. Yet let us say that it is at all times
difficult to know *what* he is, or how to account of him
and receive him! The most significant feature in the
history of an epoch is the manner it has of welcoming

a Great Man. Ever, to the true instincts of men, there is something godlike in him. Whether they shall take him to be a god, to be a prophet, or what they shall take him to be? that is ever a grand question; by their way of answering that, we shall see, as through a little window, into the very heart of these men's spiritual condition. For at bottom the Great Man, as he comes from the hand of Nature, is ever the same kind of thing: Odin, Luther, Johnson, Burns; I hope to make it appear that these are all originally of one stuff; that only by the world's reception of them, and the shapes they assume, are they so immeasurably diverse. The worship of Odin astonishes us, — to fall prostrate before the Great Man, into *deliquium* [1] of love and wonder over him, and feel in their hearts that he was a denizen of the skies, a god! This was imperfect enough: but to welcome, for example, a Burns as we did, was that what we can call perfect? The most precious gift that Heaven can give to the Earth; a man of ' genius ' as we call it; the Soul of a Man actually sent down from the skies with a God's-message to us, — this we waste away as an idle artificial firework, sent to amuse us a little, and sink it into ashes, wreck and ineffectuality : *such* reception of a Great Man I do not call very perfect either! Looking into the heart of the thing, one may perhaps call that of Burns a still uglier phenomenon, betokening still sadder imperfections in mankind's ways, than the Scandinavian method itself! To fall into mere unreasoning *deliquium* of love and admiration, was not good; but such unreasoning, nay irrational supercilious no-love at all is perhaps still worse!

[1] Melting, swooning.

— It is a thing forever changing, this of Hero-worship:
different in each age, difficult to do well in any age.
Indeed the heart of the whole business of the age, one
may say, is to do it well.

We have chosen Mahomet not as the most eminent
Prophet; but as the one we are freest to speak of. He
is by no means the truest of Prophets; but I do esteem
him a true one. Farther, as there is no danger of our
becoming, any of us, Mahometans, I mean to say all
the good of him I justly can. It is the way to get at
his secret: let us try to understand what *he* meant
with the world; what the world meant and means
with him, will then be a more answerable question.
Our current hypothesis about Mahomet, that he was
a scheming Impostor, a Falsehood incarnate, that his
religion is a mere mass of quackery and fatuity, begins really to be now untenable to any one. The lies,
which well-meaning zeal has heaped round this man,
are disgraceful to ourselves only. When Pocock [1]
inquired of Grotius,[2] Where the proof was of that
story of the pigeon, trained to pick peas from Mahomet's ear, and pass for an angel dictating to him?
Grotius answered that there was no proof! It is
really time to dismiss all that. The word this man
spoke has been the life-guidance now of a hundred-
and-eighty millions of men these twelve-hundred years.
These hundred-and-eighty millions were made by God
as well as we. A greater number of God's creatures

---

[1] A very distinguished scholar of Oriental literature and history (1604–1691). His *Specimen Historiæ Arabum* (1649) was the
fruit of many years of scholarly activity in the Orient.

[2] Hugo de Groot (1583–1645), Dutch jurist and scholar.

believe in Mahomet's word at this hour, than in any other word whatever. Are we to suppose that it was a miserable piece of spiritual legerdemain, this which so many creatures of the Almighty have lived by and died by? I, for my part, cannot form any such supposition. I will believe most things sooner than that. One would be entirely at a loss what to think of this world at all, if quackery so grew and were sanctioned here.

Alas, such theories are very lamentable. If we would attain to knowledge of anything in God's true Creation, let us disbelieve them wholly! They are the product of an Age of Scepticism; [1] they indicate the saddest spiritual paralysis, and mere death-life of the souls of men: more godless theory, I think, was never promulgated in this Earth. A false man found a religion? Why, a false man cannot build a brick house! If he do not know and follow *truly* the properties of mortar, burnt clay and what else he works in, it is no house that he makes, but a rubbish-heap. It will not stand for twelve centuries, to lodge a hundred-and-eighty millions; it will fall straightway. A man must conform himself to Nature's laws, *be* verily in communion with Nature and the truth of things, or Nature will answer him, No, not at all! Speciosities are specious — ah me! — a Cagliostro,[2] many Cagliostros, prominent world-leaders, do pros-

[1] Carlyle so names the eighteenth century. See p. 237.

[2] Giuseppe Balsamo (1743–1795). He styled himself Count Cagliostro, and prospered for a while in an extraordinarily successful career of charlatanism. The best account of his proceedings is in Carlyle's essays on *Cagliostro* and *The Diamond Necklace*.

per by their quackery, for a day. It is like a forged
bank-note; they get it passed out of *their* worthless
hands : others, not they, have to smart for it. Nature
bursts-up in fire-flames, French Revolutions and suchlike, proclaiming with terrible veracity that forged
notes are forged.

But of a Great Man especially, of him I will venture to assert that it is incredible he should have been
other than true. It seems to me the primary foundation of him, and of all that can lie in him, this. No
Mirabeau,[1] Napoleon, Burns, Cromwell, no man adequate to do anything, but is first of all in right earnest about it; what I call a sincere man. I should say
sincerity, a deep, great, genuine sincerity, is the first
characteristic of all men in any way heroic. Not the
sincerity that calls itself sincere; ah no, that is a very
poor matter indeed ; — a shallow braggart conscious
sincerity; oftenest self-conceit mainly. The Great
Man's sincerity is of the kind he cannot speak of, is
not conscious of : nay, I suppose, he is conscious rather
of *in*sincerity; for what man can walk accurately by
the law of truth for one day? No, the Great Man does
not boast himself sincere, far from that; perhaps does
not ask himself if he is so : I would say rather, his
sincerity does not depend on himself ; he cannot help
being sincere! The great Fact of Existence is great
to him. Fly as he will, he cannot get out of the awful
presence of this Reality. His mind is so made ; he is

[1] 1749–1791. The ablest and most influential member of the
French Assembly at the time of the Revolution. He was President of the Jacobin Club, but opposed the headlong radicalism
that it developed. See Carlyle's *Essay on Mirabeau* (1837).

great by that, first of all. Fearful and wonderful, real
as Life, real as Death, is this Universe to him. Though
all men should forget its truth, and walk in a vain
show, he cannot. At all moments the Flame-image
glares-in upon him ; undeniable, there, there ! — I wish
you to take this as my primary definition of a Great
Man. A little man may have this, it is competent to
all men that God has made : but a Great Man cannot
be without it.

Such a man is what we call an *original* man ; he
comes to us at first-hand. A messenger he, sent from
the Infinite Unknown [1] with tidings to us. We may
call him Poet, Prophet, God ; — in one way or other, we
all feel that the words he utters are as no other man's
words. Direct from the Inner Fact of things ; — he
lives, and has to live, in daily communion with that.
Hearsays cannot hide it from him ; he is blind, homeless, miserable, following [2] hearsays ; *it* glares-in upon
him. Really his utterances, are they not a kind of ' revelation ; ' — what we must call such for want of some
other name ? It is from the heart of the world that he
comes ; he is a portion of the primal reality of things.
God has made many revelations : but this man too, has
not God made him, the latest and newest of all ? The
' inspiration of the Almighty giveth *him* understanding : ' we must listen before all to him.

This Mahomet, then, we will in no wise consider as
an Inanity and Theatricality, a poor conscious ambitious schemer ; we cannot conceive him so. The rude
message he delivered was a real one withal; an earnest

---

[1] Comp. pp. 10, 11.   [2] Conditional, = " if he follow."

confused voice from the unknown Deep. The man's words were not false, nor his workings here below; no Inanity and Simulacrum; a fiery mass of Life cast-up from the great bosom of Nature herself. To *kindle* the world; the world's Maker had ordered it so. Neither can the faults, imperfections, insincerities even, of Mahomet, if such were never so well proved against him, shake this primary fact about him.

On the whole, we make too much of faults; the details of the business hide the real centre of it. Faults? The greatest of faults, I should say, is to be conscious of none. Readers of the Bible above all, one would think, might know better. Who is called there ' the man according to God's own heart' ? David, the Hebrew King, had fallen into sins enough; blackest crimes; there was no want of sins. And thereupon the unbelievers sneer and ask, Is this your man according to God's heart? The sneer, I must say, seems to me but a shallow one. What are faults, what are the outward details of a life; if the inner secret of it, the remorse, temptations, true, oftenbaffled, never-ended struggle of it, be forgotten? ' It is not in man that walketh to direct his steps.' Of all acts, is not, for a man, *repentance* the most divine? The deadliest sin, I say, were that same supercilious consciousness of no sin; — that is death; the heart so conscious is divorced from sincerity, humility and fact; is dead: it is ' pure ' as dead dry sand is pure. David's life and history, as written for us in those Psalms of his, I consider to be the truest emblem ever given of a man's moral progress and warfare here below. All earnest souls will ever discern in it the faithful struggle of an earnest human soul towards what is good and best. Struggle often baffled, sore baffled, down as into entire wreck; yet a struggle never ended; ever, with tears, repentance, true unconquerable purpose, begun anew. Poor human nature! Is not a man's walking, in truth, always that: ' a succession of falls'? Man can do no other. In this wild element of a Life, he has to struggle onwards; now fallen, deep-abased; and ever, with tears, repentance, with bleeding heart, he has to rise again, struggle again still onwards. That his struggle *be* a faithful unconquerable one: that is the question of questions. We will put-up with many sad details, if the soul of it were true. Details by themselves will never teach us what it is. I believe we misestimate Mahomet's faults even as faults: but the secret of him will never be got by dwelling there. We will leave all this behind us; and assuring ourselves that he did mean some true thing, ask candidly what it was or might be.

These Arabs Mahomet was born among are certainly a notable people. Their country itself is notable; the fit habitation for such a race. Savage inaccessible rock-mountains, great grim deserts, alternating with beautiful strips of verdure: wherever water is, there is greenness, beauty; odoriferous balm-shrubs, date-trees, frankincense-trees. Consider that wide waste horizon of sand, empty, silent, like a sand-sea, dividing habitable place from habitable. You are all alone there, left alone with the Universe; by day a fierce sun blazing down on it with intolerable

radiance; by night the great deep Heaven with its
stars. Such a country is fit for a swift-handed, deep-
hearted race of men. There is something most agile,
active, and yet most meditative, enthusiastic in the
Arab character. The Persians are called the French
of the East; we will call the Arabs Oriental Italians.
A gifted noble people; a people of wild strong feelings, and of iron restraint over these : the characteristic of noblemindedness, of genius. The wild Bedouin
welcomes the stranger to his tent, as one having right
to all that is there; were it his worst enemy, he will
slay his foal to treat him, will serve him with sacred
hospitality for three days, will set him fairly on his
way ; — and then, by another law as sacred, kill him
if he can. In words too, as in action. They are not
a loquacious people, taciturn rather; but eloquent,
gifted when they do speak. An earnest, truthful kind
of men. They are, we know, of Jewish kindred :
but with that deadly terrible earnestness of the Jews,
they seem to combine something graceful, brilliant,
which is not Jewish. They had 'Poetic contests'
among them before the time of Mahomet. Sale [1] says,
at Ocadh, in the South of Arabia, there were yearly
fairs, and there, when the merchandising was done,
Poets sang for prizes : — the wild people gathered to
hear that.

One Jewish quality these Arabs manifest; the outcome of many or of all high qualities : what we may
call religiosity. From of old they had been zealous wor-

[1] 1690–1736. To his translation of the *Koran* (1734) he pre-
fixed a *Preliminary Discourse* on Arab history, religion, etc. His
interpretation of Mahomet's character is friendly.

shippers, according to their light. They worshipped
the stars, as Sabeans;[1] worshipped many natural objects, — recognised them as symbols, immediate man-
ifestations, of the Maker of Nature. It was wrong;
and yet not wholly wrong. All God's works are still
in a sense symbols of God. Do we not, as I urged,
still account it a merit to recognise a certain inexhaustible significance, 'poetic beauty' as we name it, in all
natural objects whatsoever? A man is a poet, and
honoured, for doing that, and speaking or singing
it, — a kind of diluted worship. They had many Prophets, these Arabs; Teachers each to his tribe, each
according to the light he had. But indeed, have we
not from of old the noblest of proofs, still palpable to
every one of us, of what devoutness and noblemindedness had dwelt in these rustic thoughtful peoples?
Biblical critics seem agreed that our own *Book of Job*
was written in that region of the world. I call that,
apart from all theories about it, one of the grandest
things ever written with pen. One feels, indeed, as if
it were not Hebrew; such a noble universality, different from noble patriotism or sectarianism, reigns in it.
A noble Book; all men's Book! It is our first, oldest statement of the never-ending Problem, — man's
destiny, and God's ways with him here in this earth.
And all in such free flowing outlines; grand in its sincerity, in its simplicity; in its epic melody, and repose
of reconcilement. There is the seeing eye, the mildly
understanding heart. So *true* everyway; true eyesight
and vision for all things; material things no less than
spiritual: the Horse, — 'hast thou clothed his neck

with *thunder?*'—he '*laughs* at the shaking of the spear!' Such living likenesses were never since drawn. Sublime sorrow, sublime reconciliation; oldest choral melody as of the heart of mankind;—so soft, and great; as the summer midnight, as the world with its seas and stars! There is nothing written, I think, in the Bible or out of it, of equal literary merit. —

To the idolatrous Arabs one of the most ancient universal objects of worship was that Black Stone, still kept in the building called Caabah [1] at Mecca. Diodorus Siculus [2] mentions this Caabah in a way not to be mistaken, as the oldest, most honoured temple in his time; that is, some half-century before our Era. Silvestre de Sacy says there is some likelihood that the Black Stone is an aerolite. In that case, some man might *see* it fall out of Heaven! It stands now beside the Well Zemzem; the Caabah is built over both. A Well is in all places a beautiful affecting object, gushing out like life from the hard earth;—still more so in those hot dry countries, where it is the first condition of being. The Well Zemzem has its name from the bubbling sound of the waters, *zem-zem;* they think it is the Well which Hagar [3] found with her little

---

[1] A cubical structure, "twenty-seven cubits" (about forty feet) each way, in the centre of the court of the great Mosque at Mecca. Into the wall, at a height convenient for kissing, is built the famous Black Stone (probably a meteorite), an object of supreme veneration.

[2] Historian, first century B. C. His *Historical Library* is a history of the world to B. C. 60.

[3] Hagar, the maid of Abraham's wife, Sarah, bore a son, Ishmael, to Abraham. After the birth of Sarah's son, Isaac, Hagar and Ishmael at the demand of Sarah were cast out into the wilderness. When they were perishing for lack of water, "God

Ishmael in the wilderness : the aerolite and it have
been sacred now, and had a Caabah over them, for
thousands of years. A curious object, that Caabah !
There it stands at this hour, in the black cloth-cover-
ing the Sultan sends it yearly ; ' twenty-seven cubits
high ; ' with circuit, with double circuit of pillars,
with festoon-rows of lamps and quaint ornaments; the
lamps will be lighted again *this* night, — to glitter
again under the stars. An authentic fragment of the
oldest Past. It is the *Keblah* [1] of all Moslem: from
Delhi all onwards to Morocco,[2] the eyes of innumerable praying men are turned towards *it* five times,
this day and all days : one of the notablest centres in
the Habitation of Men.

It had been from the sacredness attached to this
Caabah Stone and Hagar's Well, from the pilgrimings
of all tribes of Arabs thither, that Mecca [3] took its
rise as a Town. A great town once, though much de-
cayed now. It has no natural advantage for a town ;
stands in a sandy hollow amid bare barren hills, at a
distance from the sea ; its provisions, its very bread,
have to be imported. But so many pilgrims needed
lodgings : and then all places of pilgrimage do, from
the first, become places of trade. The first day pilgrims meet, merchants have also met ; where men see

opened her eyes, and she saw a well of water ; and she . . . gave
the lad drink. . . . and he grew, and dwelt in the wilderness."
Cf. Genesis xxi, 19, 20. And see also chaps. xvi, xvii, xxi, xxv, entire.

[1] The direction toward which the face is turned in prayer.

[2] The whole Moslem world, from British India to Western
Africa.

[3] In western Arabia, a little over forty miles inland from the
Red Sea.

themselves assembled for one object, they find that
they can accomplish other objects which depend on
meeting together. Mecca became the Fair of all Arabia. And thereby indeed the chief staple and ware-
house of whatever Commerce there was between the
Indian and the Western countries, Syria, Egypt, even
Italy. It had at one time a population of 100,000;
buyers, forwarders of those Eastern and Western products; importers for their own behoof of provisions
and corn. The government was a kind of irregular
aristocratic republic, not without a touch of theocracy.
Ten Men of a chief tribe, chosen in some rough way,
were Governors of Mecca, and Keepers of the Caabah.
The Koreish were the chief tribe in Mahomet's time;
his own family was of that tribe. The rest of the
Nation, fractioned and cut-asunder by deserts, lived
under similar rude patriarchal governments by one or
several: herdsmen, carriers, traders, generally robbers
too; being oftenest at war one with another, or with all:
held together by no open bond, if it were not this meeting at the Caabah, where all forms of Arab Idolatry
assembled in common adoration; — held mainly by the
inward indissoluble bond of a common blood and language. In this way had the Arabs lived for long ages,
unnoticed by the world; a people of great qualities,
unconsciously waiting for the day when they should
become notable to all the world. Their Idolatries
appear to have been in a tottering state; much was
getting into confusion and fermentation among them.
Obscure tidings of the most important Event ever trans-
acted in this world, the Life and Death of the Divine
Man in Judea, at once the symptom and cause of im-

measurable change to all people in the world, had in
the course of centuries reached into Arabia too; and
could not but, of itself, have produced fermentation
there.

It was among this Arab people, so circumstanced, in
the year 570 of our Era, that the man Mahomet was
born. He was of the family of Hashem, of the Koreish
tribe as we said; though poor, connected with the chief
persons of his country. Almost at [1] his birth he lost
his Father; at the age of six years his Mother too, a
woman noted for her beauty, her worth and sense: he
fell to the charge of his Grandfather, an old man,
a hundred years old. A good old man: Mahomet's
Father, Abdallah, had been his youngest favourite son.
He saw in Mahomet, with his old life-worn eyes, a century old, the lost Abdallah come back again, all that
was left of Abdallah. He loved the little orphan Boy
greatly; used to say, They must take care of that
beautiful little Boy, nothing in their kindred was more
precious than he. At his death, while the boy was still
but two years old,[2] he left him in charge to Abu
Thaleb the eldest of the Uncles, as to him that now
was head of the house. By this Uncle, a just and
rational man as everything betokens, Mahomet was
brought-up in the best Arab way.

Mahomet, as he grew up, accompanied his Uncle on
trading journeys and suchlike; in his eighteenth year

[1] In fact, two months before.
[2] This is not, as appears at first sight, inconsistent with the
statement above about his mother; not the mother, but the
grandfather, as head of the house, became guardian immediately
upon the father's death.

one finds him a fighter following his Uncle in war.
But perhaps the most significant of all his journeys is
one we find noted as of some years' earlier date : a
journey to the Fairs of Syria. The young man here
first came in contact with a quite foreign world, —
with one foreign element of endless moment to him :
the Christian Religion. I know not what to make of
that ' Sergius, the Nestorian Monk,' whom Abu Thaleb
and he are said to have lodged with; or how much
any monk could have taught one still so young. Probably enough it is greatly exaggerated, this of the Nestorian [1] Monk. Mahomet was only fourteen; had no
language but his own : much in Syria must have been
a strange unintelligible whirlpool to him. But the
eyes of the lad were open ; glimpses of many things
would doubtless be taken-in, and lie very enigmatic as
yet, which were to ripen in a strange way into views,
into beliefs and insights one day. These journeys to
Syria were probably the beginning of much to Mahomet.

One other circumstance we must not forget : that
he had no school-learning ; of the thing we call school-
learning none at all. The art of writing was but just
introduced into Arabia ; it seems to be the true opinion that Mahomet never could write ! Life in the
Desert, with its experiences, was all his education.
What of this infinite Universe he, from his dim place,
with his own eyes and thoughts, could take in, so
much and no more of it was he to know. Curious, if
we will reflect on it, this of having no books. Except
by what he could see for himself, or hear of by uncer-

---

[1] The Nestorians were a sect of the Early Church, so named
from Nestorius, their most conspicuous representative.

tain rumour of speech in the obscure Arabian Desert, he could know nothing. The wisdom that had been before him or at a distance from him in the world, was in a manner as good as not there for him. Of the great brother souls, flame-beacons through so many lands and times, no one directly communicates with this great soul. He is alone there, deep down in the bosom of the Wilderness; has to grow up so, — alone with Nature and his own Thoughts.

But, from an early age, he had been remarked as a thoughtful man. His companions named him '*Al Amin*, The Faithful.' A man of truth and fidelity; true in what he did, in what he spake and thought. They noted that *he* always meant something. A man rather taciturn in speech; silent when there was nothing to be said; but pertinent, wise, sincere, when he did speak; always throwing light on the matter. This is the only sort of speech *worth* speaking! Through life we find him to have been regarded as an altogether solid, brotherly, genuine man. A serious, sincere character; yet amiable, cordial, companionable, jocose even; — a good laugh in him withal: there are men whose laugh is as untrue as anything about them; who cannot laugh. One hears of Mahomet's beauty: his fine sagacious honest face, brown florid complexion, beaming black eyes; — I somehow like too that vein on the brow, which swelled-up black when he was in anger: like the '*horse-shoe* vein' in Scott's *Redgauntlet*. It was a kind of feature in the Hashem family, this black swelling vein in the brow; Mahomet had it prominent, as would appear. A spontaneous, passionate, yet just, true-meaning man! Full of wild faculty, fire and light; of wild worth, all uncultured; working out his life-task in the depths of the Desert there.

How he was placed with Kadijah, a rich Widow, as her Steward, and travelled in her business, again to the Fairs of Syria; how he managed all, as one can well understand, with fidelity, adroitness; how her gratitude, her regard for him grew: the story of their marriage [1] is altogether a graceful intelligible one, as told us by the Arab authors. He was twenty-five; she forty, though still beautiful. He seems to have lived in a most affectionate, peaceable, wholesome way with this wedded benefactress; loving her truly, and her alone. It goes greatly against the impostor theory, the fact that he lived in this entirely unexceptionable, entirely quiet and commonplace way, till the heat of his years was done. He was forty before he talked of any mission from Heaven. All his irregularities, real and supposed, date from after his fiftieth year, when the good Kadijah died. All his ' ambition,' seemingly, had been, hitherto, to live an honest life; his ' fame,' the mere good opinion of neighbours that knew him, had been sufficient hitherto. Not till he was already getting old, the prurient heat of his life all burnt out, and *peace* growing to be the chief thing this world could give him, did he start on the ' career of ambition ;' and, belying all his past character and exist-ence, set up as a wretched empty charlatan to acquire what he could now no longer enjoy! For my share, I have no faith whatever in that.

Ah no: this deep-hearted Son of the Wilderness,

[1] In 595 or 596.

with his beaming black eyes and open social deep soul, had other thoughts in him than ambition. A silent great soul; he was one of those who cannot *but* be in earnest; whom Nature herself has appointed to be sincere. While others walk in formulas and hearsays, contented enough to dwell there, this man could not screen himself in formulas; he was alone with his own soul and the reality of things. The great Mystery of Existence, as I said, glared-in upon him, with its terrors, with its splendours; no hearsays could hide that unspeakable fact. "Here am I!" Such *sincerity*, as we named it, has in very truth something of divine. The word of such a man is a Voice direct from Nature's own Heart. Men do and must listen to that as to nothing else;—all else is wind in comparison. From of old, a thousand thoughts, in his pilgrimings and wanderings, had been in this man: What am I? What *is* this unfathomable Thing I live in, which men name Universe? What is Life; what is Death? What am I to believe? What am I to do? The grim rocks of Mount Hara,[1] of Mount Sinai,[2] the stern sandy solitudes answered not. The great Heaven rolling silent overhead, with its blue-glancing stars, answered not. There was no answer. The man's own soul and what of God's inspiration dwelt there, had to answer!

It is the thing which all men have to ask themselves; which we too have to ask, and answer. This wild man felt it to be of *infinite* moment; all other things of no

[1] Near Mecca.

[2] In the southern part of the peninsula east of the Gulf of Suez. See Genesis xix, for the experiences of another Hero-Prophet on its "grim rocks."

moment whatever in comparison. The jargon of argumentative Greek Sects, vague traditions of Jews, the
stupid routine of Arab Idolatry : there was no answer
in these. A Hero, as I repeat, has this first distinction,
which indeed we may call first and last, the Alpha and
Omega of his whole Heroism, That he looks through
the shows of things into *things*. Use and wont, respectable hearsay, respectable formula: all these are
good, or are not good. There is something behind and
beyond all these, which all these must correspond with,
be the image of, or they are — *Idolatries ;* 'bits of
black wood pretending to be God ;' to the earnest
soul a mockery and abomination. Idolatries never so
gilded waited on by heads of the Koreish, will do nothing for this man. Though all men walk by them,
what good is it? The great Reality stands glaring
there upon *him*. He there has to answer it, or perish
miserably. Now, even now, or else through all Eternity
never ! Answer it ; *thou* must find an answer. — Ambition ? What could all Arabia do for this man ; with
the crown of Greek Heraclius,[1] of Persian Chosroes,
and all crowns in the Earth ; — what could they all do
for him? It was not of the Earth he wanted to hear
tell ; it was of the Heaven above and of the Hell
beneath. All crowns and sovereignties whatsoever,
where would *they* in a few brief years be? To be
Sheik[2] of Mecca or Arabia, and have a bit of gilt
wood put into your hand, — will that be one's salva

---

[1] Byzantine Emperor from 610 to 641. He defeated the Persians under Chosroes II, in the Battle of Nineveh, 627, the fifth
year of the Mohammedan era.

[2] Tribal head ; also a religious dignitary.

tion? I decidedly think not. We will leave it altogether, this impostor hypothesis, as not credible; not very tolerable even, worthy chiefly of dismissal by us.

Mahomet had been wont to retire yearly, during the month Ramadhan, into solitude and silence; as indeed was the Arab custom; a praiseworthy custom, which such a man, above all, would find natural and useful. Communing with his own heart, in the silence of the mountains; himself silent; open to the 'small still voices:' it was a right natural custom! Mahomet was in his fortieth year, when having withdrawn to a cavern in Mount Hara, near Mecca, during this Ramadhan,[1] to pass the month in prayer, and meditation on those great questions, he one day told his wife Kadijah, who with his household was with him or near him this year, That by the unspeakable special favour of Heaven he had now found it all out; was in doubt and darkness no longer, but saw it all. That all these Idols and Formulas were nothing, miserable bits of wood; that there was One God in and over all; and we must leave all Idols, and look to Him. That God is great; and that there is nothing else great! He is the Reality. Wooden Idols are not real; He is real. He made us at first, sustains us yet; we and all things are but the shadow of Him; a transitory garment veiling the Eternal Splendour. '*Allah akbar*, God is great;'—and then also '*Islam*,'[2] That we must *submit* to God. That our whole strength lies in

---

[1] The days of this month, which comes at various seasons of the year, according to the lunar calendar, are observed by all Mussulmans as an absolute fast from dawn to sunset.

[2] Resignation, surrendering. See *New Eng. Dict.*

resigned submission to Him, whatsoever He do to us.
For this world, and for the other! The thing He sends
to us, were it death and worse than death, shall be
good, shall be best; we resign ourselves to God.—
'If this be *Islam*,' says Goethe, ' do we not all live in
Islam?' Yes, all of us that have any moral life; we
all live so. It has ever been held the highest wisdom
for a man not merely to submit to Necessity, — Necessity will make him submit, — but to know and believe
well that the stern thing which Necessity had ordered
was the wisest, the best, the thing wanted there. To
cease his frantic pretension of scanning this great
God's-world in his small fraction of a brain; to know
that it *had* verily, though deep beyond his soundings, a
Just Law, that the soul of it was Good ;— that his part
in it was to conform to the Law of the Whole, and in
devout silence follow that; not questioning it, obeying
it as unquestionable.

I say, this is yet the only true morality known. A
man is right and invincible, virtuous and on the road
towards sure conquest, precisely while he joins himself to the great deep Law of the World, in spite of
all superficial laws, temporary appearances, profit-and-
loss calculations; he is victorious while he coöperates
with that great central Law, not victorious otherwise :
— and surely his first chance of coöperating with it,
or getting into the course of it, is to know with his
whole soul that it *is;* that it is good, and alone good!
This is the soul of Islam; it is properly the soul
of Christianity; — for Islam is definable as a confused form of Christianity; had Christianity not been,
neither had it been. Christianity also commands us,

before all, to be resigned to God. We are to take no
counsel with flesh-and-blood ; give ear to no vain cav-
ils, vain sorrows and wishes : to know that we know
nothing ; that the worst and cruelest to our eyes is
not what it seems ; that we have to receive whatsoever befalls us as sent from God above, and say, It
is good and wise, God is great ! " Though He slay me,
yet will I trust in Him." Islam means in its way Denial of Self, Annihilation of Self. This is yet the highest Wisdom that Heaven has revealed to our Earth.

Such light had come, as it could, to illuminate the
darkness of this wild Arab soul. A confused dazzling
splendour as of life and Heaven, in the great darkness which threatened to be death : he called it revelation and the angel Gabriel ; [1] — who of us yet can
know what to call it ? It is the ' inspiration of the
Almighty that giveth us understanding.' To *know ;*
to get into the truth of anything, is ever a mystic act,
— of which the best Logics can but babble on the
surface. ' Is not Belief the true god-announcing Miracle ? ' says Novalis. — That Mahomet's whole soul,
set in flame with this grand Truth vouchsafed him,
should feel as if it were important and the only important thing, was very natural. That Providence
had unspeakably honoured *him* by revealing it, saving him from death and darkness ; that he therefore
was bound to make known the same to all creatures :
this is what was meant by ' Mahomet is the Prophet
of God ; ' this too is not without its true meaning. —

The good Kadijah, we can fancy, listened to him

[1] Who was said to have brought the *Koran* to Mahomet from
Heaven.

with wonder, with doubt: at length she answered: Yes, it was *true* this that he said. One can fancy too the boundless gratitude of Mahomet; and how of all the kindnesses she had done him, this of believing the earnest struggling word he now spoke was the greatest. 'It is certain,' says Novalis, 'my Conviction gains infinitely, the moment another soul will believe in it.' It is a boundless favour. — He never forgot this good Kadijah. Long afterwards, Ayesha his young favourite wife, a woman who indeed distinguished herself among the Moslem, by all manner of qualities, through her whole long life; this young brilliant Ayesha was, one day, questioning him: "Now am not I better than Kadijah? She was a widow; old, and had lost her looks: you love me better than you did her?" — "No, by Allah!" answered Mahomet: "No, by Allah! She believed in me when none else would believe. In the whole world I had but one friend, and she was that!" — Seid, his Slave, also believed in him; these with his young Cousin Ali, Abu Thaleb's son, were his first converts.

He spoke of his Doctrine to this man and that; but the most treated it with ridicule, with indifference; in three years, I think, he had gained but thirteen followers. His progress was slow enough. His encouragement to go on, was altogether the usual encouragement that such a man in such a case meets. After some three years of small success, he invited forty of his chief kindred to an entertainment; and there stood up and told them what his pretension was: that he had this thing to promulgate abroad to all men; that it was the highest thing, the one thing: which of them would second him in that? Amid the doubt and silence of all, young Ali, as yet a lad of sixteen, impatient of the silence, started-up, and exclaimed in passionate fierce language, That he would! The assembly, among whom was Abu Thaleb, Ali's Father, could not be unfriendly to Mahomet; yet the sight there, of one unlettered elderly man, with a lad of sixteen, deciding on such an enterprise against all mankind, appeared ridiculous to them; the assembly broke-up in laughter. Nevertheless it proved not a laughable thing; it was a very serious thing! As for this young Ali, one cannot but like him. A noble-minded creature, as he shows himself, now and always afterwards; full of affection, of fiery daring. Something chivalrous in him; brave as a lion; yet with a grace, a truth and affection worthy of Christian knighthood. He died by assassination in the Mosque at Bagdad; a death occasioned by his own generous fairness, confidence in the fairness of others: he said, If the wound proved not unto death, they must pardon the Assassin; but if it did, then they must slay him straightway, that so they two in the same hour might appear before God, and see which side of that quarrel was the just one!

Mahomet naturally gave offence to the Koreish, Keepers of the Caabah, superintendents of the Idols. One or two men of influence had joined him: the thing spread slowly, but it was spreading. Naturally he gave offence to everybody: Who is this that pretends to be wiser than we all; that rebukes us all, as mere fools and worshippers of wood! Abu Thaleb the good Uncle spoke with him: Could he not be silent about all that; believe it all for himself, and not trouble others, anger the chief men, endanger him self and them all, talking of it? Mahomet answered: If the Sun stood on his right hand and the Moon on his left, ordering him to hold his peace, he could not obey! No: there was something in this Truth he had got which was of Nature herself; equal in rank to Sun, or Moon, or whatsoever thing Nature had made. It would speak itself there, so long as the Almighty allowed it, in spite of Sun and Moon, and all Koreish and all men and things. It must do that, and could do no other. Mahomet answered so; and, they say, ' burst into tears.' Burst into tears: he felt that Abu Thaleb was good to him; that the task he had got was no soft, but a stern and great one.

He went on speaking to who would listen to him; publishing his Doctrine among the pilgrims as they came to Mecca; gaining adherents in this place and that. Continual contradiction, hatred, open or secret danger attended him. His powerful relations protected Mahomet himself; but by and by, on his own advice, all his adherents had to quit Mecca, and seek refuge in Abyssinia over the sea.[1] The Koreish grew ever angrier; laid plots, and swore oaths among them, to put Mahomet to death with their own hands. Abu Thaleb was dead, the good Kadijah was dead. Mahomet is not solicitous of sympathy from us; but his outlook at this time was one of the dismalest. He had to hide in caverns, escape in disguise; fly hither and thither; homeless, in continual peril of his life. More than once it seemed all-over with him; more than once it turned on a straw, some rider's horse

[1] Red Sea.

taking fright or the like, whether Mahomet and his Doctrine had not ended there, and not been heard of at all. But it was not to end so.

In the thirteenth year of his mission, finding his enemies all banded against him, forty sworn men, one out of every tribe, waiting to take his life, and no continuance possible at Mecca for him any longer, Mahomet fled to the place then called Yathreb, where he had gained some adherents ; [1] the place they now call Medina, or *'Medinat al Nabi*, the City of the Prophet,' from that circumstance. It lay some 200 miles off,[2] through rocks and deserts ; not without great difficulty, in such mood as we may fancy, he escaped thither, and found welcome. The whole East dates its era from this Flight, *Hegira* as they name it : the Year 1 of this Hegira is 622 of our Era, the fifty-third of Mahomet's life. He was now becoming an old man ; his friends sinking round him one by one ; his path desolate, encompassed with danger : unless he could find hope in his own heart, the outward face of things was but hopeless for him. It is so with all men in the like case. Hitherto Mahomet had professed to publish his Religion by the way of preaching and persuasion alone. But now, driven foully out of his native country, since unjust men had not only given no ear to his earnest Heaven's-message, the deep cry of his heart, but would not even let him live if he kept speaking it, — the wild Son of the Desert resolved to defend himself, like a man and Arab. If the Koreish will

---

[1] In 620 Mahomet converted six pilgrims from Yathreb, which city two years later accepted him as a true Prophet.

[2] Toward the north.

have it so, they shall have it. Tidings, felt to be of infinite moment to them and all men, they would not listen to these; would trample them down by sheer violence, steel and murder: well, let steel try it then! Ten years more this Mahomet had; all of fighting, of breathless impetuous toil and struggle;[1] with what result we know.

Much has been said of Mahomet's propagating his Religion by the sword. It is no doubt far nobler what we have to boast of the Christian Religion, that it propagated itself peaceably in the way of preaching and conviction. Yet withal, if we take this for an argument of the truth or falsehood of a religion, there is a radical mistake in it. The sword indeed: but where will you get your sword! Every new opinion, at its starting, is precisely in a *minority of one*. In one man's head alone, there it dwells as yet. One man alone of the whole world believes it; there is one man against all men. That *he* take a sword, and try to propagate with that, will do little for him. You must first get your sword! On the whole, a thing will propagate itself as it can. We do not find, of the Christian Religion either, that it always disdained the sword, when once it had got one. Charlemagne's conversion of the Saxons[2] was not by preaching. I care little about the

---

[1] In 629 he marched on Mecca with 10,000 followers and destroyed the idols about the Caabah in the Mosque. In 632 he made a pilgrimage to Mecca at the head of 100,000 converts. He died soon after, in the same year.

[2] Charlemagne (742–814) was at war with the Saxons for over thirty years. He was determined to Christianize them no less than to conquer them in battle. St. Lebuin, impatient at his slow progress in converting them, threatened them with **Charlemagne's**

sword: I will allow a thing to struggle for itself in
this world, with any sword or tongue or implement it
has, or can lay hold of. We will let it preach, and
pamphleteer, and fight, and to the uttermost bestir itself, and do, beak and claws, whatsoever is in it; very
sure that it will, in the long-run, conquer nothing which
does not deserve to be conquered. What is better than
itself, it cannot put away, but only what is worse. In
this great Duel, Nature herself is umpire, and can do
no wrong: the thing which is deepest-rooted in Nature,
what we call *truest*, that thing and not the other will
be found growing at last.

Here however, in reference to much that there is in
Mahomet and his success, we are to remember what
an umpire Nature is; what a greatness, composure of
depth and tolerance there is in her. You take wheat
to cast into the Earth's bosom: your wheat may be
mixed with chaff, chopped straw, barn-sweepings, dust
and all imaginable rubbish; no matter: you cast it
into the kind just Earth; she grows the wheat, — the
whole rubbish she silently absorbs, shrouds *it* in, says
nothing of the rubbish. The yellow wheat is growing
there; the good Earth is silent about all the rest, —
has silently turned all the rest to some benefit too,
and makes no complaint about it! So everywhere in
Nature! She is true and not a lie; and yet so great,
and just, and motherly in her truth. She requires of a
thing only that it *be* genuine of heart; she will protect

sword. In retaliation the destruction of churches became the
accompaniment of Saxon revolt. Charlemagne established gar-
risons all over the country, and (777) made Christian baptism
compulsory.

it if so; will not, if not so. <u>There is a soul of truth in</u> <u>all the things she ever gave harbour to</u>. Alas, is not this the history of all highest Truth that comes or ever came into the world? The *body* of them all is imperfection, an element of light *in* darkness: to us they have to come embodied in mere Logic, in some merely *scientific* Theorem of the Universe; which *cannot* be complete; which cannot but be found, one day, *in*complete, erroneous, and so die and disappear. The body of all Truth dies; and yet in all, I say, there is a soul which never dies; which in new and ever-nobler embodiment lives immortal as man himself! It is the way with Nature. The genuine essence of Truth never dies. That it be genuine, a voice from the great Deep of Nature, there is the point at Nature's judgment-seat. What *we* call pure or impure, is not with her the final question. Not how much chaff is in you; but whether you have any wheat. Pure? I might say to many a man : Yes, you are pure; pure enough; but you are chaff, — insincere hypothesis, hearsay, formality; you never were in contact with the great heart of the Universe at all; you are properly neither pure nor impure; you *are* nothing, Nature has no business with you.

Mahomet's Creed we called a kind of Christianity; and really, if we look at the wild rapt earnestness with which it was believed and laid to heart, I should say a better kind than that of those miserable Syrian Sects, with their vain janglings about *Homoiousion* and *Homoousion*, [1] the head full of worthless noise, the

---

[1] ὅμοιος = similar, ὁμός = same, + οὐσία = essence. These "vain logical janglings" of the fourth century were over the question of whether Christ and God were of similar essence or the same essence.

heart empty and dead! The truth of it is embedded in portentous error and falsehood; but the truth of it makes it be believed, not the falsehood: it succeeded by its truth. A bastard kind of Christianity, but a living kind; with a heart-life in it; not dead, chopping barren logic merely! Out of all that rubbish of Arab idolatries, argumentative theologies, traditions, subtleties, rumours and hypotheses of Greeks and Jews, with their idle wiredrawings, this wild man of the Desert, with his wild sincere heart, earnest as death and life, with his great flashing natural eyesight, had seen into the kernel of the matter. Idolatry is nothing: these Wooden Idols of yours, ' ye rub them with oil and wax, and the flies stick on them,' — these are wood, I tell you! They can do nothing for you; they are an impotent blasphemous pretence; a horror and abomination, if ye knew them. God alone is; God alone has power; He made us, He can kill us and keep us alive: ' *Allah akbar*, God is great.' Understand that His will is the best for you; that howsoever sore to flesh-and-blood, you will find it the wisest, best: you are bound to take it so; in this world and in the next, you have no other thing that you can do!

And now if the wild idolatrous men did believe this, and with their fiery hearts lay hold of it to do it, in what form soever it came to them, I say it was well worthy of being believed. In one form or the other, I say it is still the one thing worthy of being believed by all men. Man does hereby become the high-priest of this Temple of a World. He is in harmony with the Decrees of the Author of this World; coöperating with them, not vainly withstanding them : I know, to this day, no better definition of Duty than that same. All that is *right* includes itself in this of co-operating with the real Tendency of the World : you succeed by this (the World's Tendency will succeed), you are good, and in the right course there. *Homoi-ousion*, *Homoousion*, vain logical jangle, then or before or at any time, may jangle itself out, and go whither and how it likes : his is the *thing* it all struggles to mean, if it would mean anything. If it do not succeed in meaning this, it means nothing. Not that Abstractions, logical Propositions, be correctly worded or incorrectly ; but that living concrete Sons of Adam do lay this to heart : that is the important point. Islam devoured all these vain jangling Sects; and I think had right to do so. It was a Reality, direct from the great Heart of Nature once more. Arab idolatries, Syrian formulas, whatsoever was not equally real, had to go up in flame, — mere dead *fuel*, in various senses, for this which was *fire*.

It was during these wild warfarings and strugglings, especially after the Flight to[1] Mecca, that Mahomet dictated at intervals his Sacred Book, which they name *Koran* or *Reading*, 'Thing to be read.' This is the Work he and his disciples made so much of, asking all the world, Is not that a miracle? The Mahometans regard their Koran with a reverence which few Christians pay even to their Bible. It is admitted everywhere as the standard of all law and all practice; the thing to be gone-upon in speculation and life : the message sent direct out of Heaven, which this Earth

[1] Obviously a mere slip. See p. 83.

has to conform to, and walk by ; the thing to be read.
Their Judges decide by it; all Moslem are bound to
study it, seek in it for the light of their life. They
have mosques where it is all read daily ; thirty relays
of priests take it up in succession, get through the
whole each day. There, for twelve-hundred years, has
the voice of this Book, at all moments, kept sounding
through the ears and the hearts of so many men. We
hear of Mahometan Doctors that had read it seventy-
thousand times !

Very curious : if one sought for ‘ discrepancies of
national taste,’ here surely were the most eminent
instance of that ! We also can read the Koran ; our
Translation of it, by Sale, is known to be a very fair
one. I must say, it is as toilsome reading as I ever
undertook. A wearisome confused jumble, crude, incondite;[1] endless iterations, long-windedness, entanglement ; most crude, incondite ; — insupportable stupidity, in short ! Nothing but a sense of duty could carry
any European through the Koran. We read in it, as
we might in the State-Paper Office, unreadable masses
of lumber, that perhaps we may get some glimpses of
a remarkable man. It is true we have it under disadvantages : the Arabs see more method in it than we
Mahomet's followers found the Koran lying all in
fractions, as it had been written-down at first promulgation ; much of it, they say, on shoulder-blades of mutton,[2]
flung pellmell into a chest : and they published it,
without any discoverable order as to time or otherwise ; — merely trying, as would seem, and this not

[1] Disordered, rude.
[2] Also on flat stones, bits of leather, palm leaves, etc.

very strictly, to put the longest chapters first. The
real beginning of it, in that way, lies almost at the end :
for the earliest portions were the shortest. Read in its
historical sequence it perhaps would not be so bad.
Much of it, too, they say, is rhythmic; a kind of wild
chanting song, in the original. This may be a great
point; much perhaps has been lost in the Translation
here. Yet with every allowance, one feels it difficult to
see how any mortal ever could consider this Koran as
a Book written in Heaven, too good for the Earth; as
a well-written book, or indeed as a *book* at all; and
not a bewildered rhapsody; *written*, so far as writing
goes, as badly as almost any book ever was! So much
for national discrepancies, and the standard of taste.

Yet I should say, it was not unintelligible how the
Arabs might so love it. When once you get this confused coil of a Koran fairly off your hands, and have
it behind you at a distance, the essential type of it
begins to disclose itself; and in this there is a merit
quite other than the literary one. If a book come
from the heart, it will contrive to reach other hearts ;
all art and authorcraft are of small amount to that.
One would say the primary character of the Koran is
this of its *genuineness*, of its being a *bona-fide* book.
Prideaux,[1] I know, and others have represented it as
a mere bundle of juggleries; chapter after chapter
got-up to excuse and varnish the author's successive
sins, forward his ambitions and quackeries : but really
it is time to dismiss all that. I do not assert Ma-

---

[1] English clergyman and scholar (1648–1724). A most vigorous exponent of the "impostor hypothesis," in *The True Nature
of Imposture fully Displayed in the Life of Mahomet* (1697).

homet's continual sincerity: who is continually sincere? But I confess I can make nothing of the critic, in
these times, who would accuse him of deceit *prepense ;*
of conscious deceit generally, or perhaps at all ; — still
more, of living in a mere element of conscious deceit,
and writing this Koran as a forger and juggler would
have done! Every candid eye, I think, will read the
Koran far otherwise than so. It is the confused fer-
ment of a great rude human soul ; rude, untutored,
that cannot even read ; but fervent, earnest, struggling vehemently to utter itself in words. With a
kind of breathless intensity he strives to utter himself ; the thoughts crowd on him pellmell : for very
multitude of things to say, he can get nothing said.
The meaning that is in him shapes itself into no form
of composition, is stated in no sequence, method,
or coherence ; — they are not *shaped* at all, these
thoughts of his ; flung-out unshaped, as they struggle
and tumble there, in their chaotic inarticulate state.
We said 'stupid :' yet natural stupidity is by no
means the character of Mahomet's Book ; it is natural
uncultivation rather. The man has not studied speaking ; in the haste and pressure of continual fighting,
has not time to mature himself into fit speech. The
panting breathless haste and vehemence of a man
struggling in the thick of battle for life and salvation ;
this is the mood he is in! A headlong haste ; for very
magnitude of meaning, he cannot get himself articulated into words. The successive utterances of a soul
in that mood, coloured by the various vicissitudes of
three-and-twenty years ; now well uttered, now worse :
this is the Koran.

For we are to consider Mahomet, through these three-and-twenty years, as the centre of a world wholly in conflict. Battles with the Koreish and Heathen, quarrels among his own people, backslidings of his own wild heart; all this kept him in a perpetual whirl, his soul knowing rest no more. In wakeful nights, as one may fancy, the wild soul of the man, tossing amid these vortices, would hail any light of a decision for them as a veritable light from Heaven ; *any* making-up of his mind, so blessed, indispensable for him there, would seem the inspiration of a Gabriel. Forger and juggler ? No, no ! This great fiery heart, seething, simmering like a great furnace of thoughts, was not a juggler's. His Life was a Fact to him; this God's Universe an awful Fact and Reality. He has faults enough. The man was an uncultured semi-barbarous Son of Nature, much of the Bedouin still clinging to him : we must take him for that. But for a wretched Simulacrum, a hungry Impostor without eyes or heart, practising for a mess of pottage such blasphemous swindlery, forgery of celestial documents, continual high-treason against his Maker and Self, we will not and cannot take him.

Sincerity, in all senses, seems to me the merit of the Koran ; what had rendered it precious to the wild Arab men. It is, after all, the first and last merit in a book ; gives rise to merits of all kinds, — nay, at bottom, it alone can give rise to merit of any kind. Curiously, through these incondite masses of tradition, vituperation, complaint, ejaculation in the Koran, a vein of true direct insight, of what we might almost call poetry, is found straggling. The body of the Book is

made-up of mere tradition, and as it were vehement
enthusiastic extempore preaching. He returns forever
to the old stories of the Prophets as they went current
in the Arab memory: how Prophet after Prophet,
the Prophet Abraham, the Prophet Hud, the Prophet
Moses, Christian and other real and fabulous Prophets,
had come to this Tribe and to that, warning men of
their sin; and been received by them even as he
Mahomet was, — which is a great solace to him. These
things he repeats ten, perhaps twenty times; again
and ever again, with wearisome iteration; has never
done repeating them. A brave Samuel Johnson, in
his forlorn garret, might con-over the Biographies of
Authors in that way! This is the great staple of the
Koran. But curiously, through all this, comes ever
and anon some glance as of the real thinker and seer.
He has actually an eye for the world, this Mahomet:
with a certain directness and rugged vigour, he brings
home still, to our heart, the thing his own heart has
been opened to. I make but little of his praises of
Allah, which many praise; they are borrowed I suppose
mainly from the Hebrew, at least they are far surpassed
there. But the eye that flashes direct into the heart
of things, and *sees* the truth of them; this is to me a
highly interesting object. Great Nature's own gift;
which she bestows on all; but which only one in the
thousand does not cast sorrowfully away: it is what
I call sincerity of vision; the test of a sincere heart.

Mahomet can work no miracles; he often answers
impatiently: I can work no miracles. I? 'I am a
Public Preacher;'[1] appointed to preach this doctrine

---

[1] Mahomet always declared that it was his sole divine com-
mission to preach the oneness of God.

to all creatures. Yet the world, as we can see, had
really from of old been all one great miracle to him.
Look over the world, says he; is it not wonderful, the
work of Allah; wholly 'a sign to you,' if your eyes
were open! This Earth, God made it for you; 'appointed paths in it;' you can live in it, go to and fro
on it. — The clouds in the dry country of Arabia, to
Mahomet they are very wonderful: Great clouds, he
says, born in the deep bosom of the Upper Immensity,
where do they come from! They hang there, the great
black monsters; pour-down their rain-deluges 'to revive a dead earth,' and grass springs, and 'tall leafy
palm-trees with their date-clusters hanging round. Is
not that a sign?' Your cattle too, — Allah made
them; serviceable dumb creatures; they change the
grass into milk; you have your clothing from them,
very strange creatures; they come ranking home at
evening-time, 'and,' adds he, 'and are a credit to
you!' Ships also, — he talks often about ships: Huge
moving mountains, they spread-out their cloth wings,
go bounding through the water there, Heaven's wind
driving them; anon they lie motionless, God has
withdrawn the wind, they lie dead, and cannot stir!
Miracles? cries he: What miracle would you have?
Are not you yourselves there? God made *you*, 'shaped
you out of a little clay.' Ye were small once; a few
years ago ye were not at all. Ye have beauty, strength,
thoughts, 'ye have compassion on one another.' Old
age comes-on you, and gray hairs; your strength fades
into feebleness; ye sink down, and again are not.
'Ye have compassion on one another:' this struck me
much: Allah might have made you having no compas-

sion on one another, — how had it been then ! This is
a great direct thought, a glance at first-hand into the
very fact of things. Rude vestiges of poetic genius,
of whatsoever is best and truest, are visible in this
man. A strong untutored intellect; eyesight, heart:
a strong wild man, — might have shaped himself into
Poet, King, Priest, any kind of Hero.

To his eyes it is forever clear that this world wholly
is miraculous. He sees what, as we said once before,
all great thinkers, the rude Scandinavians themselves,
in one way or other, have contrived to see : That this
so solid-looking material world is, at bottom, in very
deed, Nothing; is a visual and tactual Manifestation
of God's power and presence, — a shadow hung-out
by Him, on the bosom of the void Infinite; nothing
more. The mountains, he says, these great rock-mountains, they shall dissipate themselves 'like clouds ;'
melt into the Blue as clouds do, and not be ! He figures the Earth, in the Arab fashion, Sale tells us, as
an immense Plain or flat Plate of ground, the mountains are set on that to *steady* it. At the Last Day
they shall disappear 'like clouds ;' the whole Earth
shall go spinning, whirl itself off into wreck, and as
dust and vapour vanish in the Inane. Allah with-
draws his hand from it, and it ceases to be. The universal empire of Allah, presence everywhere of an unspeakable Power, a Splendour, and a Terror not to be
named, as the true force, essence and reality, in all
things whatsoever, was continually clear to this man.
What a modern talks-of by the name, Forces of Nature, Laws of Nature ; and does not figure as a divine
thing ; not even as one thing at all, but as a set of

things, undivine enough, — saleable, curious, good for
propelling steamships! With our Sciences and Cyclo-
pædias, we are apt to forget the *divineness*, in those
laboratories of ours. We ought not to forget it! That
once well forgotten, I know not what else were worth
remembering. Most sciences, I think, were then a very
dead thing; withered, contentious, empty; — a thistle
in late autumn. The best science, without this, is but
as the dead *timber;* it is not the growing tree and
forest, — which gives ever-new timber, among other
things! Man cannot *know* either, unless he can *worship* in some way. His knowledge is a pedantry, and
dead thistle, otherwise.

Much has been said and written about the sensuality of Mahomet's Religion; more than was just. The
indulgences, criminal to us, which he permitted, were
not of his appointment; he found them practised,
unquestioned from immemorial time in Arabia; what
he did was to curtail them, restrict them, not on one
but on many sides. His Religion is not an easy one:
with rigorous fasts, lavations,[1] strict complex formulas,
prayers five times a day, and abstinence from wine,[2]
it did not 'succeed by being an easy religion.' As if
indeed any religion, or cause holding of religion, could
succeed by that! It is a calumny on men to say that
they are roused to heroic action by ease, hope of pleasure, recompense, — sugar-plums of any kind, in this
world or the next! In the meanest mortal there lies

---

[1] Purification, of both body and clothes, before any religious
act.

[2] Also pilgrimages to Mecca, and the giving of alms (see p.
101).

something nobler. The poor swearing soldier, hired to be shot, has his 'honour of a soldier,' different from drill-regulations and the shilling a day. It is not to taste sweet things, but to do noble and true things, and vindicate himself under God's Heaven as a god-made Man, that the poorest son of Adam dimly longs. Show him the way of doing that, the dullest daydrudge kindles into a hero. They wrong man greatly who say he is to be seduced by ease. Difficulty, abnegation, martyrdom, death are the *allurements* that act on the heart of man. Kindle the inner genial life of him, you have a flame that burns-up all lower considerations. Not happiness, but something higher : one sees this even in the frivolous classes, with their ' point of honour' and the like. Not by flattering our appetites ; no, by awakening the Heroic that slumbers in every heart, can any Religion gain followers.

Mahomet himself, after all that can be said about him, was not a sensual man. We shall err widely if we consider this man as a common voluptuary, intent mainly on base enjoyments, — nay on enjoyments of any kind. His household was of the frugalest; his common diet barley-bread and water: sometimes for months there was not a fire once lighted on his hearth. They record with just pride that he would mend his own shoes, patch his own cloak. A poor, hard-toiling, ill-provided man ; careless of what vulgar men toil for. Not a bad man, I should say ; something better in him than *hunger* of any sort, — or these wild Arab men, fighting and jostling three-and-twenty years at his hand, in close contact with him always, would not have reverenced him so ! They were wild men, burst

ing ever and anon into quarrel, into all kinds of fierce
sincerity ; without right worth and manhood, no man
could have commanded them. They called him Prophet, you say ? Why, he stood there face to face with
them ; bare, not enshrined in any mystery ; visibly
clouting his own cloak, cobbling his own shoes ; fighting, counselling, ordering in the midst of them : they
must have seen what kind of a man he *was*, let him be
called what you like ! No emperor with his tiaras was
obeyed as this man in a cloak of his own clouting. During three-and-twenty years of rough actual trial. I find
something of a veritable Hero necessary for that, of
itself.

His last words are a prayer ; broken ejaculations of
a heart struggling-up, in trembling hope, towards its
Maker. We cannot say that his religion made him
worse ; it made him better ; good, not bad. Generous
things are recorded of him : when he lost his Daughter, the thing he answered is, in his own dialect, everyway sincere, and yet equivalent to that of Christians,
'The Lord giveth, and the Lord taketh away ; blessed
be the name of the Lord.' He answered in like manner of Seid, his emancipated well-beloved Slave, the
second of the believers. Seid had fallen in the war of Tabûc,[1] the first of Mahomet's fightings with the Greeks.
Mahomet said, It was well ; Seid had done his Master's work, Seid had now gone to his Master : it was
all well with Seid. Yet Seid's daughter found him
weeping over the body ; — the old gray-haired man
melting in tears ! " What do I see ? " said she. —
" You see a friend weeping over his friend." — He

[1] In the year 630. Tabûc is a valley in Arabia.

went out for the last time into the mosque, two days
before his death ; asked, If he had injured any man ?
Let his own back bear the stripes. If he owed any
man ? A voice answered, " Yes, me three drachms,"
borrowed on such an occasion. Mahomet ordered them
to be paid : " Better be in shame now," said he, " than
at the Day of Judgment." — You remember Kadijah,
and the " No, by Allah ! " Traits of that kind show
us the genuine man, the brother of us all, brought
visible through twelve centuries, — the veritable Son
of our common Mother.

Withal I like Mahomet for his total freedom from
cant. He is a rough self-helping son of the wilderness ;
does not pretend to be what he is not. There is no osten-
tatious pride in him ; but neither does he go much
upon humility : he is there as he can be, in cloak and
shoes of his own clouting ; speaks plainly to all manner of Persian Kings, Greek Emperors, what it is they
are bound to do ; knows well enough, about himself,
' the respect due unto thee.' In a life-and-death war
with Bedouins, cruel things could not fail; but neither
are acts of mercy, of noble natural pity and generosity wanting. Mahomet makes no apology for the one,
no boast of the other. They were each the free dictate
of his heart; each called-for, there and then. Not a
mealy-mouthed man ! A candid ferocity, if the case
call for it, is in him ; he does not mince matters ! The
War of Tabûc is a thing he often speaks of : his men
refused, many of them, to march on that occasion ;
pleaded the heat of the weather, the harvest, and so
forth ; he can never forget that. Your harvest ? It
lasts for a day. What will become of your harvest

LIBRARY OF

Western Union College

LE MARS, IOWA

through all Eternity? Hot weather? Yes, it was hot;
'but Hell will be hotter!' Sometimes a rough sar-
casm turns-up: He says to the unbelievers, Ye shall
have the just measure of your deeds at that Great
Day. They will be weighed-out to you; ye shall not
have short weight! — Everywhere he fixes the matter
in his eye; he *sees* it: his heart, now and then, is as
if struck dumb by the greatness of it. 'Assuredly,' he
says: that word, in the Koran, is written-down sometimes as a sentence by itself: 'Assuredly.'

No *Dilettantism* in this Mahomet; it is a business of Reprobation and Salvation with him, of Time
and Eternity: he is in deadly earnest about it!
Dilettantism, hypothesis, speculation, a kind of ama-
teur-search for Truth, toying and coquetting with
Truth: this is the sorest sin. The root of all other
imaginable sins. It consists in the heart and soul of
the man never having been *open* to Truth; — 'living
in a vain show.' Such a man not only utters and produces falsehoods, but *is* himself a falsehood. The rational moral principle, spark of the Divinity, is sunk
deep in him, in quiet paralysis of life-death. The
very falsehoods of Mahomet are truer than the truths
of such a man. He is the insincere man: smooth-
polished, respectable in some times and places;
inoffensive, says nothing harsh to anybody; most
cleanly, — just as carbonic acid is, which is death and
poison.

[1] As Carlyle uses this word, in the sense of dabbling frivo-
lously or carelessly with things that ought to be taken seriously,
it is quite far away from the original sense of dilettante, a
delighter in fine art, etc.

We will not praise Mahomet's moral precepts as always of the superfinest sort; yet it can be said that there is always a tendency to good in them; that they are the true dictates of a heart aiming towards what is just and true. The sublime forgiveness of Christianity, turning of the other cheek when the one has been smitten, is not here: you *are* to revenge yourself, but it is to be in measure, not overmuch, or beyond justice. On the other hand, Islam, like any great Faith, and insight into the essence of man, is a perfect equaliser of men: the soul of one believer outweighs all earthly kingships; all men, according to Islam too, are equal. Mahomet insists not on the propriety of giving alms, but on the necessity of it: he marks-down by law how much you are to give, and it is at your peril if you neglect. The tenth part of a man's annual income, whatever that may be, is the *property* of the poor, of those that are afflicted and need help. Good all this: the natural voice of humanity, of pity and equity dwelling in the heart of this wild Son of Nature speaks *so*.

Mahomet's Paradise is sensual, his Hell sensual: true; in the one and the other there is enough that shocks all spiritual feeling in us. But we are to recollect that the Arabs already had it so; that Mahomet, in whatever he changed of it, softened and diminished all this. The worst sensualities, too, are the work of doctors, followers of his, not his work. In the Koran there is really very little said about the joys of Paradise; they are intimated rather than insisted on. Nor is it forgotten that the highest joys even there shall be spiritual; the pure Presence of

the Highest, this shall infinitely transcend all other
joys. He says, ' Your salutation shall be, Peace.'
Salam, Have Peace!—the thing that all rational
souls long for, and seek, vainly here below, as the one
blessing. ' Ye shall sit on seats, facing one another:
all grudges shall be taken away out of your hearts.'
All grudges! Ye shall love one another freely; for
each of you, in the eyes of his brothers, there will be
Heaven enough!

In reference to this of the sensual Paradise and
Mahomet's sensuality, the sorest chapter of all for us,
there were many things to be said; which it is not
convenient to enter upon here. Two remarks only I
shall make, and therewith leave it to your candour.
The first is furnished me by Goethe; it is a casual
hint of his which seems well worth taking note of. In
one of his Delineations, in *Meister's Travels* it is, the
hero comes-upon a Society of men with very strange
ways, one of which was this: " We require," says the
Master, " that each of our people shall restrict himself
in one direction," shall go right against his desire in
one matter, and *make* himself do the thing he does
not wish, " should we allow him the greater latitude on
all other sides." There seems to me a great justness
in this. Enjoying things which are pleasant; that
is not the evil: it is the reducing of our moral self to
slavery by them that is. Let a man assert withal that
he is king over his habitudes; that he could and
would shake them off, on cause shown: this is an excellent law. The Month Ramadhan for the Moslem,
much in Mahomet's Religion, much in his own Life,
bears in that direction; if not by forethought, or clear

purpose of moral improvement on his part, then by a certain healthy manful instinct, which is as good.

But there is another thing to be said about the Mahometan Heaven and Hell. This namely, that, however gross and material they may be, they are an emblem of an everlasting truth, not always so well remembered elsewhere. That gross sensual Paradise of his; that horrible flaming Hell; the great enormous Day of Judgment he perpetually insists on: what is all this but a rude shadow, in the rude Bedouin imagination, of that grand spiritual Fact, and Beginning of Facts, which it is ill for us too if we do not all know and feel: the Infinite Nature of Duty? That man's actions here are of *infinite* moment to him, and never die or end at all; that man, with his little life, reaches upwards high as Heaven, downwards low as Hell, and in his threescore years of Time holds an Eternity fearfully and wonderfully hidden: all this had burnt itself, as in flame-characters, into the wild Arab soul. As in flame and lightning, it stands written there; awful, unspeakable, ever present to him. With bursting earnestness, with a fierce savage sincerity, half-articulating, not able to articulate, he strives to speak it, bodies it forth in that Heaven and that Hell. Bodied forth in what way you will, it is the first of all truths. It is venerable under all embodiments. What is the chief end of man here below? Mahomet has answered this question, in a way that might put some of *us* to shame! He does not, like a Bentham,[1] a Paley,[2] take Right and Wrong, and cal-

---

[1] Utilitarian philosopher (1748–1832).

[2] English clergyman (1743–1805), expounder of utilitarian morals.

culate the profit and loss, ultimate pleasure of the one
and of the other; and summing all up by addition and
subtraction into a net result, ask you, Whether on the
whole the Right does not preponderate considerably?
No; it is not *better* to do the one than the other; the
one is to the other as life is to death, — as Heaven is to
Hell. The one must in nowise be done, the other in nowise left undone. You shall not measure them; they are
incommensurable: the one is death eternal to a man,
the other is life eternal. Benthamee Utility, virtue by
Profit and Loss; [1] reducing this God's-world to a dead
brute Steam-engine, the infinite celestial Soul of Man
to a kind of Hay-balance for weighing hay and thistles
on, pleasures and pains on: — If you ask me which
gives, Mahomet or they, the beggarlier and falser view
of Man and his Destinies in this Universe, I will answer, It is not Mahomet! — —

On the whole, we will repeat that this Religion of Mahomet's is a kind of Christianity; has a genuine element of what is spiritually highest looking through it,
not to be hidden by all its imperfections. The Scandinavian God *Wish*, the god of all rude men, — this has
been enlarged into a Heaven by Mahomet; but a
Heaven symbolical of sacred Duty, and to be earned
by faith and welldoing, by valiant action and a divine
patience which is still more valiant. It is Scandinavian
Paganism, and a truly celestial element superadded to
that. Call it not false; look not at the falsehood of it,

---

[1] "Utility the test and measure of virtue," "the greatest
happiness of the greatest number," are phrases of Benthamee
utility. One of Bentham's books is *The Theory of Penalties and
Rewards* (1811).

look at the truth of it. For these twelve centuries, it has been the religion and life-guidance of the fifth part of the whole kindred of Mankind. Above all things, it has been a religion heartily *believed*. These Arabs believe their religion, and try to live by it! No Christians, since the early ages, or only perhaps the English Puritans in modern times, have ever stood by their Faith as the Moslem do by theirs,—believing it wholly, fronting Time with it, and Eternity with it. This night the watchman on the streets of Cairo when he cries, "Who goes?" will hear from the passenger, along with his answer, "There is no God but God." *Allah akbar, Islam*, sounds through the souls, and whole daily existence, of these dusky millions. Zealous missionaries preach it abroad among Malays, black Papuans, brutal Idolaters;—displacing what is worse, nothing that is better or good.

To the Arab Nation it was as a birth from darkness into light; Arabia first became alive by means of it. A poor shepherd people, roaming unnoticed in its deserts since the creation of the world : a Hero-Prophet was sent down to them with a word they could believe : see, the unnoticed becomes world-notable, the small has grown world-great; within one century afterwards, Arabia is at Grenada on this hand, at Delhi on that; — glancing in valour and splendour and the light of genius, Arabia shines through long ages over a great section of the world. Belief is great, life-giving. The history of a Nation becomes fruitful, soul-elevating, great, so soon as it believes. These Arabs, the man Mahomet, and that one century,—is it not as if a spark had fallen, one spark, on a world of what seemed black unnoticeable sand; but lo, the sand proves explosive powder, blazes heaven-high from Delhi to Grenada! I said, the Great Man was always as lightning out of Heaven; the rest of men waited for him like fuel, and then they too would flame.

LECTURE III

THE Hero as Divinity, the Hero as Prophet, are productions of old ages; not to be repeated in the new.
They presuppose a certain rudeness of conception,
which the progress of mere scientific knowledge puts
an end to. There needs to be, as it were, a world
vacant, or almost vacant of scientific forms, if men in
their loving wonder are to fancy their fellow-man either
a god or one speaking with the voice of a god. Divinity and Prophet are past. We are now to see our Hero
in the less ambitious, but also less questionable, character of Poet; a character which does not pass. The
Poet is a heroic figure belonging to all ages; whom
all ages possess, when once he is produced, whom the
newest age as the oldest may produce; — and will produce, always when Nature pleases. Let Nature send a
Hero-soul; in no age is it other than possible that he
may be shaped into a Poet.

Hero, Prophet, Poet, — many different names, in
different times and places, do we give to Great Men;
according to varieties we note in them, according to
the sphere in which they have displayed themselves!
We might give many more names, on this same principle. I will remark again, however, as a fact not

unimportant to be understood, that the different *sphere*
constitutes the grand origin of such distinction; that
the Hero can be Poet, Prophet, King, Priest or what
you will, according to the kind of world he finds himself born into. I confess, I have no notion of a truly
great man that could not be *all* sorts of men. The
Poet who could merely sit on a chair, and compose stanzas, would never make a stanza worth much. He could
not sing the Heroic warrior, unless he himself were at
least a Heroic warrior too. I fancy there is in him the
Politician, the Thinker, Legislator, Philósopher; — in
one or the other degree, he could have been, he is all
these. So too I cannot understand how a Mirabeau,
with that great glowing heart, with the fire that was
in it, with the bursting tears that were in it, could not
have written verses, tragedies, poems, and touched all
hearts in that way, had his course of life and education
led him thitherward. The grand fundamental character is that of Great Man; that the man be great.
Napoleon has words in him which are like Austerlitz
Battles.[1] Louis Fourteenth's[2] Marshals are a kind of
poetical men withal; the things Turenne[3] says are full
of sagacity and geniality, like sayings of Samuel Johnson. The great heart, the clear deep-seeing eye: there
it lies; no man whatever, in what province soever, can
prosper at all without these. Petrarch and Boccaccio[4]

---

[1] See p. 333, n. 4.   [2] See p. 255, n. 1.

[3] 1611–1675; France's greatest general except Napoleon.

[4] The chief initiators of the revival of classical learning in the
fourteenth century. Boccaccio (1313–1375), best known by his
Decameron, was the author of the earliest Life of Dante. Petrarch (or Petrarca, 1304–1374), important as the first of modern

did diplomatic messages, it seems, quite well: one can easily believe it; they had done things a little harder than these! Burns, a gifted song-writer, might have made a still better Mirabeau. Shakspeare, — one knows not what *he* could not have made, in the supreme degree.

True, there are aptitudes of Nature too. Nature does not make all great men, more than all other men, in the self-same mould. Varieties of aptitude doubtless; but infinitely more of circumstance; and far oftenest it is the *latter* only that are looked to. But it is as with common men in the learning of trades. You take any man, as yet a vague capability of a man, who could be any kind of craftsman; and make him into a smith, a carpenter, a mason: he is then and thenceforth that and nothing else. And if, as Addison complains, you sometimes see a street-porter staggering under his load on spindle-shanks, and near at hand a tailor with the frame of a Samson handling a bit of cloth and small Whitechapel needle, — it cannot be considered that aptitude of Nature alone has been consulted here either! — The Great Man also, to what shall he be bound apprentice? Given your Hero, is he to become Conqueror, King, Philosopher, Poet? It is an inexplicably complex controversial-calculation between the world and him! He will read the world and its laws; the world with its laws will be there to be read. What the world, on *this* matter, shall permit and bid is, as we said, the most important fact about the world. —

classical scholars, is remembered mainly for his sonnets addressed to Laura (cf. *Rom. and Jul.*, II, iv, 41).

Poet and Prophet differ greatly in our loose modern notions of them. In some old languages, again, the titles are synonymous; *Vates* means both Prophet and Poet: and indeed at all times, Prophet and Poet, well understood, have much kindred of meaning. Fundamentally indeed they are still the same; in this most important respect especially, That they have penetrated both of them into the sacred mystery of the Universe; what Goethe calls ' the open secret.' " Which is the great secret? " asks one. — " The *open* secret," — open to all, seen by almost none! That divine mystery, which lies everywhere in all Beings, ' the Divine Idea of the World, that which lies at the bottom of Appearance,' as Fichte [1] styles it; of which all Appearance, from the starry sky to the grass of the field, but especially the Appearance of Man and his work, is but the *vesture*, the embodiment that renders it visible. This divine mystery *is* in all times and in all places; veritably is. In most times and places it is greatly overlooked; and the Universe, definable always in one or the other dialect, as the realised Thought of God, is considered a trivial, inert, commonplace matter, — as if, says the Satirist,[2] it were a dead thing, which some upholsterer had put together! It could do no good, at present, to *speak* much about this; but it is a pity for every one of us if we do not know it, live ever in the knowledge of it.

[1] See p. 217, 218.

[2] Carlyle, as here, has a trick, sometimes perplexing to the beginner, of introducing his own opinions and sayings as if quoted from other (fictitious) persons, — most notable among whom is Professor Diogenes Teufelsdröckh, whose " Life and Opinions " constitute the subject matter of *Sartor Resartus.*

Really a most mournful pity ; — a failure to live at all, if we live otherwise!

But now, I say, whoever may forget this divine mystery, the *Vates*, whether Prophet or Poet, has penetrated into it ; is a man sent hither to make it more impressively known to us. That always is his message ; he is to reveal that to us, — that sacred mystery which he more than others lives ever present with. While others forget it, he knows it ; — I might say, he has been driven to know it ; without consent asked of *him*, he finds himself living in it, bound to live in it. Once more, here is no Hearsay, but a direct Insight and Belief; this man too could not help being a sincere man! Whosoever may live in the shows of things, it is for him a necessity of nature to live in the very fact of things. A man once more, in earnest with the Universe, though all others were but toying with it. He is a *Vates*, first of all, in virtue of being sincere. So far Poet and Prophet, participators in the ' open secret,' are one.

With respect to their distinction again: The *Vates* Prophet, we might say, has seized that sacred mystery rather on the moral side, as Good and Evil, Duty and Prohibition ; the *Vates* Poet on what the Germans call the æsthetic side, as Beautiful, and the like. The one we may call a revealer of what we are to do, the other of what we are to love. But indeed these two provinces run into one another, and cannot be disjoined. The Prophet too has his eye on what we are to love : how else shall he know what it is we are to do? The highest Voice ever heard on this earth said withal, " Consider the lilies of the field ; they toil not,

neither do they spin : yet Solomon in all his glory was
not arrayed like one of these." [1] A glance, that, into
the deepest deep of Beauty. 'The lilies of the field,'
— dressed finer than earthly princes, springing-up
there in the humble furrow-field ; a beautiful *eye*
looking-out on you, from the great inner Sea of
Beauty ! How could the rude Earth make these if
her Essence, rugged as she looks and is, were not inwardly Beauty ? In this point of view, too, a saying
of Goethe's, which has staggered several, may have
meaning : 'The Beautiful,' he intimates, ' is higher
than the Good ; the Beautiful includes in it the Good.'
The *true* Beautiful ; which however, I have said somewhere, ' differs from the *false* as Heaven does from
Vauxhall ! ' [2] So much for the distinction and identity
of Poet and Prophet. —

In ancient and also in modern periods we find a
few Poets who are accounted perfect ; whom it were
a kind of treason to find fault with. This is noteworthy ; this is right : yet in strictness it is only an
illusion. At bottom, clearly enough, there is no perfect
Poet ! A vein of Poetry exists in the hearts of all men ;
no man is made altogether of Poetry. We are all poets
when we *read* a poem well. The 'imagination that
shudders at the Hell of Dante,' is not that the same
faculty, weaker in degree, as Dante's own ? No one
but Shakspeare can embody, out of *Saxo Grammati-*

---

[1] Sermon on the Mount, Matt. vi, 28–29.
[2] A famous place of amusement in London, on the Thames,
above Westminster, 1661–1859. The *Spectator*, No. 383, " Sir
Roger at Vauxhall," and *Vanity Fair*, vol. i, ch. vi, give glimpses
of the amusements there.

cus, the story of *Hamlet* as Shakspeare did : but every one models some kind of story out of it; every one embodies it better or worse. We need not spend time in defining. Where there is no specific difference, as between round and square, all definition must be more or less arbitrary. A man that has *so* much more of the poetic element developed in him as to have become noticeable, will be called Poet by his neighbours. World-Poets too, those whom we are to take for perfect Poets, are settled by critics in the same way. One who rises *so* far above the general level of Poets will, to such and such critics, seem a Universal Poet; as he ought to do. And yet it is, and must be, an arbitrary distinction. All Poets, all men, have some touches of the Universal; no man is wholly made of that. Most Poets are very soon forgotten : but not the noblest Shakspeare or Homer of them can be remembered *forever ;* — a day comes when he too is not !

Nevertheless, you will say, there must be a difference between true Poetry and true speech not poetical : what is the difference? On this point many things have been written, especially by late German Critics, some of which are not very intelligible at first. They say, for example, that the Poet has an *infinitude* in him; communicates an *Unendlichkeit*, a certain character of 'infinitude,' to whatsoever he delineates. This, though not very precise, yet on so vague a matter is worth remembering : if well meditated, some meaning will gradually be found in it. For my own part, I find considerable meaning in the old vulgar distinction of Poetry being *metrical*, having music in it, being a Song. Truly, if pressed to give a definition, one might say this as soon as anything else: If your delineation be authentically *musical*, musical not in word only, but in heart and substance, in all the thoughts and utterances of it, in the whole conception of it, then it will be poetical; if not, not. — Musical: how much lies in that! A *musical* thought is one spoken by a mind that has penetrated into the inmost heart of the thing; detected the inmost mystery of it, namely the *melody* that lies hidden in it; the inward harmony of coherence which is its soul, whereby it exists, and has a right to be, here in this world. All inmost things, we may say, are melodious; naturally utter themselves in Song. The meaning of Song goes deep. Who is there that, in logical words, can express the effect music has on us? A kind of inarticulate unfathomable speech, which leads us to the edge of the Infinite, and lets us for moments gaze into that!

Nay all speech, even the commonest speech, has something of song in it: not a parish in the world but has its parish-accent; — the rhythm or *tune* to which the people there *sing* what they have to say! Accent is a kind of chanting; all men have accent of their own, — though they only *notice* that of others. Observe too how all passionate language does of itself become musical, — with a finer music than the mere accent; the speech of a man even in zealous anger becomes a chant, a song. All deep things are Song. It seems somehow the very central essence of us, Song; as if all the rest were but wrappages and hulls! The primal element of us; of us, and of all things. The Greeks fabled of Sphere-Harmonies: it was the feeling they had of the inner structure of Nature: that the soul of all her voices and utterances was perfect music. Poetry, therefore, we will call *musical Thought*. The Poet is he who *thinks* in that manner. At bottom, it turns still on power of intellect; it is a man's sincerity and depth of vision that makes him a Poet See deep enough, and you see musically; the heart of Nature *being* everywhere music, if you can only reach it.

The *Vates* Poet, with his melodious Apocalypse of Nature, seems to hold a poor rank among us, in comparison with the *Vates* Prophet; his function, and our esteem of him for his function, alike slight. The Hero taken as Divinity; the Hero taken as Prophet; then next the Hero taken only as Poet: does it not look as if our estimate of the Great Man, epoch after epoch, were continually diminishing? We take him first for a god, then for one god-inspired; and now in the next stage of it, his most miraculous word gains from us only the recognition that he is a Poet, beautiful verse-maker, man of genius, or suchlike! — It looks so; but I persuade myself that intrinsically it is not so. If we consider well, it will perhaps appear that in man still there is the *same* altogether peculiar admiration for the Heroic Gift, by what name soever called, that there at any time was.

I should say, if we do not now reckon a Great Man literally divine, it is that our notions of God, of the supreme unattainable Fountain of Splendour, Wisdom, and Heroism, are ever rising *higher;* not altogether that our reverence for these qualities, as manifested in our like, is getting lower. This is worth taking thought of. Sceptical Dilettantism, the curse of these ages, a

curse which will not last forever, does indeed in this
the highest province of human things, as in all provinces, make sad work; and our reverence for great
men, all crippled, blinded, paralytic as it is, comes-out
in poor plight, hardly recognisable. Men worship the
shows of great men; the most disbelieve that there is
any reality of great men to worship. The dreariest, fatalest faith; believing which, one would literally despair
of human things. Nevertheless look, for example, at
Napoleon! A Corsican lieutenant of artillery; that is
the show of *him:* yet is he not obeyed, *worshipped* after
his sort, as all the Tiaraed and Diademed of the world
put together could not be? High Duchesses, and ostlers
of inns, gather round the Scottish rustic, Burns;—a
strange feeling dwelling in each that they never heard
a man like this; that, on the whole, this is the man!
In the secret heart of these people it still dimly reveals
itself, though there is no accredited way of uttering it
at present, that this rustic, with his black brows and
flashing sun-eyes, and strange words moving laughter
and tears, is of a dignity far beyond all others, incommensurable with all others. Do not we feel it so? But
now, were Dilettantism, Scepticism, Triviality, and all
that sorrowful brood, cast-out of us,—as, by God's
blessing, they shall one day be; were faith in the shows
of things entirely swept-out, replaced by clear faith in
the *things*, so that a man acted on the impulse of that
only, and counted the other non-extant; what a new
livelier feeling towards this Burns were it!

Nay here in these ages, such as they are, have we
not two mere Poets, if not deified, yet we may say
beatified? Shakspeare and Dante are Saints of Poetry;

really, if we will think of it, *canonised*, so that it is
impiety to meddle with them. The unguided instinct
of the world, working across all these perverse impedi-
ments, has arrived at such result. Dante and Shakspeare are a peculiar Two. They dwell apart, in a
kind of royal solitude ; none equal, none second to
them : in the general feeling of the world, a certain
transcendentalism, a glory as of complete perfection,
invests these two. They *are* canonised, though no Pope
or Cardinals took hand in doing it ! Such, in spite of
every perverting influence, in the most unheroic times,
is still our indestructible reverence for heroism. — We
will look a little at these Two, the Poet Dante and the
Poet Shakspeare : what little it is permitted us to say
here of the Hero as Poet will most fitly arrange itself
in that fashion.

Many volumes have been written by way of commentary on Dante and his Book ; yet, on the whole, with
no great result. His Biography is, as it were, irrecov-
erably lost for us. An unimportant, wandering, sorrow-
stricken man, not much note was taken of him while he
lived ; and the most of that has vanished, in the long
space that now intervenes. It is five centuries since he
ceased writing and living here. After all commentaries,
the Book itself is mainly what we know of him. The
Book ; — and one might add that Portrait commonly
attributed to Giotto, [1] which, looking on it, you cannot

---

[1] The most famous artist of his time (1276–1337), friend of
Dante. What portrait Carlyle had in mind here it is impossible
to say with certainty. The only portrait now "commonly attributed to Giotto," was at that time unknown. See add. note.

help inclining to think genuine, whoever did it. To me it is a most touching face; perhaps of all faces that I know, the most so. Lonely there, painted as on vacancy, with the simple laurel wound round it; the deathless sorrow and pain, the known victory which is also deathless; — significant of the whole history of Dante! I think it is the mournfulest face that ever was painted from reality; an altogether tragic, heart-affecting face. There is in it, as a foundation of it, the softness, tenderness, gentle affection as of a child; but all this is as if congealed into sharp contradiction, into abnegation, isolation, proud hopeless pain. A soft ethereal soul looking-out so stern, implacable, grim-trenchant, as from imprisonment of thick-ribbed ice! Withal it is a silent pain too, a silent scornful one: the lip is curled in a kind of godlike disdain of the thing that is eating-out his heart, — as if it were withal a mean insignificant thing, as if he whom it had power to torture and strangle were greater than it. The face of one wholly in protest, and life-long unsur-rendering battle, against the world. Affection all converted into indignation: an implacable indignation; slow, equable, silent, like that of a god! The eye too, it looks-out as in a kind of *surprise*, a kind of inquiry, Why the world was of such a sort? This is Dante: so he looks, this ' voice of ten silent centuries,' and sings us ' his mystic unfathomable song.'

The little that we know of Dante's [1] Life corresponds well enough with this Portrait and this Book. He was born at Florence, in the upper class of society, in the

---

[1] His full name was Durante Alighieri, called Dante "for short."

DANTE ALIGHIERI
The Bargello Portrait

Drawn by Mr. Seymour Kirkup before it was retouched by Marini.

year 1265. His education was the best then going; much school-divinity, Aristotelean logic, some Latin classics, — no inconsiderable insight into certain provinces of things : and Dante, with his earnest intelligent nature, we need not doubt, learned better than most all that was learnable. He has a clear cultivated understanding, and of great subtlety; this best fruit of education he had contrived to realise from these scholastics. He knows accurately and well what lies close to him; but, in such a time, without printed books or free intercourse, he could not know well what was distant : the small clear light, most luminous for what is near, breaks itself into singular *chiaroscuro* striking on what is far off. This was Dante's learning from the schools. In life, he had gone through the usual destinies ; been twice out campaigning as a soldier for the Florentine State, been on embassy; had in his thirty-fifth year, by natural gradation of talent and service, become one of the Chief Magistrates of Florence. He had met in boyhood a certain Beatrice Portinari,[1] a beautiful little girl of his own age and rank, and grown-up thenceforth in partial sight of her, in some distant intercourse with her. All readers know his graceful affecting account of this; and then of their being parted; of her being wedded to

[1] The tradition that Beatrice was of the Portinari family dates from Boccaccio's *Life of Dante*. Modern scholarship is inclined to doubt the authority of that statement, and accordingly of other statements frequently made about her, and even in fact whether " Beatrice " was her real name or a poetical invention of Dante. The story, " graceful, affecting " beyond almost all else in literature, is beautifully told in *La Vita Nuova* (The New Life), Dante's first book.

another, and of her death soon after. She makes a great figure in Dante's Poem; seems to have made a great figure in his life. Of all beings it might seem as if she, held apart from him, far apart at last in the dim Eternity, were the only one he had ever with his whole strength of affection loved. She died: Dante himself was wedded; but it seems not happily, far from happily.[1] I fancy, the rigorous earnest man, with his keen excitabilities, was not altogether easy to make happy.

We will not complain of Dante's miseries: had all gone right with him as he wished it, he might have been Prior,[2] Podestà, or whatsoever they call it, of Florence, well accepted among neighbours, — and the world had wanted one of the most notable words ever spoken or sung. Florence would have had another prosperous Lord Mayor; and the ten dumb centuries continued voiceless, and the ten other listening centuries (for there will be ten of them and more) had no *Divina Commedia* to hear! We will complain of nothing. A nobler destiny was appointed for this Dante; and he, struggling like a man led towards death and crucifixion, could not help fulfilling it. Give *him* the choice of his happiness! He knew not, more than we do, what was really happy, what was really miserable.

[1] Not altogether proven. The only evidence is the statement of the gossiping Boccaccio, and the facts that no mention of his wife occurs in Dante's works, and that she did not accompany him into exile.

[2] He *was* Prior for one term (two months) in 1300, but not Podestà, a higher rank in the Florentine municipal government. See next paragraph.

In Dante's Priorship, the Guelf-Ghibelline, Bianchi-Neri,[1] or some other confused disturbances rose to such a height, that Dante, whose party had seemed the stronger, was with his friends cast unexpectedly forth into banishment; doomed thenceforth to a life of woe and wandering. His property was all confiscated and more; he had the fiercest feeling that it was entirely unjust, nefarious in the sight of God and man. He tried what was in him to get reinstated; tried even by warlike surprisal, with arms in his hand: but it would not do; bad only had become worse. There is a record,[2] I believe, still extant in the Florence Archives, dooming this Dante, wheresoever caught, to be burnt alive. Burnt alive; so it stands, they say: a very curious civic document. Another curious document, some considerable number of years later, is a Letter of Dante's to the Florentine Magistrates, written in answer to a milder proposal of theirs, that he should return on condition of apologising and paying a fine. He answers, with fixed stern pride: " If I cannot return without calling myself guilty, I will never return, *nunquam revertar.*"[3]

[1] The Guelphs and Ghibellines (the words derived from two German family names) in medieval history were the parties respectively of the Pope and the people, and the Emperor and the aristocracy. The Guelph party in Florence, being in the ascendency, became subdivided into Bianchi (Whites), the moderate party, and Neri (Blacks), the violent. The Pope's interference on behalf of the Blacks resulted in the banishment from Florence of the Whites, among whom was Dante (1302).

[2] Dated March 10, 1302, forty days after the sentence of Dante and his fellow Priors to pay fines, upon conviction of various crimes.

[3] Some doubt has been thrown on the authenticity of this letter.

For Dante there was now no home in this world. He wandered from patron to patron, from place to place ; proving, in his own bitter words, ' How hard is the path, *Come è duro calle.*' [1] The wretched are not cheerful company. Dante, poor and banished, with his proud earnest nature, with his moody humours, was not a man to conciliate men. Petrarch reports of him that being at Can della Scala's court, and blamed one day for his gloom and taciturnity, he answered in no courtier-like way. Della Scala [2] stood among his courtiers, with mimes and buffoons (*nebulones ac histriones*) making him heartily merry ; when turning to Dante, he said : " Is it not strange, now, that this poor fool should make himself so entertaining ; while you a wise man sit there day after day, and have nothing to amuse us with at all ? " Dante answered bitterly : " No, not strange ; your Highness is to recollect the Proverb, *Like to Like ;* "— given the amuser, the amusee must also be given ! Such a man, with his proud silent ways, with his sarcasms and sorrows, was not made to succeed at court. By degrees, it came to be evident to him that he had no longer any resting-place, or hope of benefit, in this earth. The earthly world had cast him forth, to wander, wander ; no living heart to love him now ; for his sore miseries there was no solace here.

[1] Thou shalt have proof how savoreth of salt
The bread of others, and how hard a road
The going down and up another's stairs.

Par. XVII, 58–60.

(This and the following quotations are from Longfellow's translation.)

[2] The name of the reigning family of Verona, 1260–1387. Dante's Patron became Lord of Verona in 1312.

The deeper naturally would the Eternal World
impress itself on him; that awful reality over which,
after all, this Time-world, with its Florences and ban-
ishments, only flutters as an unreal shadow. Florence
thou shalt never see : but Hell and Purgatory and
Heaven thou shalt surely see ! What is Florence,
Can della Scala, and the World and Life altogether?
ETERNITY : thither, of a truth, not elsewhither, art
thou and all things bound ! The great soul of Dante,
homeless on earth, made its home more and more in
that awful other world. Naturally his thoughts brooded
on that, as on the one fact important for him. Bodied or bodiless, it is the one fact important for all
men : — but to Dante, in that age, it was bodied in
fixed certainty of scientific shape ; he no more doubted
of that *Malebolge* [1] Pool, that it all lay there with its
gloomy circles, with its *alti guai*,[2] and that he himself
should see it, than we doubt that we should see Constantinople if we went thither. Dante's heart, long
filled with this, brooding over it in speechless thought
and awe, bursts forth at length into ' mystic [3] unfath-

[1] " Evil pouches." The graphic description of the place occurs in *Inf.* XVIII, 1 ff.: —

> There is a place in Hell called Malebolge,
> Wholly of stone and of an iron color,
> As is the circle that around it turns.

[2] " Deep groans," heard by Dante just within the gate of
Hell : —

> There sighs, complaints, and ululations loud
> Resounded through the air without a star,
> Whence I, at the beginning, wept thereat.
> *Inf.* III, 22-24.

[3] No better explanation of the meaning of this word could be
given than is contained in this paragraph.

omable song;' and this his *Divine Comedy*,[1] the
most remarkable of all modern Books, is the result.

It must have been a great solacement to Dante, and
was, as we can see, a proud thought for him at times,
That he, here in exile, could do this work; that no
Florence, nor no man or men, could hinder him from
doing it, or even much help him in doing it. He knew
too, partly, that it was great; the greatest a man
could do. 'If thou follow thy star, *Se tu segui tua
stella*,'[2] — so could the Hero, in his forsakenness, in
his extreme need, still say to himself: " Follow thou
thy star, thou shalt not fail of a glorious haven! "
The labour of writing, we find, and indeed could know
otherwise, was great and painful for him; he says,
This Book, ' which has made me lean for many years.'[3]

---

[1] So entitled because, beginning in trouble and confusion in the
Inferno, it reaches a prosperous and happy issue in the *Paradiso*.

[2] The words of Dante's friend and teacher, Brunetto Latini,
whom he finds in Hell : —

> If thou thy star do follow,
>
> Thou canst not fail thee of a glorious port,
>
> If well I judged in the life beautiful.   *Inf.* xv, 55–57.

He continues with an invective against the Florentines, and
Dante responds with a tender expression of gratitude for what
Latini taught him in life.

[3] If e'er it happen that the Poem Sacred,

> To which both heaven and earth have set their hand,
>
> So that it many a year hath made me lean,

O'ercome the cruelty that bars me out

> From the fair sheepfold, where a lamb I slumbered,
>
> .   .   .   .
>
> Poet will I return, and at my font
>
> Baptismal will I take the laurel crown,
>
> > *Par.* xxv, 1–5, 8, 9.

Comp. last lines with *nunquam revertar*, p. 121.

Ah yes, it was won, all of it, with pain and sore toil,
— not in sport, but in grim earnest. His Book, as
indeed most good Books are, has been written, in
many senses, with his heart's blood. It is his whole
history, this Book. He died after finishing it; not
yet very old, at the age of fifty-six; — broken-hearted
rather, as is said. He lies buried in his death-city
Ravenna: *Hic claudor Dantes patriis extorris ab
oris.* The Florentines begged back his body, in a
century after; the Ravenna people would not give it.
" Here am I Dante laid, shut-out from my native
shores." [1]

I said, Dante's Poem was a Song: it is Tieck [2] who
calls it ' a mystic unfathomable Song; ' and such is
literally the character of it. Coleridge remarks very
pertinently somewhere, that wherever you find a sentence musically worded, of true rhythm and melody
in the words, there is something deep and good in the
meaning too. For body and soul, word and idea, go
strangely together here as everywhere. Song: we said
before, it was the Heroic of Speech! All *old* Poems,
Homer's and the rest, are authentically Songs. I
would say, in strictness, that all right Poems are;
that whatsoever is not *sung* is properly no Poem, but
a piece of Prose cramped into jingling lines, — to the
great injury of the grammar, to the great grief of the
reader, for most part! What we want to get at is the

---

[1] Epitaph long supposed to have been composed by Dante
himself. Dante's remains disappeared from their resting-place
in Ravenna just before they were to be transferred to Florence
in 1519. They were rediscovered accidentally in 1865.

[2] German critic and poet (1773–1853); one of the founders
of the German Romantic School of literature.

thought the man had, if he had any: why should he twist it into jingle, if he *could* speak it out plainly? It is only when the heart of him is rapt into true passion of melody, and the very tones of him, according to Coleridge's remark, become musical by the greatness, depth and music of his thoughts, that we can give him right to rhyme and sing; that we call him a Poet, and listen to him as the Heroic of Speakers, — whose speech *is* Song. Pretenders to this are many; and to an earnest reader, I doubt, it is for most part a very melancholy, not to say an insupportable business, that of reading rhyme! Rhyme that had no inward necessity to be rhymed: — it ought to have told us plainly, without any jingle, what it was aiming at. I would advise all men who *can* speak their thought, not to sing it; to understand that, in a serious time, among serious men, there is no vocation in them for singing it. Precisely as we love the true song, and are charmed by it as by something divine, so shall we hate the false song, and account it a mere wooden noise, a thing hollow, superfluous, altogether an insincere and offensive thing.

I give Dante my highest praise when I say of his *Divine Comedy* that it is, in all senses, genuinely a Song. In the very sound of it there is a *canto fermo;* [1] it proceeds as by a chant. The language, his simple *terza rima*, [2] doubtless helped him in this. One reads

[1] In church music, a "fixed song" (melody, or air) prescribed by authority of the Church to be sung without change, with whatever variations of harmony it might be accompanied.

[2] "Third rime." Dante's verse consists of eleven-syllable lines with two-syllable rimes, alternate lines riming together in groups of three, — aba bcb cdc ded, etc. See add. note.

along naturally with a sort of *lilt*. But I add, that it
could not be otherwise; for the essence and material
of the work are themselves rhythmic. Its depth, and
rapt passion and sincerity, makes it musical; — go
deep enough, there is music everywhere. A true inward symmetry, what one calls an architectural harmony, reigns in it, proportionates it all: architectural;
which also partakes of the character of music. The
three kingdoms, *Inferno, Purgatorio, Paradiso*, look-
out on one another like compartments of a great edifice; a great supernatural world-cathedral, piled-up
there, stern, solemn, awful; Dante's World of Souls!
It is, at bottom, the *sincerest* of all Poems; sincerity,
here too, we find to be the measure of worth. It came
deep out of the author's heart of hearts; and it goes
deep, and through long generations, into ours. The
people of Verona, when they saw him on the streets,
used to say, " *Eccovi l' uom ch' è stato all' Inferno*,
See, there is the man that was in Hell!" Ah yes, he
had been in Hell; — in Hell enough, in long severe
sorrow and struggle; as the like of him is pretty sure
to have been. Commedias that come-out *divine* are not
accomplished otherwise. Thought, true labour of any
kind, highest virtue itself, is it not the daughter of
Pain? Born as out of the black whirlwind; — true
effort, in fact, as of a captive struggling to free himself: that is Thought. In all ways we are ' to become
perfect through *suffering*.' [1] — But, as I say, no work
known to me is so elaborated as this of Dante's. It has

[1] For it became him, for whom are all things, and by whom are
all things, in bringing many sons unto glory, to make the captain
of their salvation perfect through sufferings. Heb. ii, 10.

all been as if molten, in the hottest furnace of his soul.
It had made him ' lean ' for many years. Not the general whole only ; every compartment of it is worked-
out, with intense earnestness, into truth, into clear
visuality. Each answers to the other ; each fits in its
place, like a marble stone accurately hewn and polished. It is the soul of Dante, and in this the soul of
the middle ages, rendered forever rhythmically visible
there. No light task ; a right intense one : but a task
which is *done*.

Perhaps one would say, *intensity*, with the much
that depends on it, is the prevailing character of Dante's
genius. Dante does not come before us as a large catholic mind, rather a narrow, and even sectarian mind :
it is partly the fruit of his age and position, but partly
too of his own nature. His greatness has, in all senses,
concentered itself into fiery emphasis and depth. He
is world-great not because he is world-wide, but because
he is world-deep. Through all objects he pierces as it
were down into the heart of Being. I know nothing so
intense as Dante. Consider, for example, to begin with
the outermost development of his intensity, consider
how he paints. He has a great power of vision ; seizes
the very type of a thing ; presents that and nothing
more. You remember that first view he gets of the
Hall of Dite : [1] *red* pinnacle, redhot cone of iron glowing through the dim immensity of gloom ; — so vivid,
so distinct, visible at once and forever ! It is as an

---

[1] Its mosques already, Master, clearly
Within there in the valley I discern
Vermilion, as if issuing from the fire
They were.   *Inf.* VIII, 70–73.

emblem of the whole genius of Dante. There is a brev-
ity, an abrupt precision in him : Tacitus [1] is not briefer,
more condensed; and then in Dante it seems a natural condensation, spontaneous to the man. One smiting word; and then there is silence, nothing more said.
His silence is more eloquent than words. It is strange
with what a sharp decisive grace he snatches the true
likeness of a matter : cuts into the matter as with a
pen of fire. Plutus, [2] the blustering giant, collapses at
Virgil's rebuke; [3] it is ' as the sails sink, the mast being suddenly broken.' Or that poor Brunetto Latini,
with the *cotto aspetto*, 'face *baked*,' parched brown and
lean; [4] and the ' fiery snow ' that falls on them there,
a ' fiery snow without wind,' slow, deliberate, never-ending! [5] Or the lids of those Tombs; square sarcopha-

---

[1] Latin historian, *c.* 55–117.

[2] The god of riches, jailer of the avaricious and prodigal in
Hell.

> " Be silent, thou accursed wolf;"
>
> . . . .
>
> Even as the sails inflated by the wind
>   Together fall involved when snaps the mast,
>   So fell the cruel monster to the earth.
>
> *Inf.* VII, 8, 13–15.

[4] And I, when he stretched forth his arm to me,
   On his baked aspect fastened so mine eyes,
   That the scorched countenance prevented not
His recognition by my intellect;
   And bowing down my face unto his own,
   I made reply, " Are you here Ser Brunetto ? "
>
> *Inf.* XV, 25–30.

[5] O'er all the sand-waste, with a gradual fall,
   Were raining down dilated flakes of fire,
   As of the snow on Alp without a wind.
>
> *Inf.* XIV, 28–30.

guses, in that silent dim-burning Hall, each with its Soul
in torment ; the lids laid open there ; they are to be
shut at the Day of Judgment, through Eternity.   And
how Farinata rises ; and how Cavalcante falls — at
hearing of his Son, and the past tense '*fue*' *!* [1] The
very movements in Dante have something brief ; swift,
decisive, almost military.   It is of the inmost essence
of his genius, this sort of painting.   The fiery, swift
Italian nature of the man, so silent, passionate, with
its quick abrupt movements, its silent 'pale rages,'
speaks itself in these things.

[1] For flames between the sepulchres were scattered,
  By which they so intensely heated were,
  That iron more so asks not any art.
All of their coverings uplifted were,
  And from them issued forth such dire laments,
  Sooth seemed they of the wretched and tormented.
                                        Inf. ix, 118–123.

"Behold there Farinata who has risen ;
From the waist upwards wholly shalt thou see him."
I had already fixed mine eyes on his,
  And he uprose erect with breast and front
  E'en as if Hell he had in great despite.   *Inf.* x, 32–36.

"Where is my son ? and why is he not with thee ?"
And I to him [Cavalcante]: "I come not of myself ;
  He who is waiting yonder leads me here,
  Whom in disdain perhaps your Guido had."
    .   .   .   .
Upstarting suddenly, he cried out : "How
  Saidst thou, — he had ? Is he not still alive ?
  Does not the sweet light strike upon his eyes ?"
When he became aware of some delay,
  Which I before my answer made, supine
  He fell again and forth appeared no more.
                                  Inf. x, 60–63, 67–72.
Carlyle's memory has substituted '*fue*' =was, for '*ebbe*' = had.

For though this of painting is one of the outermost developments of a man, it comes like all else from the essential faculty of him; it is physiognomical of the whole man. Find a man whose words paint you a likeness, you have found a man worth something; mark his manner of doing it, as very characteristic of him. In the first place, he could not have discerned the object at all, or seen the vital type of it, unless he had, what we may call, *sympathised* with it, — had sympathy in him to bestow on objects. He must have been *sincere* about it too; sincere and sympathetic: a man without worth cannot give you the likeness of any object; he dwells in vague outwardness, fallacy and trivial hearsay, about all objects. And indeed may we not say that intellect altogether expresses itself in this power of discerning what an object is? Whatsoever of faculty a man's mind may have will come out here. Is it even of business, a matter to be done? The gifted man is he who *sees* the essential point, and leaves all the rest aside as surplusage: it is his faculty too, the man of business's faculty, that he discern the true *likeness*, not the false superficial one, of the thing he has got to work in. And how much of *morality* is in the kind of insight we get of anything; 'the eye seeing in all things what it brought with it the faculty of seeing'! To the mean eye all things are trivial, as certainly as to the jaundiced they are yellow. Raphael, the Painters tell us, is the best of all Portrait-painters withal. No most gifted eye can exhaust the significance of any object. In the commonest human face there lies more than Raphael will take-away with him.

Dante's painting is not graphic only, brief, true, and of a vividness as of fire in dark night; taken on the wider scale, it is everyway noble, and the outcome of a great soul. Francesca and her Lover,[1] what qualities in that! A thing woven as out of rainbows, on a ground of eternal black. A small flute-voice of infinite wail speaks there, into our very heart of hearts. A touch of womanhood in it too: *della bella persona, che mi fu tolta;* and how, even in the Pit of woe, it is a solace that *he* will never part from her![2] Saddest tragedy in these *alti guai.* And the racking winds, in that *aer bruno,*[3] whirl them away again, to wail forever! — Strange to think: Dante was the friend of this poor Francesca's father;[4] Francesca herself may have sat upon the Poet's knee, as a

---

[1] Paolo, Francesca da Rimini's lover, had been deceitfully pointed out to her as her future husband, and to him she gave her love. Too late she found out that he had come only as representative of his brother, an ill-appearing cripple, whom her father caused her to marry. The husband, finding the lovers together one day not long after, in a burst of jealous anger slew them both.

[2] Love, that on gentle heart doth swiftly seize,

  Seized this man *for the person beautiful*
  That was ta'en from me, and still the mode offends me.

Love, that exempts no one beloved from loving,

  Seized me with pleasure of this man so strongly,
  That, as thou seest, it doth not yet desert me;

Love has conducted us unto one death;

  Caïna waiteth him who quenched our life!

Inf. v, 100–107.

[3] "Brown air;" used to describe the approach of evening, *Inf.* II, 1. Dante calls the air of this circle of Hell where carnal sinners are punished *aer maligno* and *tenebroso*, v, 86, and VI, 11.

[4] Nephew, say later scholars.

bright innocent little child. Infinite pity,[1] yet also
infinite rigour of law: it is so Nature is made; it is
so Dante discerned that she was made. What a paltry
notion is that of his *Divine Comedy's* being a poor
splenetic impotent terrestrial libel; putting those into
Hell whom he could not be avenged-upon on earth!
I suppose if ever pity, tender as a mother's, was in
the heart of any man, it was in Dante's. But a man
who does not know rigour cannot pity either. His
very pity will be cowardly, egoistic, — sentimentality,
or little better. I know not in the world an affection
equal to that of Dante. It is a tenderness, a trembling, longing, pitying love: like the wail of Æolean
harps, soft, soft; like a child's young heart; — and
then that stern, sore-saddened heart! These longings
of his towards his Beatrice;[2] their meeting together

[1] Francesca having told her story, the canto ends: —

> And all the while one spirit uttered this,
> The other one did weep so, that, for pity,
> I swooned away as if I had been dying,
> And fell, even as a dead body falls.   v, 139–142.

[2] E. g., in *Purg.* XXVII, where Dante, fearing to pass through
the fire, is encouraged by Virgil: —

> " Now look thou, Son,
> 'Twixt Beatrice and thee there is this wall."
> .   .   .   .
> Even thus, my obduracy being softened,
> I turned to my wise Guide, hearing the name
> That in my memory evermore is welling.
> Whereat he wagged his head, and said : " How now ?
> Shall we stay on this side ? " then smiled as one
> Doth at a child who 's vanquished by an apple.
> .   .   .   .

I

in the *Paradiso;* [1] his gazing in her pure transfig‧
ured eyes, [2] her that had been purified by death so
long, separated from him so far : — one likens it to
the song of angels ; it is among the purest utterances
of affection, perhaps the very purest, that ever came
out of a human soul.

For the *intense* Dante is intense in all things ; he
has got into the essence of all. His intellectual in‧
sight as painter, on occasion too as reasoner, is but
the result of all other sorts of intensity. Morally
great, above all, we must call him ; it is the begin‧
ning of all. His scorn, his grief are as transcendent
as his love; — as indeed, what are they but the

> And my sweet Father, to encourage me,
> Discoursing still of Beatrice went on,
> Saying : " Her eyes I seem to see already ! "
> > 35, 36, 40–45, 52–54.

[1] Their first meeting is in the Earthly Paradise, on the top of the
Mountain of Purgatory (*Purg.* xxx), where, although her face is
veiled, Dante's spirit " Of ancient love the mighty influence felt."

[2] So steadfast and attentive were mine eyes
> In satisfying their decennial thirst,
> That all my other senses were extinct,
> And upon this side and on that they had
> Walls of indifference, so the holy smile
> Drew them unto itself with the old net.
> > *Purg.* xxxii, 1–6.

Virgil, who has guided Dante through Hell and Purgatory,
leaves him, for the last third of his journey, to Beatrice, who
is portrayed in the *Paradiso* with constantly increasing beauty
and splendor. Dante abundantly fulfills the promise at the end
of the *Vita Nuova:* "So that if it shall be the pleasure of Him,
through whom all things live, that my life shall continue some‧
what longer, I hope to say of her what never yet was said of
any woman."

inverse or *converse* of his love? '*A Dio spiacenti ed a' nemici sui*, Hateful to God and to the enemies of God:' lofty scorn, unappeasable silent reprobation and aversion; '*Non ragionam di lor*, We will not speak of *them*, look only and pass.' Or think of this; 'They have not the *hope* to die, *Non han speranza di morte*.'[1] One day, it had risen sternly benign on the scathed heart of Dante, that he, wretched, never-resting, worn as he was, would full surely *die;* 'that Destiny itself could not doom him not to die.' Such words are in this man. For rigour, earnestness and depth, he is not to be paralleled in the modern world; to seek his parallel we must go into the Hebrew Bible, and live with the antique Prophets there.

I do not agree with much modern criticism, in greatly preferring the *Inferno* to the two other parts of the Divine *Commedia*. Such preference belongs, I imagine, to our general Byronism of taste, and is like to be a transient feeling. The *Purgatorio* and *Paradiso*, especially the former, one would almost say, is even more excellent than it. It is a noble thing that *Purgatorio*, 'Mountain of Purification;' an emblem of the noblest conception of that age. If Sin is so fatal, and Hell is and must be so rigorous, awful, yet in Repentance too is man purified; Repentance is the grand Christian act. It is beautiful how Dante works it out. The *tremolar dell' onde*, that 'trembling' of

---

[1] The three lines here quoted (*Inf.* III, 63, 51, 46) relate to
    " that caitiff choir
Of Angels, who have not rebellious been,
Nor faithful were to God, but were for self." 37–39.
Carlyle's lively sympathy with Dante's scorn reflects his own uncompromising positiveness.

the ocean-waves, under the first pure gleam of morning,[1] dawning afar on the wandering Two, is as the type of an altered mood. Hope has now dawned; never-dying Hope, if in company still with heavy sorrow. The obscure sojourn of dæmons and reprobate is underfoot; a soft breathing of penitence mounts higher and higher, to the Throne of Mercy itself. " Pray for me," the denizens of that Mount of Pain all say to him. "Tell my Giovanna to pray for me," my daughter Giovanna; " I think her mother loves me no more!"[2] They toil painfully up by that winding steep, 'bent-down like corbels of a building,'[3] some of them, — crushed-together so 'for the sin of pride;' yet nevertheless in years, in ages and æons, they shall have reached the top, which is Heaven's gate, and by Mercy shall have been admitted in. The joy too of all, when one has prevailed;

[1] The dawn was vanquishing the matin hour
   Which fled before it, so that from afar
   I recognized the trembling of the sea.
                              Purg. I, 115–117.

[2] When thou shalt be beyond the waters wide,
   Tell my Giovanna that she pray for me,
   Where answer to the innocent is made.
  I do not think her mother loves me more,
   Since she has laid aside her wimple white,
   Which she, unhappy, needs must wish again.
                              Purg. VIII, 70–72.

[3] As to sustain a ceiling or a roof,
   In place of corbel, oftentimes, a figure
   Is seen to join its knees unto its breast,
  Which makes of the unreal real anguish
   Arise in him who sees it; fashioned thus
   Beheld I those, when I had ta'en good heed.
                              Purg. X, 130–135.

the whole Mountain shakes with joy, and a psalm of praise rises,[1] when one soul has perfected repentance and got its sin and misery left behind! I call all this a noble embodiment of a true noble thought.

But indeed the Three compartments mutually support one another, are indispensable to one another. The *Paradiso*, a kind of inarticulate music to me, is the redeeming side of the *Inferno;* the *Inferno* without it were untrue. All three make-up the true Unseen World, as figured in the Christianity of the Middle Ages; a thing forever memorable, forever true in the essence of it, to all men. It was perhaps delineated in no human soul with such depth of veracity as in this of Dante's; a man *sent* to sing it, to keep it long memorable. Very notable with what brief simplicity he passes out of the every-day reality, into the Invisible one; and in the second or third stanza, we find ourselves in the World of Spirits; and dwell there, as among things palpable, indubitable! To Dante they *were* so; the real world, as it is called, and its facts, was but the threshold to an infinitely higher Fact of a World. At bottom, the one was as *preter*natural as the other. Has not each man a soul? He will not only be a spirit, but is one. To the earnest Dante it is all one visible Fact; he believes it, sees it; is the Poet of it in virtue of that. Sincerity, I say again, is the saving merit, now as always.

[1] *Purg.* xx (124-141) tells of the occurrence; xxi gives the explanation : —

> It trembles here, whenever any soul
> Feels itself pure, so that it soars, or moves
> To mount aloft, and such a cry attends it. 58-60.

Dante's Hell, Purgatory, Paradise, are a symbol
withal, an emblematic representation of his Belief
about this Universe : — some Critic in a future age,
like those Scandinavian ones the other day, who has
ceased altogether to think as Dante did, may find this
too all an ' Allegory,' perhaps an idle Allegory ! It is
a sublime embodiment, or sublimest, of the soul of
Christianity. It expresses, as in huge worldwide architectural emblems, how the Christian Dante felt Good
and Evil to be the two polar elements of this Creation,
on which it all turns ; that these two differ not by
preferability of one to the other, but by incompatibility
absolute and infinite ; that the one is excellent and
high as light and Heaven, the other hideous, black as
Gehenna and the Pit of Hell ! Everlasting Justice,
yet with Penitence, with everlasting Pity, — all Christianism, as Dante and the Middle Ages had it, is
emblemed here. Emblemed : and yet, as I urged the
other day, with what entire truth of purpose ; how
unconscious of any embleming ! Hell, Purgatory, Paradise : these things were not fashioned as emblems ;
was there, in our Modern European Mind, any thought
at all of their being emblems ! Were they not indubitable awful facts ; the whole heart of man taking them
for practically true, all Nature everywhere confirming
them ? So is it always in these things. Men do not
believe an Allegory. The future Critic, whatever his
new thought may be, who considers this of Dante to
have been all got-up as an Allegory, will commit one
sore mistake ! — Paganism we recognised as a veracious
expression of the earnest awe-struck feeling of man
towards the Universe ; veracious, true once, and still

not without worth for us. But mark here the difference of Paganism and Christianism; one great difference. Paganism emblemed chiefly the Operations of Nature; the destinies, efforts, combinations, vicissitudes of things and men in this world; Christianism emblemed the Law of Human Duty, the Moral Law of Man. One was for the sensuous nature: a rude helpless utterance of the *first* Thought of men, — the chief recognised virtue, Courage, Superiority to Fear. The other was not for the sensuous nature, but for the moral. What a progress is here, if in that one respect only! —

And so in this Dante, as we said, had ten silent centuries, in a very strange way, found a voice. The *Divina Commedia* is of Dante's writing; yet in truth *it* belongs to ten Christian centuries, only the finishing of it is Dante's. So always. The craftsman there, the smith with that metal of his, with these tools, with these cunning methods, — how little of all he does is properly *his* work! All past inventive men work there with him; — as indeed with all of us, in all things. Dante is the spokesman of the Middle Ages; the Thought they lived by stands here, in everlasting music. These sublime ideas of his, terrible and beautiful, are the fruit of the Christian Meditation of all the good men who had gone before him. Precious they; but also is not he precious? Much, had not he spoken, would have been dumb; not dead, yet living voiceless.

On the whole, is it not an utterance, this mystic Song, at once of one of the greatest human souls, and of the highest thing that Europe had hitherto realised

for itself? Christianism, as Dante sings it, is another
than Paganism in the rude Norse mind; another than
'Bastard Christianism' half-articulately spoken in the
Arab Desert, seven-hundred years before!—The noble
idea made *real* hitherto among men, is sung, and
emblemed-forth abidingly, by one of the noblest men.
In the one sense and in the other, are we not right
glad to possess it? As I calculate, it may last yet for
long thousands of years. For the thing that is uttered
from the inmost parts of a man's soul, differs altogether
from what is uttered by the outer part. The outer
is of the day, under the empire of mode; the outer
passes away, in swift endless changes; the inmost is
the same yesterday, today and forever. True souls,
in all generations of the world, who look on this Dante,
will find a brotherhood in him; the deep sincerity of
his thoughts, his woes and hopes, will speak likewise
to their sincerity; they will feel that this Dante too
was a brother. Napoleon in Saint-Helena is charmed
with the genial veracity of old Homer. The oldest Hebrew Prophet, under a vesture the most diverse from
ours, does yet, because he speaks from the heart of
man, speak to all men's hearts. It is the one sole
secret of continuing long memorable. Dante, for depth
of sincerity, is like an antique Prophet too; his words,
like theirs, come from his very heart. One need not
wonder if it were predicted that his Poem might be
the most enduring thing our Europe has yet made;
for nothing so endures as a truly spoken word. All
cathedrals, pontificalities, brass and stone, and outer
arrangement never so lasting, are brief in comparison
to an unfathomable heart-song like this: one feels as

if it might survive, still of importance to men, when these had all sunk into new irrecognisable combinations, and had ceased individually to be. Europe has made much ; great cities, great empires, encyclopædias, creeds, bodies of opinion and practice: but it has made little of the class of Dante's Thought. Homer yet *is*, veritably present face to face with every open soul of us ; and Greece, where is *it?* Desolate for thousands of years ; away, vanished ; a bewildered heap of stones and rubbish, the life and existence of it all gone. Like a dream ; like the dust of King Agamemnon ! Greece was ; Greece, except in the *words* it spoke, is not.

The uses of this Dante? We will not say much about his ' uses.' A human soul who has once got into that primal element of *Song*, and sung-forth fitly somewhat therefrom, has worked in the *depths* of our existence ; feeding through long times the life-*roots* of all excellent human things whatsoever, — in a way that ' utilities ' will not succeed well in calculating ! We will not estimate the Sun by the quantity of gas-light it saves us ; Dante shall be invaluable, or of no value. One remark I may make: the contrast in this respect between the Hero-Poet and the Hero-Prophet. In a hundred years, Mahomet, as we saw, had his Arabians at Grenada and at Delhi ; Dante's Italians seem to be yet very much where they were. Shall we say, then, Dante's effect on the world was small in comparison ? Not so; his arena is far more restricted; but also it is far nobler, clearer ; — perhaps not less but more important. Mahomet speaks to great masses of men, in the coarse dialect adapted to such ; a dialect filled with inconsistencies, crudities, follies: on the great masses alone can he act, and there with good and with evil strangely blended. Dante speaks to the noble, the pure and great, in all times and places. Neither does he grow obsolete, as the other does. Dante burns as a pure star, fixed there in the firmament, at which the great and the high of all ages kindle themselves: he is the possession of all the chosen of the world for un-counted time. Dante, one calculates, may long survive Mahomet. In this way the balance may be made straight again.

But, at any rate, it is not by what is called their effect on the world, by what *we* can judge of their ef-fect there, that a man and his work are measured. Effect? Influence? Utility? Let a man *do* his work; the fruit of it is the care of Another than he. It will grow its own fruit; and whether embodied in Caliph Thrones and Arabian Conquests, so that it 'fills all Morning and Evening Newspapers,' and all Histories, which are a kind of distilled Newspapers; or not em-bodied so at all;—what matters that? That is not the real fruit of it! The Arabian Caliph, in so far only as he did something, was something. If the great Cause of Man, and Man's work in God's Earth, got no furtherance from the Arabian Caliph, then no mat-ter how many scimetars he drew, how many gold pias-ters pocketed, and what uproar and blaring he made in this world,—*he* was but a loud-sounding inanity and futility; at bottom, he *was* not at all. Let us honour the great empire of *Silence*, once more! The boundless treasury which we do *not* jingle in our pockets, or count up and present before men! It is perhaps, of all things,

the usefulest for each of us to do, in these loud
times. —— ——

As Dante, the Italian man, was sent into our world
to embody musically the Religion of the Middle Ages,
the Religion of our Modern Europe, its Inner Life;
so Shakspeare, we may say, embodies for us the Outer
Life of our Europe as developed then, its chivalries,
courtesies, humours, ambitions, what practical way of
thinking, acting, looking at the world, men then had.
As in Homer we may still construe Old Greece; so in
Shakspeare and Dante, after thousands of years, what
our modern Europe was, in Faith and in Practice, will
still be legible. Dante has given us the Faith or Soul;
Shakspeare, in a not less noble way, has given us the
Practice or body. This latter also we were to have; a
man was sent for it, the man Shakspeare. Just when
that chivalry way of life had reached its last finish, and
was on the point of breaking down into slow or swift
dissolution, as we now see it everywhere, this other sovereign Poet, with his seeing eye, with his perennial
singing voice, was sent to take note of it, to give long-
enduring record of it. Two fit men: Dante, deep, fierce
as the central fire of the world; Shakspeare, wide, placid, far-seeing, as the Sun, the upper light of the world.
Italy produced the one world-voice; we English had
the honour of producing the other.

Curious enough how, as it were by mere accident,
this man came to us. I think always, so great, quiet,
complete and self-sufficing is this Shakspeare, had the
Warwickshire Squire not prosecuted him for deer-
stealing, we had perhaps never heard of him as a

Poet! The woods and skies, the rustic Life of Man
in Stratford there, had been enough for this man!
But indeed that strange outbudding of our whole English Existence, which we call the Elizabethan Era,
did not it too come as of its own accord? The 'Tree
Igdrasil' buds and withers by its own laws, — too
deep for our scanning. Yet it does bud and wither,
and every bough and leaf of it is there, by fixed eternal laws; not a Sir Thomas Lucy [1] but comes at the
hour fit for him. Curious, I say, and not sufficiently
considered: how everything does coöperate with all;
not a leaf rotting on the highway but is indissoluble
portion of solar and stellar systems; no thought, word
or act of man but has sprung withal out of all men,
and works sooner or later, recognisably or irrecognis-
ably, on all men! It is all a Tree: circulation of sap
and influences, mutual communication of every minutest leaf with the lowest talon of a root, with every
other greatest and minutest portion of the whole. The
Tree Igdrasil, that has its roots down in the Kingdoms
of Hela and Death, and whose boughs overspread the
highest Heaven! —

In some sense it may be said that this glorious Elizabethan Era with its Shakspeare, as the outcome and
flowerage of all which had preceded it, is itself attri-
butable to the Catholicism of the Middle Ages. The
Christian Faith, which was the theme of Dante's
Song, had produced this Practical Life which Shakspeare was to sing. For Religion then, as it now and
always is, was the soul of Practice; the primary vital
fact in men's life. And remark here, as rather curi-

---

[1] The "Warwickshire Squire" afore-mentioned.

ous, that Middle-Age Catholicism was abolished, so far as Acts of Parliament could abolish it, before Shakspeare, the noblest product of it, made his appearance. He did make his appearance nevertheless. Nature at her own time, with Catholicism or what else might be necessary, sent him forth; taking small thought of Acts of Parliament. King-Henrys,[1] Queen-Elizabeths[1] go their way; and Nature too goes hers. Acts of Parliament, on the whole, are small, notwithstanding the noise they make. What Act of Parliament, debate at St. Stephen's,[2] on the hustings[3] or elsewhere, was it that brought this Shakspeare into being? No dining at Freemasons' Tavern,[4] opening subscription-lists, selling of shares, and infinite other jangling and true or false endeavouring! This Elizabethan Era, and all its nobleness and blessedness, came without proclamation, preparation of ours. Priceless Shakspeare was the free gift of Nature; given altogether silently; — received altogether silently, as if it

---

[1] Mentioned as effective opponents of Roman Catholicism in England.

[2] St. Stephen's Chapel, the site of which is now occupied by St. Stephen's Hall in the Houses of Parliament, was once the meeting-place of the House of Commons.

[3] "The temporary platform from which, previous to the Ballot Act of 1872, the nomination of candidates for Parliament was made, and on which these stood while addressing the electors." *New Eng. Dict.*

[4] In London, where at a meeting of distinguished men including Carlyle, six weeks after the delivery of the present lecture, it was unanimously voted to establish a library. Subscription lists were opened, etc. The project was most successfully carried out. Obviously this sentence was added in preparing the lecture for the press.

had been a thing of little account. And yet, very literally, it is a priceless thing. One should look at that
side of matters too.

Of this Shakspeare of ours, perhaps the opinion one
sometimes hears a little idolatrously expressed is, in
fact, the right one; I think the best judgment not of
this country only, but of Europe at large, is slowly
pointing to the conclusion, That Shakspeare is the
chief of all Poets hitherto; the greatest intellect who,
in our recorded world, has left record of himself in the
way of Literature. On the whole, I know not such a
power of vision, such a faculty of thought, if we take
all the characters of it, in any other man. Such a
calmness of depth; placid joyous strength; all things
imaged in that great soul of his so true and clear, as
in a tranquil unfathomable sea! It has been said,
that in the constructing of Shakspeare's Dramas there
is, apart from all other 'faculties' as they are called,
an understanding manifested, equal to that in Bacon's
Novum Organum. That is true; and it is not a truth
that strikes every one. It would become more apparent
if we tried, any of us for himself, how, out of Shakspeare's dramatic materials, *we* could fashion such a
result! The built house seems all so fit, — everyway
as it should be, as if it came there by its own law and
the nature of things, — we forget the rude disorderly
quarry it was shaped from. The very perfection of
the house, as if Nature herself had made it, hides the
builder's merit. Perfect, more perfect than any other
man, we may call Shakspeare in this: he discerns,
knows as by instinct, what condition he works under,
what his materials are, what his own force and its

relation to them is. It is not a transitory glance of
insight that will suffice; it is deliberate illumination
of the whole matter; it is a calmly *seeing* eye; a
great intellect, in short. How a man, of some wide
thing that he has witnessed, will construct a narrative,
what kind of picture and delineation he will give of it,
— is the best measure you could get of what intellect
is in the man. Which circumstance is vital and shall
stand prominent; which unessential, fit to be suppressed; where is the true *beginning*, the true sequence
and ending? To find out this, you task the whole
force of insight that is in the man. He must *understand* the thing; according to the depth of his understanding, will the fitness of his answer be. You will
try him so. Does like join itself to like; does the
spirit of method stir in that confusion, so that its
embroilment becomes order? Can the man say, *Fiat
lux*, Let there be light;[1] and out of chaos make a
world? Precisely as there is *light* in himself, will he
accomplish this.

Or indeed we may say again, it is in what I called
Portrait-painting, delineating of men and things,
especially of men, that Shakspeare is great. All the
greatness of the man comes out decisively here. It is
unexampled, I think, that calm creative perspicacity
of Shakspeare. The thing he looks at reveals not this
or that face of it, but its inmost heart, and generic
secret: it dissolves itself as in light before him, so that
he discerns the perfect structure of it. Creative, we
said: poetic creation, what is this too but *seeing* the

[1] And God said, Let there be light: and there was light.
Gen. i, 3.

thing sufficiently? The *word* that will describe the
thing, follows of itself from such clear intense sight of
the thing. And is not Shakspeare's *morality*, his valour,
candour, tolerance, truthfulness; his whole victorious
strength and greatness, which can triumph over such
obstructions, visible there too? Great as the world!
No *twisted*, poor convex-concave[1] mirror, reflecting all
objects with its own convexities and concavities; a perfectly *level* mirror; — that is to say withal, if we will
understand it, a man justly related to all things and
men, a good man. It is truly a lordly spectacle how
this great soul takes-in all kinds of men and objects,
a Falstaff, an Othello, a Juliet, a Coriolanus; sets them
all forth to us in their round completeness; loving, just,
the equal brother of all. *Novum Organum*, and all the
intellect you will find in Bacon, is of a quite secondary
order; earthly, material, poor in comparison with this.
Among modern men, one finds, in strictness, almost
nothing of the same rank. Goethe alone, since the
days of Shakspeare, reminds me of it. Of him too you
say that he *saw* the object; you may say what he himself says of Shakspeare : ' His characters are like
watches with dial-plates of transparent crystal; they
show you the hour like others, and the inward mechanism also is all visible.'

The seeing eye! It is this that discloses the inner
harmony of things; what Nature meant, what musical
idea Nature has wrapped-up in these often rough embodiments. Something she did mean. To the seeing
eye that something were discernible. Are they base,

[1] *I. e.*, some parts of the surface convex and others concave,
so that it would give an utterly distorted reflection.

miserable things ? You can laugh over them, you can weep over them ; you can in some way or other genially relate yourself to them ; — you can, at lowest, hold your peace about them, turn away your own and others' face from them, till the hour come for practically exterminating and extinguishing them ! At bottom, it is the Poet's first gift, as it is all men's, that he have intellect enough. He will be a Poet if he have : a Poet in word ; or failing that, perhaps still better, a Poet in act. Whether he write at all ; and if so, whether in prose or in verse, will depend on accidents · who knows on what extremely trivial accidents, — perhaps on his having had a singing-master, on his being taught to sing in his boyhood ! But the faculty which enables him to discern the inner heart of things, and the harmony that dwells there (for whatsoever exists has a harmony in the heart of it, or it would not hold together and exist), is not the result of habits or accidents, but the gift of Nature herself ; the primary outfit for a Heroic Man in what sort soever. To the Poet, as to every other, we say first of all, *See*. If you cannot do that, it is of no use to keep stringing rhymes together, jingling sensibilities against each other, and *name* yourself a Poet ; there is no hope for you. If you can, there is, in prose or verse, in action or speculation, all manner of hope. The crabbed old Schoolmaster used to ask, when they brought him a new pupil, " But are ye sure he 's *not a dunce ?* " Why, really one might ask the same thing, in regard to every man proposed for whatsoever function ; and consider it as the one inquiry needful : Are ye sure he 's not a dunce ? There is, in this world, no other entirely fatal person.

For, in fact, I say the degree of vision that dwells in a man is a correct measure of the man. If called to define Shakspeare's faculty, I should say superiority of Intellect, and think I had included all under that. What indeed are faculties? We talk of faculties as if they were distinct, things separable; as if a man had intellect, imagination, fancy, &c., as he has hands, feet and arms. That is a capital error. Then again, we hear of a man's 'intellectual nature,' and of his 'moral nature,' as if these again were divisible, and existed apart. Necessities of language do perhaps prescribe such forms of utterance; we must speak, I am aware, in that way, if we are to speak at all. But words ought not to harden into things for us. It seems to me, our apprehension of this matter is, for most part, radically falsified thereby. We ought to know withal, and to keep forever in mind, that these divisions are at bottom but *names;* that man's spiritual nature, the vital Force which dwells in him, is essentially one and indivisible; that what we call imagination, fancy, understanding, and so forth, are but different figures of the same Power of Insight, all indissolubly connected with each other, physiognomically related; that if we knew one of them, we might know all of them. Morality itself, what we call the moral quality of a man, what is this but another *side* of the one vital Force whereby he is and works? All that a man does is physiognomical of him. You may see how a man would fight, by the way in which he sings; his courage, or want of courage, is visible in the word he utters, in the opinion he has formed, no less than in the stroke he strikes. He is *one;* and preaches the same Self abroad in all these ways.

Without hands a man might have feet, and could still walk: but, consider it, — without morality, intellect were impossible for him; a thoroughly immoral *man* could not know anything at all! To know a thing, what we can call knowing, a man must first *love* the thing, sympathise with it: that is, be *virtuously* related to it. If he have not the justice to put down his own selfishness at every turn, the courage to stand by the dangerous-true at every turn, how shall he know? His virtues, all of them, will lie recorded in his knowledge. Nature, with her truth, remains to the bad, to the selfish and the pusillanimous forever a sealed book: what such can know of Nature is mean, superficial, small; for the uses of the day merely. — But does not the very Fox know something of Nature? Exactly so: it knows where the geese lodge! The human Reynard, very frequent everywhere in the world, what more does he know but this and the like of this? Nay, it should be considered too, that if the Fox had not a certain vulpine *morality*, he could not even know where the geese were, or get at the geese! If he spent his time in splenetic atrabiliar reflections on his own misery, his ill usage by Nature, Fortune and other Foxes, and so forth; and had not courage, promptitude, practicality, and other suitable vulpine gifts and graces, he would catch no geese. We may say of the Fox too, that his morality and insight are of the same dimensions; different faces of the same internal unity of vulpine life! — These things are worth stating; for the contrary of them acts with

manifold very baleful perversion, in this time: what
limitations, modifications they require, your own candour will supply.

If I say, therefore, that Shakspeare is the greatest
of Intellects, I have said all concerning him. But
there is more in Shakspeare's intellect than we have
yet seen. It is what I call an unconscious intellect;
there is more virtue in it than he himself is aware of.
Novalis beautifully remarks of him, that those Dramas
of his are Products of Nature too, deep as Nature
herself. I find a great truth in this saying. Shakspeare's Art is not Artifice; the noblest worth of it
is not there by plan or precontrivance. It grows-up
from the deeps of Nature, through this noble sincere
soul, who is a voice of Nature. The latest generations
of men will find new meanings in Shakspeare, new
elucidations of their own human being; 'new harmonies with the infinite structure of the Universe;
concurrences with later ideas, affinities with the
higher powers and senses of man.' This well deserves
meditating. It is Nature's highest reward to a true
simple great soul, that he get thus to be *a part of
herself*. Such a man's works, whatsoever he with utmost conscious exertion and forethought shall accomplish, grow up withal *un*consciously, from the unknown
deeps in him; — as the oak-tree grows from the
Earth's bosom, as the mountains and waters shape
themselves; with a symmetry grounded on Nature's
own laws, comformable to all Truth whatsoever. How
much in Shakspeare lies hid; his sorrows, his silent
struggles known to himself; much that was not
known at all, not speakable at all: like *roots*, like

sap and forces working underground! Speech is great ; but Silence is greater.

Withal the joyful tranquillity of this man is notable. I will not blame Dante for his misery : it is as battle without victory; but true battle, — the first, indispensable thing. Yet I call Shakspeare greater than Dante, in that he fought truly, and did conquer. Doubt it not, he had his own sorrows : those *Sonnets* of his will even testify expressly in what deep waters he had waded, and swum struggling for his life ; — as what man like him ever failed to have to do ? It seems to me a heedless notion, our common one, that he sat like a bird on the bough ; and sang forth, free and offhand, never knowing the troubles of other men. Not so ; with no man is it so. How could a man travel forward from rustic deer-poaching to such tragedy-writing, and not fall-in with sorrows by the way ? Or, still better, how could a man delineate a Hamlet, a Coriolanus, a Macbeth, so many suffering heroic hearts, if his own heroic heart had never suffered ? — And now, in contrast with all this, observe his mirthfulness, his genuine overflowing love of laughter ! You would say, in no point does he *exaggerate* but only in laughter. Fiery objurgations, words that pierce and burn, are to be found in Shakspeare; yet he is always in measure here ; never what Johnson would remark as a specially 'good hater.' But his laughter seems to pour from him in floods ; he heaps all manner of ridiculous nicknames on the butt he is bantering, tumbles and tosses him in all sorts of horse-play ; you would say, with his whole heart laughs. And then, if not always the finest, it is always a genial laughter. Not at mere weakness, at misery or poverty; never. No man who *can* laugh, what we call laughing, will laugh at these things. It is some poor character only *desiring* to laugh, and have the credit of wit, that does so. Laughter means sympathy; good laughter is not ' the crackling of thorns under the pot.'[1] Even at stupidity and pretension this Shakspeare does not laugh otherwise than genially. Dogberry and Verges[2] tickle our very hearts ; and we dismiss them covered with explosions of laughter : but we like the poor fellows only the better for our laughing ; and hope they will get on well there, and continue Presidents of the City-watch. Such laughter, like sunshine on the deep sea, is very beautiful to me.

We have no room to speak of Shakspeare's individual works ; though perhaps there is much still waiting to be said on that head. Had we, for instance, all his plays reviewed as *Hamlet*, in *Wilhelm Meister*,[3] is ! A thing which might, one day, be done. August Wilhelm Schlegel[4] has a remark on his Historical Plays, *Henry Fifth* and the others, which is worth remembering. He calls them a kind of National Epic. Marlborough,[5] you recollect, said, he knew no English

[1] For as the crackling of thorns under a pot, so is the laughter of the fool : this also is vanity. Eccles. vii, 6.

[2] In *Much Ado*, esp. III, iii, first part, — one of the best bits of " laughter " in all literature.

[3] In *Meister's Apprenticeship*, Book IV, iii–v, xii, *passim*.

[4] Eminent German critic and poet (1767–1845).

[5] Duke of Marlborough (1650–1722), commander of the allied forces against France, 1702–1711. Won the important victory of Blenheim, 1704.

History but what he had learned from Shakspeare. There are really, if we look to it, few as memorable Histories. The great salient points are admirably seized ; all rounds itself off, into a kind of rhythmic coherence ; it is, as Schlegel says, *epic ;* — as indeed all delineation by a great thinker will be. There are right beautiful things in those Pieces, which indeed together form one beautiful thing. That battle of Agincourt[1] strikes me as one of the most perfect things, in its sort, we anywhere have of Shakspeare's. The description of the two hosts : the worn-out, jaded English ; the dread hour, big with destiny, when the battle shall begin ; and then that deathless valour : " Ye good yeomen, whose limbs were made in Eng-gland ! "[2] There is a noble Patriotism in it, — far other than the ' indifference ' you sometimes hear ascribed to Shakspeare. A true English heart breathes, calm and strong, through the whole business ; not boisterous, protrusive ; all the better for that. There is a sound in it like the ring of steel. This man too had a right stroke in him, had it come to that !

But I will say, of Shakspeare's works generally, that we have no full impress of him there ; even as full as we have of many men. His works are so many

[1] *Hen. V*, IV ; Agincourt is in northern France, SE of Calais; there Henry V with 15,000 English completely defeated 60,000 French in 1415.

[2] From the splendid and famous speech before Harfleur :—

> Once more unto the breach, dear friends, once more;
> Or close the wall up with our English dead.
>
> · · · · · · · · · ·
>
>   And you, good yeomen,
> Whose limbs were made in England, show us here
> The mettle of your pasture.   III, i.

windows, through which we see a glimpse of the world
that was in him. All his works seem, comparatively
speaking, cursory, imperfect, written under cramping
circumstances; giving only here and there a note of
the full utterance of the man. Passages there are that
come upon you like splendour out of Heaven; bursts
of radiance, illuminating the very heart of the thing:
you say, " That is *true*, spoken once and forever;
wheresoever and whensoever there is an open human
soul, that will be recognised as true!" Such bursts,
however, make us feel that the surrounding matter is
not radiant; that it is, in part, temporary, conventional. Alas, Shakspeare had to write for the Globe
Playhouse : his great soul had to crush itself, as it
could, into that and no other mould. It was with him,
then, as it is with us all. No man works save under
conditions. The sculptor cannot set his own free
Thought before us; but his Thought as he could trans-
late it into the stone that was given, with the tools
that were given. *Disjecta membra* [1] are all that we
find of any Poet, or of any man.

Whoever looks intelligently at this Shakspeare may
recognise that he too was a *Prophet*, in his way; of
an insight analogous to the Prophetic, though he took
it up in another strain. Nature seemed to this man
also divine; *un*speakable, deep as Tophet, high as
Heaven : ' We are such stuff as Dreams are made of!'
That scroll [2] in Westminster Abbey, which few read

[1] Scattered parts.
[2] Held in the left hand of the statue of Shakespeare. On it is
inscribed a somewhat inaccurate version of a part of Prospero's
famous speech in *The Tempest*, IV, i, 152 ff. : —

with understanding, is of the depth of any seer. But the man sang; did not preach, except musically. We called Dante the melodious Priest of Middle-Age Catholicism. May we not call Shakspeare the still more melodious Priest of a *true* Catholicism, the 'Universal Church' of the Future and of all times? No narrow superstition, harsh asceticism, intolerance, fanatical fierceness or perversion: a Revelation, so far as it goes, that such a thousandfold hidden beauty and divineness dwells in all Nature; which let all men worship as they can! We may say without offence, that there rises a kind of universal Psalm out of this Shakspeare too; not unfit to make itself heard among the still more sacred Psalms. Not in disharmony with these, if we understood them, but in harmony! — I cannot call this Shakspeare a 'Sceptic,' as some do; his indifference to the creeds and theological quarrels of his time misleading them. No: neither unpatriotic, though he says little about his Patriotism; nor sceptic, though he says little about his Faith. Such 'indifference' was the fruit of his greatness withal: his whole heart was in his own grand sphere of worship (we may call it such); these other controversies, vitally important to other men, were not vital to him.

But call it worship, call it what you will, is it not a right glorious thing, and set of things, this that Shak-

> The cloud-capp'd towers, the gorgeous palaces,
> The solemn temples, the great globe itself,
> Yea, all which it inherit, shall dissolve
> And, like this insubstantial pageant faded,
> Leave not a rack behind. We are such stuff
> As dreams are made on, and our little life
> Is rounded with a sleep.

speare has brought us? For myself, I feel that there
is actually a kind of sacredness in the fact of such a
man being sent into this Earth. Is he not an eye to
us all; a blessed heaven-sent Bringer of Light? —
And, at bottom, was it not perhaps far better that
this Shakspeare, everyway an unconscious man, was
conscious of no Heavenly message? He did not feel,
like Mahomet, because he saw into those internal
Splendours, that he specially was the ' Prophet of
God :' and was he not greater than Mahomet in that?
Greater; and also, if we compute strictly, as we did
in Dante's case, more successful. It was intrinsically
an error that notion of Mahomet's, of his supreme
Prophethood; and has come down to us inextricably
involved in error to this day; dragging along with it
such a coil of fables, impurities, intolerances, as makes
it a questionable step for me here and now to say, as
I have done, that Mahomet was a true Speaker at all,
and not rather an ambitious charlatan, perversity and
simulacrum; no Speaker, but a Babbler! Even in
Arabia, as I compute, Mahomet will have exhausted
himself and become obsolete, while this Shakspeare,
this Dante may still be young; — while this Shakspeare
may still pretend to be a Priest of Mankind, of Arabia
as of other places, for unlimited periods to come!

Compared with any speaker or singer one knows,
even with Æschylus [1] or Homer, why should he not
for veracity and universality, last like them? He is
sincere as they; reaches deep down like them, to the
universal and perennial. But as for Mahomet, I think

[1] Greatest of Greek dramatists (525–456 B. C.), author of
Prometheus Bound, The Seven against Thebes, Agamemnon.

it had been better for him *not* to be so conscious!
Alas, poor Mahomet; all that he was *conscious* of
was a mere error; a futility and triviality, — as indeed
such ever is. The truly great in him too was the unconscious: that he was a wild Arab lion of the desert,
and did speak-out with that great thunder-voice of his,
not by words which he *thought* to be great, but by
actions, by feelings, by a history which *were* great!
His Koran has become a stupid piece of prolix absurd-
ity; we do not believe, like him, that God wrote that!
The Great Man here too, as always, is a Force of
Nature: whatsoever is truly great in him springs-up
from the *in*articulate deeps.

Well: this is our poor Warwickshire Peasant, who
rose to be Manager of a Playhouse, so that he could
live without begging; whom the Earl of Southampton
cast some kind glances on; whom Sir Thomas Lucy,
many thanks to him, was for sending to the Tread-
mill![1] We did not account him a god, like Odin,
while he dwelt with us; — on which point there were
much to be said. But I will say rather, or repeat:
In spite of the sad state Hero-worship now lies in,
consider what this Shakspeare has actually become
among us. Which Englishman we ever made, in this
land of ours, which million of Englishmen, would we
not give-up rather than the Stratford Peasant? There
is no regiment of highest Dignitaries that we would
sell him for. He is the grandest thing we have yet
done. For our honour among foreign nations, as an

[1] Used in prisons of Carlyle's time as an instrument of discipline, to provide "labor" for prisoners.

ornament to our English Household, what item is
there that we would not surrender rather than him?
Consider now, if they asked us, Will you give-up
your Indian Empire or your Shakspeare, you English;
never have had any Indian Empire, or never have had
any Shakspeare? Really it were a grave question.
Official persons would answer doubtless in official language; but we, for our part too, should not we be
forced to answer: Indian Empire, or no Indian Empire; we cannot do without Shakspeare! Indian
Empire will go, at any rate, some day; but this Shakspeare does not go, he lasts forever with us; we cannot give-up our Shakspeare!

Nay, apart from spiritualities; and considering
him merely as a real, marketable, tangibly-useful possession. England, before long, this Island of ours,
will hold but a small fraction of the English: in
America, in New Holland,[1] east and west to the very
Antipodes, there will be a Saxondom covering great
spaces of the Globe. And now, what is it that can
keep all these together into virtually one Nation, so
that they do not fall-out and fight, but live at peace,
in brotherlike intercourse, helping one another? This
is justly regarded as the greatest practical problem,
the thing all manner of sovereignties and governments
are here to accomplish: what is it that will accomplish this? Acts of Parliament, administrative prime-
ministers cannot. America is parted from us, so far
as Parliament could part it. Call it not fantastic, for
there is much reality in it: Here, I say, is an English King, whom no time or chance, Parliament or
combination of Parliaments, can dethrone! This

[1] An early name for Australia.

King Shakspeare, does not he shine, in crowned sovereignty, over us all, as the noblest, gentlest, yet strongest of rallying-signs ; *in*destructible ; really more valuable in that point of view than any other means or appliance whatsoever ? We can fancy him as radiant aloft over all the Nations of Englishmen, a thousand years hence. From Paramatta,[1] from New York, wheresoever, under what sort of Parish-Constable soever, English men and women are, they will say to one another : " Yes, this Shakspeare is ours ; we produced him, we speak and think by him ; we are of one blood and kind with him." The most common-sense politician, too, if he pleases, may think of that.

Yes, truly, it is a great thing for a Nation that it get an articulate voice ; that it produce a man who will speak-forth melodiously what the heart of it means ! Italy, for example, poor Italy lies dismembered, scattered asunder, not appearing in any protocol or treaty as a unity at all ; yet the noble Italy is actually *one :* Italy produced its Dante ; Italy can speak ! The Czar of all the Russias, he is strong with so many bayonets, Cossacks and cannons ; and does a great feat in keeping such a tract of Earth politically together ; but he cannot yet speak. Something great in him, but it is a dumb greatness. He has had no voice of genius, to be heard of all men and times. He must learn to speak. He is a great dumb monster hitherto. His cannons and Cossacks will all have rusted into nonentity, while that Dante's voice is still audible. The Nation that has a Dante is bound together as no dumb Russia can be. — We must here end what we had to say of the *Hero-Poet.*

[1] In New South Wales, Australia.

LECTURE IV

THE HERO AS PRIEST. LUTHER ; REFORMATION :
KNOX ; PURITANISM

[Friday, 15th May 1840.]

OUR present discourse is to be of the Great Man as
Priest. We have repeatedly endeavoured to explain
that all sorts of Heroes are intrinsically of the same
material; that given a great soul, open to the Divine
Significance of Life, then there is given a man fit to
speak of this, to sing of this, to fight and work for this,
in a great, victorious, enduring manner; there is given
a Hero, — the outward shape of whom will depend on
the time and the environment he finds himself in. The
Priest too, as I understand it, is a kind of Prophet; in
him too there is required to be a light of inspiration,
as we must name it. He presides over the worship of
the people; is the Uniter of them with the Unseen
Holy. He is the spiritual Captain of the people; as the
Prophet is their spiritual King with many captains:
he guides them heavenward, by wise guidance through
this Earth and its work. The ideal of him is, that he too
be what we can call a voice from the unseen Heaven;
interpreting, even as the Prophet did, and in a more
familiar manner unfolding the same to men. The unseen Heaven, — the ' open secret of the Universe,'—
which so few have an eye for! He is the Prophet shorn
of his more awful splendour; burning with mild equa-

ble radiance, as the enlightener of daily life. This, I say, is the ideal of a Priest. So in old times; so in these, and in all times. One knows very well that, in reducing ideals to practice, great latitude of tolerance is needful; very great. But a Priest who is not this at all, who does not any longer aim or try to be this, is a character — of whom we had rather not speak in this place.

Luther and Knox were by express vocation Priests, and did faithfully perform that function in its common sense. Yet it will suit us better here to consider them chiefly in their historical character, rather as Reformers than Priests. There have been other Priests perhaps equally notable, in calmer times, for doing faithfully the office of a Leader of Worship; bringing down, by faithful heroism in that kind, a light from Heaven into the daily life of their people; leading them forward, as under God's guidance, in the way wherein they were to go. But when this same *way* was a rough one, of battle, confusion and danger, the spiritual Captain, who led through that, becomes, especially to us who live under the fruit of his leading, more notable than any other. He is the warfaring and battling Priest; who led his people, not to quiet faithful labour as in smooth times, but to faithful valorous conflict, in times all violent, dismembered: a more perilous service, and a more memorable one, be it higher or not. These two men we will account our best Priests, inasmuch as they were our best Reformers. Nay I may ask, Is not every true Reformer, by the nature of him, a *Priest* first of all? He appeals to Heaven's invisible justice against Earth's visible force; knows that it, the invisible, is strong and alone strong. He is a believer in the divine truth of things; a *seer*, seeing through the shows of things; a worshipper, in one way or the other, of the divine truth of things; a Priest, that is. If he be not first a Priest, he will never be good for much as a Reformer.

Thus then, as we have seen Great Men, in various situations, building-up Religions, heroic Forms of human Existence in this world, Theories of Life worthy to be sung by a Dante, Practices of Life by a Shakspeare, — we are now to see the reverse process; which also is necessary, which also may be carried-on in the Heroic manner. Curious how this should be necessary: yet necessary it is. The mild shining of the Poet's light has to give place to the fierce lightning of the Reformer: unfortunately the Reformer too is a personage that cannot fail in History! The Poet indeed, with his mildness, what is he but the product and ultimate adjustment of Reform, or Prophecy, with its fierceness? No wild Saint Dominics[1] and Thebaïd Eremites,[2] there had been no melodious Dante; rough Practical Endeavour, Scandinavian and other, from Odin to Walter Raleigh,[3] from Ulfila[4] to Cranmer,[5]

[1] Domingo de Guzman (1170–1221), a Spanish Roman Catholic ecclesiastic, founder of the monastic order of Dominicans, or Preaching Friars, — called in England Black Friars.

[2] The Hermits of Thebes, in Egypt, living in solitude and privation as a religious obligation.

[3] A brilliant and versatile adventurer, explorer, poet, and prose-writer (1552–1618).

[4] See p. 28, n. 2.

[5] Archbishop of Canterbury; burned at the stake for heresy in 1556, under "Bloody Mary" (Queen of England, 1553–1558).

enabled Shakspeare to speak. Nay the finished Poet, I remark sometimes, is a symptom that his epoch itself has reached perfection and is finished; that before long there will be a new epoch, new Reformers needed.

Doubtless it were finer, could we go along always in the way of *music;* be tamed and taught by our Poets, as the rude creatures were by their Orpheus [1] of old. Or failing this rhythmic *musical* way, how good were it could we get so much as into the *equable* way; I mean, if *peaceable* Priests, reforming from day to day, would always suffice us! But it is not so; even this latter has not yet been realised. Alas, the battling Reformer too is, from time to time, a needful and inevitable phenomenon. Obstructions are never wanting: the very things that were once indispensable furtherances become obstructions; and need to be shaken-off and left behind us, — a business often of enormous difficulty. It is notable enough, surely, how a Theorem or spiritual Representation, so we may call it, which once took-in the whole Universe, and was completely satisfactory in all parts of it to the highly-discursive acute intellect of Dante, one of the greatest in the world, — had in the course of another century become dubitable to common intellects; become deniable; and is now, to every one of us, flatly incredible, obsolete as Odin's Theorem! To Dante, human Existence, and God's ways with men, were all well represented by those *Malebolges, Purgatorios;* to Luther not well. How was this? Why could not Dante's

---

[1] Whose skill in music was so great, according to the Greek myth, that he charmed the wild animals and even rocks and trees to follow him.

Catholicism continue; but Luther's Protestantism must needs follow? Alas, nothing will *continue.*

I do not make much of 'Progress of the Species,' as handled in these times of ours; nor do I think you would care to hear much about it. The talk on that subject is too often of the most extravagant, confused sort. Yet I may say, the fact itself seems certain enough; nay we can trace-out the inevitable necessity of it in the nature of things. Every man, as I have stated somewhere, is not only a learner but a doer: he learns with the mind given him what has been; but with the same mind he discovers farther, he invents and devises somewhat of his own. Absolutely without originality there is no man. No man whatever believes, or can believe, exactly what his grandfather believed: he enlarges somewhat, by fresh discovery, his view of the Universe, and consequently his Theorem of the Universe, — which is an *infinite* Universe, and can never be embraced wholly or finally by any view or Theorem, in any conceivable enlargement: he enlarges somewhat, I say; finds somewhat that was credible to his grandfather incredible to him, false to him, inconsistent with some new thing he has discovered or observed. It is the history of every man; and in the history of Mankind we see it summed-up into great historical amounts, — revolutions, new epochs. Dante's Mountain of Purgatory [1] does *not* stand 'in the ocean of the other Hemisphere,' when Columbus has once sailed thither! Men find no such thing extant in the other Hemisphere. It is not there.

[1] Located by the poet on the other side of the earth, exactly opposite Jerusalem.

It must cease to be believed to be there. So with all beliefs whatsoever in this world, — all Systems of Belief, and Systems of Practice that spring from these.

If we add now the melancholy fact, that when Belief waxes uncertain, Practice too becomes unsound, and errors, injustices and miseries everywhere more and more prevail, we shall see material enough for revolution. At all turns, a man who will *do* faithfully, needs to believe firmly. If he have to ask at every turn the world's suffrage; if he cannot dispense with the world's suffrage, and make his own suffrage serve, he is a poor eye-servant; the work committed to him will be *mis*done. Every such man is a daily contributor to the inevitable downfall. Whatsoever work he does, dishonestly, with an eye to the outward look of it, is a new offence, parent of new misery to somebody or other. Offences accumulate till they become insupportable; and are then violently burst through, cleared off as by explosion. Dante's sublime Catholicism, incredible now in theory, and defaced still worse by faithless, doubting and dishonest practice, has to be torn asunder by a Luther; Shakspeare's noble Feudalism, as beautiful as it once looked and was, has to end in a French Revolution. The accumulation of offences is, as we say, too literally *exploded*, blasted asunder volcanically; and there are long troublous periods before matters come to a settlement again.

Surely it were mournful enough to look only at this face of the matter, and find in all human opinions and arrangements merely the fact that they were uncertain, temporary, subject to the law of death! At bottom, it is not so: all death, here too we find, is but of the body, not of the essence or soul; all destruction, by violent revolution or howsoever it be, is but new creation on a wider scale. Odinism was *Valour ;* Christianism was *Humility,* a nobler kind of Valour. No thought that ever dwelt honestly as true in the heart of man but *was* an honest insight into God's truth on man's part, and *has* an essential truth in it which endures through all changes, an everlasting possession for us all. And, on the other hand, what a melancholy notion is that, which has to represent all men, in all countries and times except our own, as having spent their life in blind condemnable error, mere lost Pagans, Scandinavians, Mahometans, only that we might have the true ultimate knowledge! All generations of men were lost and wrong, only that this present little section of a generation might be saved and right. They all marched forward there, all generations since the beginning of the world, like the Russian soldiers into the ditch of Schweidnitz Fort,[1] only to fill-up the ditch with their dead bodies, that we might march-over and take the place! It is an incredible hypothesis.

Such incredible hypothesis we have seen maintained with fierce emphasis; and this or the other poor individual man, with his sect of individual men, marching as over the dead bodies of all men, towards sure victory : but when he too, with his hypothesis and ultimate infallible credo, sank into the ditch, and became a dead body, what was to be said? — Withal,

---

[1] In eastern Germany. The story of the capture of the town (1761) by the Allies (in the Seven Years' War of Frederick the Great *vs.* Austria, Russia, France, Saxony, and Sweden) is told in Carlyle's *History of Friedrich II,* Book xx, viii.

it is an important fact in the nature of man, that he tends to reckon his own insight as final, and goes upon it as such. He will always do it, I suppose, in one or the other way; but it must be in some wider, wiser way than this. Are not all true men that live, or that ever lived, soldiers of the same army, enlisted, under Heaven's captaincy, to do battle against the same enemy, the empire of Darkness and Wrong? Why should we misknow one another, fight not against the enemy but against ourselves, from mere difference of uniform? All uniforms shall be good, so they hold in them true valiant men. All fashions of arms, the Arab turban and swift scimetar, Thor's strong hammer smiting down *Jötuns*, shall be welcome. Luther's battle-voice, Dante's march-melody, all genuine things are with us, not against us. We are all under one Captain, soldiers of the same host. — Let us now look a little at this Luther's fighting; what kind of battle it was, and how he comported himself in it. Luther too was of our spiritual Heroes; a Prophet to his country and time.

As introductory to the whole, a remark about Idolatry will perhaps be in place here. One of Mahomet's characteristics, which indeed belongs to all Prophets, is unlimited implacable zeal against Idolatry. It is the grand theme of Prophets: Idolatry, the worshipping of dead Idols as the Divinity, is a thing they cannot away-with, [1] but have to denounce continually, and

---

[1] Bring no more vain oblations; incense is an abomination unto me; the new moons and sabbaths, the calling of assemblies, I cannot away with. Isaiah i, 13.

brand with inexpiable reprobation; it is the chief of
all the sins they see done under the sun.[1] This is
worth noting. We will not enter here into the theological question about Idolatry. Idol is *Eidolon*, a
thing seen, a symbol. It is not God, but a Symbol of
God; and perhaps one may question whether any
the most benighted mortal ever took it for more than
a Symbol. I fancy, he did not think that the poor
image his own hands had made *was* God; but that
God was emblemed by it, that God was in it some
way or other. And now in this sense, one may ask, Is
not all worship whatsoever a worship by Symbols, by
eidola, or things seen? Whether *seen*, rendered visible
as an image or picture to the bodily eye; or visible
only to the inward eye, to the imagination, to the
intellect: this makes a superficial, but no substantial
difference. It is still a Thing Seen, significant of
Godhead; an Idol. The most rigorous Puritan has
his Confession of Faith, and intellectual Representation of Divine things, and worships thereby; thereby
is worship first made possible for him. All creeds,
liturgies, religious forms, conceptions that fitly invest
religious feelings, are in this sense *eidola*, things seen.
All worship whatsoever must proceed by Symbols, by
Idols: — we may say, all Idolatry is comparative, and
the worst Idolatry is only *more* idolatrous.

Where, then, lies the evil of it? Some fatal evil
must lie in it, or earnest prophetic men would not on
all hands so reprobate it. Why is Idolatry so hateful
to Prophets? It seems to me as if, in the worship of

[1] I have seen all the works that are done under the sun; and,
behold, all is vanity and vexation of spirit. Eccles. i, 14.

those poor wooden symbols, the thing that had chiefly provoked the Prophet, and filled his inmost soul with indignation and aversion, was not exactly what suggested itself to his own thought, and came out of him in words to others, as the thing. The rudest heathen that worshipped Canopus, or the Caabah Black-Stone, he, as we saw, was superior to the horse that worshipped nothing at all! Nay there was a kind of lasting merit in that poor act of his; analogous to what is still meritorious in Poets: recognition of a certain endless *divine* beauty and significance in stars and all natural objects whatsoever. Why should the Prophet so mercilessly condemn him? The poorest mortal worshipping his Fetish,[1] while his heart is full of it, may be an object of pity, of contempt and avoidance, if you will; but cannot surely be an object of hatred. Let his heart *be* honestly full of it, the whole space of his dark narrow mind illuminated thereby; in one word, let him entirely *believe* in his Fetish, — it will then be, I should say, if not well with him, yet as well as it can readily be made to be, and you will leave him alone, unmolested there.

But here enters the fatal circumstance of Idolatry, that, in the era of the Prophets, no man's mind *is* any longer honestly filled with his Idol or Symbol. Before the Prophet can arise who, seeing through it, knows it to be mere wood, many men must have begun dimly to doubt that it was little more. Condemnable Idolatry is *insincere* Idolatry. Doubt has eaten-out the heart of it: a human soul is seen clinging spasmodically to

[1] Any object worshipped or feared as possessing mysterious or supernatural powers.

an Ark of the Covenant, which it half-feels now to
have become a Phantasm. This is one of the balefulest
sights. Souls are no longer *filled* with their Fetish;
but only pretend to be filled, and would fain make
themselves feel that they are filled. " You do not believe," said Coleridge; "you only believe that you
believe." It is the final scene in all kinds of Worship
and Symbolism; the sure symptom that death is now
nigh. It is equivalent to what we call Formulism, and
Worship of Formulas, in these days of ours. No more
immoral act can be done by a human creature; for it
is the beginning of all immorality, or rather it is the
impossibility henceforth of any morality whatsoever:
the innermost moral soul is paralysed thereby, cast into
fatal magnetic sleep! Men are no longer *sincere* men.
I do not wonder that the earnest man denounces this,
brands it, prosecutes it with inextinguishable aversion.
He and it, all good and it, are at death-feud. Blamable Idolatry is *Cant*, and even what one may call Sincere-Cant. Sincere-Cant: that is worth thinking of!
Every sort of Worship ends with this phasis.

I find Luther to have been a Breaker of Idols, no
less than any other Prophet. The wooden gods of the
Koreish, made of timber and bees-wax, were not more
hateful to Mahomet than Tetzel's [1] Pardons of Sin,
made of sheepskin and ink, were to Luther. It is the
property of every Hero, in every time, in every place

[1] A Dominican preacher (1455–1519), who was so (financially)
efficient a seller of indulgences that he was employed in that
capacity by the Pope almost continuously from 1502 to 1518.
His personal morals were by no means above reproach. He was
suspended in 1518. The Council of Trent repudiated the principle of selling indulgences. See p. 31, n. 2.

and situation, that he come back to reality; that he stand upon things, and not shows of things. According as he loves, and venerates, articulately or with deep speechless thought, the awful realities of things, so will the hollow shows of things, however regular, decorous, accredited by Koreishes or Conclaves, be intolerable and detestable to him. Protestantism too is the work of a Prophet: the prophet-work of that sixteenth century. The first stroke of honest demolition to an ancient thing grown false and idolatrous; preparatory afar off to a new thing, which shall be true, and authentically divine! —

At first view it might seem as if Protestantism were entirely destructive to this that we call Hero-worship, and represent as the basis of all possible good, religious or social, for mankind. One often hears it said that Protestantism introduced a new era, radically different from any the world had ever seen before: the era of 'private judgment,' as they call it. By this revolt against the Pope, every man became his own Pope; and learnt, among other things, that he must never trust any Pope, or spiritual Hero-captain, any more! Whereby, is not spiritual union, all hierarchy and subordination among men, henceforth an impossibility? So we hear it said. — Now I need not deny that Protestantism was a revolt against spiritual sovereignties, Popes and much else. Nay I will grant that English Puritanism, revolt against earthly sovereignties, was the second act of it; that the enormous French Revolution itself was the third act, whereby all sovereignties earthly and spiritual were, as might seem, abolished or made sure of abolition. Protestantism is the grand

root from which our whole subsequent European History branches out. For the spiritual will always body
itself forth in the temporal history of men ; the spiritual is the beginning of the temporal. And now, sure
enough, the cry is everywhere for Liberty and Equality,
Independence and so forth ; instead of *Kings*, Ballot-
boxes and Electoral suffrages : it seems made out that
any Hero-sovereign, or loyal obedience of men to a
man, in things temporal or things spiritual, has passed
away forever from the world. I should despair of
the world altogether, if so. One of my deepest con-
victions is, that it is not so. Without sovereigns, true
sovereigns, temporal and spiritual, I see nothing possible but an anarchy; the hatefulest of things. But I
find Protestantism, whatever anarchic democracy it
have produced, to be the beginning of new genuine
sovereignty and order. I find it to be a revolt against
false sovereigns ; the painful but indispensable first
preparative for *true* sovereigns getting place among
us ! This is worth explaining a little.

Let us remark, therefore, in the first place, that
this of ' private judgment ' is, at bottom, not a new
thing in the world, but only new at that epoch of the
world. There is nothing generically new or peculiar
in the Reformation ; it was a return to Truth and
Reality in opposition to Falsehood and Semblance, as
all kinds of Improvement and genuine Teaching are
and have been. Liberty of private judgment, if we
will consider it, must at all times have existed in the
world. Dante had not put-out his eyes, or tied shackles
on himself ; he was at home in that Catholicism of
his, a free-seeing soul in it, — if many a poor Hog-

straten,[1] Tetzel and Dr. Eck [1] had now become slaves in it. Liberty of judgment ? No iron chain, or outward force of any kind, could ever compel the soul of a man to believe or to disbelieve : it is his own indefeasible light, that judgment of his ; he will reign, and believe there, by the grace of God alone ! The sorriest sophistical Bellarmine,[2] preaching sightless faith and passive obedience, must first, by some kind of *conviction*, have abdicated his right to be convinced. His ' private judgment ' indicated that, as the advisablest step *he* could take. The right of private judgment will subsist, in full force, wherever true men subsist. A true man *believes* with his whole judgment, with all the illumination and discernment that is in him, and has always so believed. A false man, only struggling to ' believe that he believes,' will naturally manage it in some other way. Protestantism said to this latter, Woe ! and to the former, Well done ! At bottom, it was no new saying ; it was a return to all old sayings that ever had been said. Be genuine, be sincere : that was, once more, the meaning of it. Mahomet believed with his whole mind ; Odin with his whole mind, — he, and all *true* Followers of Odinism. They, by their private judgment, had ' judged ' — *so*.

And now I venture to assert, that the exercise of private judgment, faithfully gone about, does by no means necessarily end in selfish independence, isola-

---

[1] Hogstraten or (Hoogstraten), a Dominican monk, and Eck, a professor of theology, both contemporaries of Luther, were enthusiastic haters of him and his doctrines.

[2] Cardinal, Archbishop, Librarian of the Vatican (1542–1621); a zealous champion of Roman Catholic orthodoxy.

tion ; but rather ends necessarily in the opposite of that. It is not honest inquiry that makes anarchy ; but it is error, insincerity, half-belief and untruth that make it. A man protesting against error is on the way towards uniting himself with all men that believe in truth. There is no communion possible among men who believe only in hearsays. The heart of each is lying dead ; has no power of sympathy even with *things*, — or he would believe *them* and not hearsays. No sympathy even with things; how much less with his fellow-men ! He cannot unite with men ; he is an anarchic man. Only in a world of sincere men is unity possible ; — and there, in the longrun, it is as good as *certain*.

For observe one thing, a thing too often left out of view, or rather altogether lost sight of, in this controversy : That it is not necessary a man should himself have *discovered* the truth he is to believe in, and never so *sincerely* to believe in. A Great Man, we said, was always sincere, as the first condition of him. But a man need not be great in order to be sincere ; that is not the necessity of Nature and all Time, but only of certain corrupt unfortunate epochs of Time. A man an believe, and make his own, in the most genuine way, what he has received from another ; — and with boundless gratitude to that other ! The merit of *originality* is not novelty ; it is sincerity. The believing man is the original man ; whatsoever he believes, he believes it for himself, not for another. Every son of Adam can become a sincere man, an original man, in this sense ; no mortal is doomed to be an insincere man. Whole ages, what we call ages of Faith, are ori-

ginal; all men in them, or the most of men in them,
sincere. These are the great and fruitful ages: every
worker, in all spheres, is a worker not on semblance
but on substance; every work issues in a result: the
general sum of such work is great; for all of it, as
genuine, tends towards one goal; all of it is *additive*,
none of it subtractive. There is true union, true kingship, loyalty, all true and blessed things, so far as the
poor Earth can produce blessedness for men.

Hero-worship? Ah me, that a man be self-subsistent,
original, true, or what we call it, is surely the farthest
in the world from indisposing him to reverence and
believe other men's truth! It only disposes, necessi-
tates and invincibly compels him to *dis*believe other
men's dead formulas, hearsays and untruths. A man
embraces truth with his eyes open, and because his
eyes are open: does he need to shut them before he
can love his Teacher of truth? He alone can love, with
a right gratitude and genuine loyalty of soul, the
Hero-Teacher who has delivered him out of darkness
into light. Is not such a one a true Hero and Serpent-
queller; worthy of all reverence! The black monster,
Falsehood, our one enemy in this world, lies prostrate
by his valour; it was he that conquered the world for
us!— See, accordingly, was not Luther himself reverenced as a true Pope, or Spiritual Father, *being*
verily such? Napoleon, from amid boundless revolt of
Sansculottism, [1] became a King. Hero-worship never
dies, nor can die. Loyalty and Sovereignty are everlasting in the world: — and there is this in them, that
they are grounded not on garnitures and semblances,

[1] See p. 275, n. 1.

but on realities and sincerities. Not by shutting your eyes, your 'private judgment;' no, but by opening them, and by having something to see! Luther's message was deposition and abolition to all false Popes and Potentates, but life and strength, though afar off, to new genuine ones.

All this of Liberty and Equality, Electoral suf frages, Independence and so forth, we will take, therefore, to be a temporary phenomenon, by no means a final one. Though likely to last a long time, with sad enough embroilments for us all, we must welcome it, as the penalty of sins that are past, the pledge of inestimable benefits that are coming. In all ways, it behoved men to quit simulacra and return to fact; cost what it might, that did behove to be done. With spurious Popes, and Believers having no private judgment, — quacks pretending to command over dupes, — what can you do? Misery and mischief only. You cannot make an association out of insincere men; you cannot build an edifice except by plummet and level, — at *right*-angles to one another! In all this wild revolutionary work, from Protestantism downwards, I see the blessedest result preparing itself: not abolition of Hero-worship, but rather what I would call a whole World of Heroes. If Hero mean *sincere man*, why may not every one of us be a Hero? A world all sincere, a believing world: the like has been; the like will again be, — cannot help being. That were the right sort of Worshippers for Heroes: never could the truly Better be so reverenced as where all were True and Good! — But we must hasten to Luther and his Life.

Luther's birthplace was Eisleben [1] in Saxony; he came into the world there on the 10th of November 1483. It was an accident that gave this honour to Eisleben. His parents, poor mine-labourers in a village of that region, named Mohra, had gone to the Eisleben Winter-Fair : in the tumult of this scene the Frau Luther was taken with travail, found refuge in some poor house there, and the boy she bore was named MARTIN LUTHER. Strange enough to reflect upon it. This poor Frau Luther, she had gone with her husband to make her small merchandisings ; perhaps to sell the lock of yarn she had been spinning, to buy the small winter-necessaries for her narrow hut or household ; in the whole world, that day, there was not a more entirely unimportant-looking pair of people than this Miner and his Wife. And yet what were all Emperors, Popes and Potentates, in comparison ? There was born here, once more, a Mighty Man ; whose light was to flame as the beacon over long centuries and epochs of the world ; the whole world and its history was waiting for this man. It is strange, it is great. It leads us back to another Birth-hour, in a still meaner environment, Eighteen Hundred years ago, — of which it is fit that we *say* nothing, that we think only in silence ; for what words are there ! The Age of Miracles past ? The Age of Miracles is forever here ! —

I find it altogether suitable to Luther's function in this Earth, and doubtless wisely ordered to that end by the Providence presiding over him and us and all things, that he was born poor, and brought-up poor,

[1] Thirty-nine miles about WNW of Leipzig.

one of the poorest of men. He had to beg, as the school-children in those times did ; singing for alms and bread, from door to door. Hardship, rigorous Necessity was the poor boy's companion ; no man nor no thing would put-on a false face to flatter Martin Luther. Among things, not among the shows of things, had he to grow. A boy of rude figure, yet with weak health, with his large greedy soul, full of all faculty and sensibility, he suffered greatly. But it was his task to get acquainted with *realities*, and keep acquainted with them, at whatever cost : his task was to bring the whole world back to reality, for it had dwelt too long with semblance ! A youth nursed-up in wintry whirlwinds, in desolate darkness and difficulty, that he may step-forth at last from his stormy Scandinavia, strong as a true man, as a god : a Christian Odin, — a right Thor once more, with his thunder-hammer, to smite asunder ugly enough *Jötuns* and Giant-monsters !

Perhaps the turning incident of his life, we may fancy, was that death of his friend Alexis, by lightning, at the gate of Erfurt. Luther had struggled-up through boyhood, better and worse ; displaying, in spite of all hindrances, the largest intellect, eager to learn : his father judging doubtless that he might promote himself in the world, set him upon the study of Law. This was the path to rise ; Luther, with little will in it either way, had consented : he was now nineteen years of age. Alexis and he had been to see the old Luther people at Mansfeldt ; [1] were got back

[1] Where Luther's father had become a member of the town council.

again near Erfurt,[1] when a thunderstorm came on ;
the bolt struck Alexis, he fell dead at Luther's feet.
What is this Life of ours ? — gone in a moment,
burnt-up like a scroll, into the blank Eternity ! What
are all earthly preferments, Chancellorships, Kingships ? They lie shrunk together — there ! The Earth
has opened on them ; in a moment they are not, and
Eternity is. Luther, struck to the heart, determined
to devote himself to God and God's service alone. In
spite of all dissuasions from his father and others, he
became a Monk [2] in the Augustine Convent at Erfurt.

This was probably the first light-point in the history
of Luther, his purer will now first decisively uttering
itself ; but, for the present, it was still as one light-
point in an element all of darkness. He says he was
a pious monk, *ich bin ein frommer Mönch gewesen ;*
faithfully, painfully struggling to work-out the truth
of this high act of his ; but it was to little purpose.
His misery had not lessened ; had rather, as it were,
increased into infinitude. The drudgeries he had to
do, as novice in his Convent, all sorts of slave-work,
were not his grievance : the deep earnest soul of the
man had fallen into all manner of black scruples, dubi-
tations ; he believed himself likely to die soon, and
far worse than die. One hears with a new interest for
poor Luther that, at this time, he lived in terror of the
unspeakable misery ; fancied that he was doomed to
eternal reprobation. Was it not the humble sincere
nature of the man ? What was he, that he should be
raised to Heaven ! He that had known only misery,

---

[1] Where Luther had entered the university in 1501.
[2] 1505.

and mean slavery: the news was too blessed to be
credible. It could not become clear to him how, by
fasts, vigils, formalities and mass-work, a man's soul
could be saved. He fell into the blackest wretchedness;
had to wander staggering as on the verge of bottomless
Despair.

It must have been a most blessed discovery, that of
an old Latin Bible which he found in the Erfurt
Library about this time. He had never seen the Book
before.[1] It taught him another lesson than that of
fasts and vigils. A brother monk too, of pious experience, was helpful. Luther learned now that a man was
saved not by singing masses, but by the infinite grace
of God: a more credible hypothesis. He gradually
got himself founded, as on the rock. No wonder he
should venerate the Bible, which had brought this
blessed help to him. He prized it as the Word of the
Highest must be prized by such a man. He determined
to hold by that; as through life and to death he firmly
did.

This, then, is his deliverance from darkness, his final
triumph over darkness, what we call his conversion;
for himself the most important of all epochs. That he
should now grow daily in peace and clearness; that,
unfolding now the great talents and virtues implanted
in him, he should rise to importance in his Convent,
in his country, and be found more and more useful in
all honest business of life, is a natural result. He was

[1] Luther had followed the usual university course with the study
of law (see p. 180). Outside the ranks of teachers and students
of theology, the Bible was much less known than the Church
Fathers, who were considered of equal, if not greater, authority
and importance.

sent on missions by his Augustine Order, as a man of
talent and fidelity fit to do their business well : the
Elector of Saxony, Friedrich, named the Wise, a truly
wise and just prince, had cast his eye on him as a valuable person ; made him Professor in his new University of Wittenberg,[1] Preacher too at Wittenberg ;
in both which capacities, as in all duties he did, this
Luther, in the peaceable sphere of common life, was
gaining more and more esteem with all good men.

It was in his twenty-seventh year that he first saw
Rome ; being sent thither, as I said, on mission from
his Convent. Pope Julius the Second, and what was
going-on at Rome, must have filled the mind of Luther
with amazement. He had come as to the Sacred City,
throne of God's Highpriest on Earth ; and he found
it — what we know ![2] Many thoughts it must have
given the man ; many which we have no record of,
which perhaps he did not himself know how to utter.
This Rome, this scene of false priests, clothed not in
the beauty of holiness, but in far other vesture, is
false : but what is it to Luther? A mean man he,
how shall he reform a world ? That was far from his
thoughts. A humble, solitary man, why should he at
all meddle with the world? It was the task of quite
higher men than he. His business was to guide his
own footsteps wisely through the world. Let him do
his own obscure duty in it well ; the rest, horrible and
dismal as it looks, is in God's hand, not in his.

[1] Founded 1502. Shakespeare's Hamlet and Horatio were
Wittenberg students.
[2] Unequaled in all Europe for every sort of debauchery and
corruption.

It is curious to reflect what might have been the issue, had Roman Popery happened to pass this Luther by; to go on in its great wasteful orbit, and not come athwart his little path, and force him to assault it! Conceivable enough that, in this case, he might have held his peace about the abuses of Rome; left Providence, and God on high, to deal with them! A modest quiet man; not prompt he to attack irreverently persons in authority. His clear task, as I say, was to do his own duty; to walk wisely in this world of confused wickedness, and save his own soul alive. But the Roman Highpriesthood did come athwart him: afar off at Wittenberg he, Luther, could not get lived[1] in honesty for it; he remonstrated, resisted, came to extremity; was struck-at, struck again, and so it came to wager of battle between them! This is worth attending to in Luther's history. Perhaps no man of so humble, peaceable a disposition ever filled the world with contention. We cannot but see that he would have loved privacy, quiet diligence in the shade; that it was against his will he ever became a notoriety. Notoriety: what would that do for him? The goal of his march through this world was the Infinite Heaven; an indubitable goal for him: in a few years, he should either have attained that, or lost it forever! We will say nothing at all, I think, of that sorrowfulest of theories, of its being some mean shopkeeper grudge, of the Augustine Monk against the Dominican, that first kindled the wrath of Luther, and produced the Pro-

---

[1] The idiom is more familiar in "get killed," "get lost," etc. See p. 326, — "could not get resigned."

testant Reformation. We will say to the people who
maintain it, if indeed any such exist now: Get first
into the sphere of thought by which it is so much as
possible to judge of Luther, or of any man like
Luther, otherwise than distractedly; we may then
begin arguing with you.

The Monk Tetzel, sent out carelessly in the way of
trade, by Leo Tenth,[1] — who merely wanted to raise
a little money, and for the rest seems to have been a
Pagan rather than a Christian, so far as he was anything, — arrived at Wittenberg, and drove his scandal-
ous trade there. Luther's flock bought Indulgences;
in the confessional of his church, people pleaded to
him that they had already got their sins pardoned.
Luther, if he would not be found wanting at his own
post, a false sluggard and coward at the very centre of
the little space of ground that was his own and no
other man's, had to step-forth against Indulgences,
and declare aloud that *they* were a futility and sorrowful mockery, that no man's sins could be pardoned by
them. It was the beginning of the whole Reformation. We know how it went; forward from this first
public challenge[2] of Tetzel, on the last day of October
1517, through remonstrance and argument; — spreading ever wider, rising ever higher; till it became
unquenchable, and enveloped all the world. Luther's

[1] Born 1475, made Cardinal at the age of thirteen, Pope in
1513, and died 1521. He was the son of Lorenzo de' Medici
"The Magnificent," and a liberal patron of art and letters.

[2] The ninety-five "theses" or statements, opposing indulgences, nailed to the door of the Castle Church in Wittenberg.
The Elector of Saxony sided with Luther, and refused Tetzel
permission to enter his domain.

heart's-desire was to have this grief and other griefs
amended; his thought was still far other than that of
introducing separation in the Church, or revolting
against the Pope, Father of Christendom. — The
elegant Pagan Pope cared little about this Monk and
his doctrines; wished, however, to have done with the
noise of him: in a space of some three years, having
tried various softer methods, he thought good to end
it by *fire*. He dooms the Monk's writings to be burnt
by the hangman, and his body to be sent bound to
Rome, — probably for a similar purpose. It was the
way they had ended with Huss,[1] with Jerome,[1] the
century before. A short argument, fire. Poor Huss:
he came to that Constance Council,[2] with all imaginable promises and safe-conducts; an earnest, not rebel-
lious kind of man: they laid him instantly in a stone
dungeon 'three-feet wide, six-feet high, seven-feet
long;' *burnt* the true voice of him out of this world;
choked it in smoke and fire. That was *not* well
done!

I, for one, pardon Luther for now altogether revolting against the Pope. The elegant Pagan, by this fire-
decree of his, had kindled into noble just wrath the
bravest heart then living in this world. The bravest,
if also one of the humblest, peaceablest; it was now
kindled. These words of mine, words of truth and
soberness, aiming faithfully, as human inability would

[1] Huss and his friend and follower, Jerome, were burned at
the stake in 1415 and 1416, respectively. Luther was astonished,
he said, to find that he was "a Hussite without knowing it;
that St. Paul and Augustine were Hussites!"

[2] The seventeenth general Council of the Church, convened at
Constance in Baden on the Rhine, in 1414.

allow, to promote God's truth on Earth, and save men's souls, you, God's vicegerent on earth, answer them by the hangman and fire? You will burn me and them, for answer to the God's-message they strove to bring you? *You* are not God's vicegerent; you are another's than his, I think! I take your Bull,[1] as an emparch-mented Lie, and burn *it*. You will do what you see good next: this is what I do. — It was on the 10th of December 1520, three years after the beginning of the business, that Luther, ' with a great concourse of people,' took this indignant step of burning the Pope's fire-decree ' at the Elster-Gate of Wittenberg.' Wittenberg looked on ' with shoutings; ' the whole world was looking on. The Pope should not have provoked that ' shout '! It was the shout of the awakening of nations. The quiet German heart, modest, patient of much, had at length got more than it could bear. Formulism, Pagan Popeism, and other Falsehood and corrupt Semblance had ruled long enough: and here once more was a man found who durst tell all men that God's-world stood not on semblances but on realities; that Life was a truth, and not a lie!

At bottom, as was said above, we are to consider Luther as a Prophet Idol-breaker; a bringer-back of men to reality. It is the function of great men and teachers. Mahomet said, These idols of yours are wood; you put wax and oil on them, the flies stick on them: they are not God, I tell you, they are black wood! Luther said to the Pope, This thing of yours that you call a Pardon of Sins, it is a bit of rag-paper

---

[1] Papal decree (Lat. *bulla*=knob, seal), written on parchment with a leaden seal appended with a cord.

with ink. It *is* nothing else; it, and so much like it, is nothing else. God alone can pardon sins. Pope-ship, spiritual Fatherhood of God's Church, is that a vain semblance, of cloth and parchment? It is an awful fact. God's Church is not a semblance, Heaven and Hell are not semblances. I stand on this, since you drive me to it. Standing on this, I a poor German Monk am stronger than you all. I stand solitary, friendless, but on God's Truth; you with your tiaras,[1] triple-hats,[1] with your treasuries and armories, thunders spiritual and temporal, stand on the Devil's Lie, and are not so strong! —

The Diet of Worms,[2] Luther's appearance there on the 17th of April 1521, may be considered as the greatest scene in Modern European History; the point, indeed, from which the whole subsequent history of civilisation takes its rise. After multiplied negotiations, disputations, it had come to this. The young Emperor Charles Fifth, with all the Princes of Germany, Papal nuncios, dignitaries spiritual and temporal, are assembled there: Luther is to appear and answer for himself, whether he will recant or not. The world's pomp and power sits there on this hand: on that, stands-up for God's Truth, one man, the poor miner Hans Luther's Son. Friends had reminded him of Huss, advised him not to go; he would not be advised. A large company of friends rode-out to meet him, with still more earnest

[1] Papal hat, encircled with three crowns and surmounted with a globe and cross. The three crowns date from the early fourteenth century. Their significance has been variously interpreted, but conclusive proof is wanting. See *The Dolphin* (Phila.), iv, No. 3, September, 1903, pp. 308, 309, 312.

[2] On the Rhine, in S. W. Germany (pron. Vōrms).

warnings; he answered, " Were there as many Devils in Worms as there are roof-tiles, I would on." The people, on the morrow, as he went to the Hall of the Diet, crowded the windows and housetops, some of them calling out to him, in solemn words, not to recant: " Whosoever denieth me before men ! " [1] they cried to him, — as in a kind of solemn petition and adjuration. Was it not in reality our petition too, the petition of the whole world, lying in dark bondage of soul, paralysed under a black spectral Nightmare and triple-hatted Chimera, calling itself Father in God, and what not: " Free us ; it rests with thee ; desert us not ! "

Luther did not desert us. His speech, of two hours, distinguished itself by its respectful, wise and honest tone ; submissive to whatsoever could lawfully claim submission, not submissive to any more than that. His writings, he said, were partly his own, partly derived from the Word of God. As to what was his own, human infirmity entered into it ; unguarded anger, blindness, many things doubtless which it were a blessing for him could he abolish altogether. But as to what stood on sound truth and the Word of God, he could not recant it. How could he ? " Confute me," he concluded, " by proofs of Scripture, or else by plain just arguments : I cannot recant otherwise. For it is neither safe nor prudent to do aught against conscience. Here stand I ; I can do no other : God assist me ! " — It is, as we say, the greatest moment in the Modern History of Men. English Puritanism, Eng-

[1] But whosoever shall deny me before men, him will I also deny before my Father which is in heaven. Matt. x, 33.

land and its Parliaments, Americas, and vast work
these two centuries ; French Revolution, Europe and
its work everywhere at present : the germ of it all lay
there : had Luther in that moment done other, it had
all been otherwise ! The European World was asking
him : Am I to sink ever lower into falsehood, stag-
nant putrescence, loathsome accursed death ; or, with
whatever paroxysm, to cast the falsehoods out of me,
and be cured and live ? —

Great wars, contentions and disunion followed out
of this Reformation ; which last down to our day, and
are yet far from ended. Great talk and crimination
has been made about these. They are lamentable,
undeniable ; but after all, what has Luther or his
cause to do with them ? It seems strange reasoning to
charge the Reformation with all this. When Hercules
turned the purifying river into King Augeas's stables,[1]
I have no doubt the confusion that resulted was considerable all around: but I think it was not Hercules's
blame ; it was some other's blame ! The Reformation
might bring what results it liked when it came, but
the Reformation simply could not help coming. To all
Popes and Popes' advocates, expostulating, lamenting
and accusing, the answer of the world is : Once for all,
your Popehood has become untrue. No matter how
good it was, how good you say it is, we cannot believe
it ; the light of our whole mind, given us to walk-by
from Heaven above, finds it henceforth a thing unbe-

[1] One of the "Twelve Labors" of Hercules. He turned the
river Alpheus through the stables, where three thousand oxen
were kept, and cleansed them in a day from the accumulations
of many years.

lievable. We will not believe it, we will not try to believe it, — we dare not! The thing is *untrue ;* we were traitors against the Giver of all Truth, if we durst pretend to think it true. Away with it ; let whatsoever likes come in the place of it : with *it* we can have no farther trade! — Luther and his Protestantism is not responsible for wars ; the false Simulacra that forced him to protest, they are responsible. Luther did what every man that God has made has not only the right, but lies under the sacred duty, to do : answered a Falsehood when it questioned him, Dost thou believe me? — No ! — At what cost soever, without counting of costs, this thing behoved to be done. Union, organisation spiritual and material, a far nobler than any Popedom or Feudalism in their truest days, I never doubt, is coming for the world ; sure to come. But on Fact alone, not on Semblance and Simulacrum, will it be able either to come, or to stand when come. With union grounded on falsehood, and ordering us to speak and act lies, we will not have anything to do. Peace ? A brutal lethargy is peaceable, the noisome grave is peaceable. We hope for a living peace, not a dead one !

And yet, in prizing justly the indispensable blessings of the New, let us not be unjust to the Old. The Old *was* true, if it no longer is. In Dante's days it needed no sophistry, self-blinding or other dishonesty, to get itself reckoned true. It was good then ; nay there is in the soul of it a deathless good. The cry of ' No Popery ' is foolish enough in these days. The speculation that Popery is on the increase, building new chapels and so forth, may pass for one of the

idlest ever started. Very curious: to count-up a few
Popish chapels, listen to a few Protestant logic-chop-
pings, — to much dull-droning drowsy inanity that still
calls itself Protestant, and say: See, Protestantism is
dead; Popeism is more alive than it, will be alive
after it! — Drowsy inanities, not a few, that call themselves Protestant are dead; but *Protestantism* has
not died yet, that I hear of! Protestantism, if we will
look, has in these days produced its Goethe, its Napoleon; German Literature and the French Revolution;
rather considerable signs of life! Nay, at bottom,
what else is alive *but* Protestantism? The life of
most else that one meets is a galvanic one merely, —
not a pleasant, not a lasting sort of life!

Popery can build new chapels; welcome to do so,
to all lengths. Popery cannot come back, any more
than Paganism can, — *which* also still lingers in some
countries. But, indeed, it is with these things, as with
the ebbing of the sea: you look at the waves oscillat-
ing hither, thither on the beach; for *minutes* you cannot tell how it is going; look in half an hour where it
is, — look in half a century where your Popehood is!
Alas, would there were no greater danger to our Europe than the poor old Pope's revival! Thor may as
soon try to revive. — And withal this oscillation has a
meaning. The poor old Popehood will not die away
entirely, as Thor has done, for some time yet; nor
ought it. We may say, the Old never dies till this
happen, Till all the soul of good that was in it have
got itself transfused into the practical New. While
a good work remains capable of being done by the
Romish form; or, what is inclusive of all, while a

pious life remains capable of being led by it, just so long, if we consider, will this or the other human soul adopt it, go about as a living witness of it. So long it will obtrude itself on the eye of us who reject it, till we in our practice too have appropriated whatsoever of truth was in it. Then, but also not till then, it will have no charm more for any man. It lasts here for a purpose. Let it last as long as it can. —

Of Luther I will add now, in reference to all these wars and bloodshed, the noticeable fact that none of them began so long as he continued living.[1] The controversy did not get to fighting so long as he was there. To me it is proof of his greatness in all senses, this fact. How seldom do we find a man that has stirred-up some vast commotion, who does not himself perish, swept-away in it! Such is the usual course of revolutionists. Luther continued, in a good degree, sovereign of this greatest revolution ; all Protestants, of what rank or function soever, looking much to him for guidance : and he held it peaceable, continued firm at the centre of it. A man to do this must have a kingly faculty : he must have the gift to discern at all turns where the true heart of the matter lies, and to plant himself courageously on that, as a strong true man, that other true men may rally round him there. He will not continue leader of men otherwise. Luther's clear deep force of judgment, his force of all sorts, of *silence*, of tolerance and moderation, among others, are very notable in these circumstances.

[1] It was not until 1537 that Luther put away finally all hope of reconciliation with the Church.

Tolerance, I say ; a very genuine kind of tolerance :
he distinguishes what is essential, and what is not ; the
unessential may go very much as it will. A complaint
comes to him that such and such a Reformed Preacher
'will not preach without a cassock.' Well, answers
Luther, what harm will a cassock do the man ? 'Let
him have a cassock to preach in ; let him have three
cassocks if he find benefit in them!' His conduct
in the matter of Karlstadt's [1] wild image-breaking ;
of the Anabaptists ; [2] of the Peasants' War, [3] shows a
noble strength, very different from spasmodic violence.
With sure prompt insight he discriminates what is
what : a strong just man, he speaks-forth what is the
wise course, and all men follow him in that. Luther's
Written Works give similar testimony of him. The
dialect of these speculations is now grown obsolete for
us ; but one still reads them with a singular attraction.
And indeed the mere grammatical diction is still
legible enough ; Luther's merit in literary history is
of the greatest : his dialect became the language of all
writing. They are not well written, these Four-and-
twenty Quartos of his ; written hastily, with quite
other than literary objects. But in no Books have I
found a more robust, genuine, I will say noble faculty
of a man than in these. A rugged honesty, homeliness,

[1] He carried Luther's views to extremes in his radical opposition to priests and churches, resulting in riotous outbreaks in
Luther's absence from Wittenberg. Luther on his return had
much difficulty in restraining these excesses.

[2] At Münster (1532). So-called as denying the validity of infant baptism and requiring adults to be baptized again (Gr. ἀνά
=again).

[3] Against the Nobles and Clergy (1525), opposed by Luther.

simplicity; a rugged sterling sense and strength. He flashes-out illumination from him; his smiting idiomatic phrases seem to cleave into the very secret of the matter. Good humour too, nay tender affection, nobleness, and depth: this man could have been a Poet too! He had to *work* an Epic Poem, not write one. I call him a great Thinker; as indeed his greatness of heart already betokens that.

Richter says of Luther's words, ' his words are half-battles.' They may be called so. The essential quality of him was, that he could fight and conquer; that he was a right piece of human Valour. No more valiant man, no mortal heart to be called *braver*, that one has record of, ever lived in that Teutonic Kindred, whose character is valour. His defiance of the ' Devils' in Worms was not a mere boast, as the like might be if now spoken. It was a faith of Luther's that there were Devils, spiritual denizens of the Pit, continually besetting men. Many times, in his writings, this turns-up; and a most small sneer has been grounded on it by some. In the room of the Wartburg [1] where he sat translating the Bible, they still show you a black spot on the wall; the strange memorial of one of these conflicts. Luther sat translating one of the Psalms; he was worn-down with long labour, with sickness, abstinence from food: there rose before him some hideous indefinable Image, which he took for the Evil One, to forbid his work: Luther started-up,

[1] Near Eisenach, an ancient residence and fortress, where, immediately after the Diet of Worms, Luther was carried by the Elector's troops for protection against violence from the Papal party : about one hundred and thirty miles NNE of Worms.

with fiend-defiance ; flung his inkstand at the spectre, and it disappeared ! The spot still remains there ; a curious monument of several things. Any apothecary's apprentice can now tell us what we are to think of this apparition, in a scientific sense : but the man's heart that dare rise defiant, face to face, against Hell itself, can give no higher proof of fearlessness. The thing he will quail before exists not on this Earth or under it. — Fearless enough ! 'The Devil is aware,' writes he on one occasion, ' that this does not proceed out of fear in me. I have seen and defied innumerable Devils. Duke George,' of Leipzig, a great enemy of his, 'Duke George is not equal to one Devil,' — far short of a Devil ! ' If I had business at Leipzig, I would ride into Leipzig, though it rained Duke-Georges for nine days running.' What a reservoir of Dukes to ride into ! —

At the same time, they err greatly who imagine that this man's courage was ferocity, mere coarse disobedient obstinacy and savagery, as many do. Far from that. There may be an absence of fear which arises from the absence of thought or affection, from the presence of hatred and stupid fury. We do not value the courage of the tiger highly ! With Luther it was far otherwise ; no accusation could be more unjust than this of mere ferocious violence brought against him. A most gentle heart withal, full of pity and love, as indeed the truly valiant heart ever is. The tiger before a *stronger* foe — flies : the tiger is not what we call valiant, only fierce and cruel. I know few things more touching than those soft breathings of affection, soft as a child's or a mother's, in this great

wild heart of Luther. So honest, unadulterated with
any cant; homely, rude in their utterance; pure as
water welling from the rock. What, in fact, was all that
downpressed mood of despair and reprobation, which
we saw in his youth, but the outcome of preëminent
thoughtful gentleness, affections too keen and fine? It is
the course such men as the poor Poet Cowper[1] fall into.
Luther to a slight observer might have seemed a timid,
weak man; modesty, affectionate shrinking tenderness
the chief distinction of him. It is a noble valour which
is roused in a heart like this, once stirred-up into
defiance, all kindled into a heavenly blaze.

In Luther's *Table-Talk*, a posthumous Book of anecdotes and sayings collected by his friends, the most
interesting now of all the Books proceeding from him,
we have many beautiful unconscious displays of the
man, and what sort of nature he had. His behaviour
at the deathbed of his little Daughter, so still, so
great and loving, is among the most affecting things.
He is resigned that his little Magdalene should die,
yet longs inexpressibly that she might live; — follows,
in awestruck thought, the flight of her little soul
through those unknown realms. Awestruck; most
heartfelt, we can see; and sincere, — for after all
dogmatic creeds and articles, he feels what nothing
it is that we know, or can know: His little Magdalene shall be with God, as God wills; for Luther too
that is all; *Islam* is all.

Once he looks-out from his solitary Patmos,[2] the

---

[1] Under the shadow of melancholia, or worse, all his life
(1731–1800).

[2] The name of an island in the Ægean Sea, where John the

Castle of Coburg,[1] in the middle of the night: The
great vault of Immensity, long flights of clouds sailing through it, — dumb, gaunt, huge: — who supports all that? " None ever saw the pillars of it; yet
it is supported." God supports it. We must know
that God is great, that God is good; and trust,
where we cannot see. — Returning home from Leipzig once, he is struck by the beauty of the harvest-
fields: How it stands, that golden yellow corn, on its
fair taper stem, its golden head bent, all rich and waving there, — the meek Earth, at God's kind bidding,
has produced it once again; the bread of man! — In
the garden at Wittenberg one evening at sunset, a
little bird has perched for the night: That little bird,
says Luther, above it are the stars and deep Heaven
of worlds; yet it has folded its little wings; gone
trustfully to rest there as in its home: the Maker of
it has given it too a home! — — Neither are mirthful
turns wanting: there is a great free human heart in
this man. The common speech of him has a rugged
nobleness, idiomatic, expressive, genuine; gleams here
and there with beautiful poetic tints. One feels him
to be a great brother man. His love of Music, indeed,
is not this, as it were, the summary of all these affections in him? Many a wild unutterability he spoke-
forth from him in the tones of his flute. The Devils
fled from his flute, he says. Death-defiance on the
one hand, and such love of music on the other; I

Apostle, in banishment " for the testimony of Jesus Christ," saw
the vision recorded in the book of Revelation.

[1] Where Luther lived for several months in 1530, and wrote
his famous hymn, *Ein feste Burg*.

could call these the two opposite poles of a great soul ; between these two all great things had room.

Luther's face is to me expressive of him ; in Kranach's [1] best portraits I find the true Luther. A rude plebeian face ; with its huge crag-like brows and bones, the emblem of rugged energy ; at first, almost a repulsive face. Yet in the eyes especially there is a wild silent sorrow ; an unnamable melancholy, the element of all gentle and fine affections ; giving to the rest the true stamp of nobleness. Laughter was in this Luther, as we said ; but tears also were there. Tears also were appointed him ; tears and hard toil. The basis of his life was Sadness, Earnestness. In his latter days, after all triumphs and victories, he expresses himself heartily weary of living ; he considers that God alone can and will regulate the course things are taking, and that perhaps the Day of Judgment is not far. As for him, he longs for one thing : that God would release him from his labour, and let him depart and be at rest. They understand little of the man who cite this in *dis*credit of him ! — I will call this Luther a true Great Man ; great in intellect, in courage, affection and integrity ; one of our most lovable and precious men. Great, not as a hewn obelisk ; but as an Alpine mountain, — so simple, honest, spontaneous, not setting-up to be great at all ; there for quite another purpose than being great! Ah yes, unsubduable granite, piercing far and wide into the Heavens : yet in the clefts of it fountains, green beautiful valleys with flowers! A right Spiritual Hero and Pro-

[1] Intimate friend of Luther (1472–1553), court painter to three Electors of Saxony.

LIBRARY OF
Western Union College
LE MARS, IOWA

phet; once more, a true Son of Nature and Fact, for whom these centuries, and many that are to come yet, will be thankful to Heaven.[1]

The most interesting phasis which the Reformation anywhere assumes, especially for us English, is that of Puritanism. In Luther's own country Protestantism soon dwindled into a rather barren affair : not a religion or faith, but rather now a theological jangling of argument, the proper seat of it not the heart; the essence of it sceptical contention : which indeed has jangled more and more, down to Voltaireism itself, — through Gustavus-Adolphus[2] contentions onward to French-Revolution ones! But in our Island there arose a Puritanism, which even got itself established as a Presbyterianism and National Church among the Scotch ; which came forth as a real business of the heart; and has produced in the world very notable fruit. In some senses, one may say it is the only phasis of Protestantism that ever got to the rank of being a Faith, a true heart-communication with Heaven, and of exhibiting itself in History as such. We must spare a few words for Knox ; himself a brave and remarkable man ; but still more important as Chief Priest and Founder, which one may consider him to be, of the Faith that became Scotland's, New England's, Oliver Cromwell's. History will have something to say about this, for some time to come !

[1] Luther died in the town of his birth, 1546, and lies buried in the church at Wittenberg on the door of which he nailed his ninety-five theses.

[2] King of Sweden from 1611 until his death in 1632 ; leader of the Protestant forces in the Thirty Years' War (1618–1648).

We may censure Puritanism as we please; and no one of us, I suppose, but would find it a very rough defective thing. But we, and all men, may understand that it was a genuine thing; for Nature has adopted it, and it has grown, and grows. I say sometimes, that all goes by wager-of-battle in this world; that *strength*, well understood, is the measure of all worth. Give a thing time; if it can succeed, it is a right thing. Look now at American Saxondom; and at that little Fact of the sailing of the Mayflower, two-hundred years ago, from Delft Haven in Holland![1] Were we of open sense as the Greeks were, we had found a Poem here: one of Nature's own Poems, such as she writes in broad facts over great continents. For it was properly the beginning of America: there were straggling settlers in America before, some material as of a body was there; but the soul of it was first this. These poor men, driven-out of their own country, not able well to live in Holland, determine on settling in the New World. Black untamed forests are there, and wild savage creatures; but not so cruel as Star-chamber[2] hangmen. They thought the Earth would yield them food, if they tilled honestly; the everlasting heaven would stretch, there too, overhead; they should be left in peace, to prepare for Eternity by living well in this world of Time; worshipping in what they thought the true, not the idolatrous way. They clubbed

[1] It was the Speedwell that sailed from Delft Haven; when she was abandoned at Plymouth (England) those of her passengers that had not lost courage were taken on board the Mayflower.

[2] An English court, abolished in 1640, that decided cases on its own arbitrary authority instead of according to common law.

their small means together; hired a ship, the little ship Mayflower, and made ready to set sail.

In Neal's *History of the Puritans* [1] is an account of the ceremony of their departure: solemnity, we might call it rather, for it was a real act of worship. Their minister went down with them to the beach, and their brethren whom they were to leave behind; all joined in solemn prayer, That God would have pity on His poor children, and *go* with them into that waste wilderness, for He also had made that, He was there also as well as here. — Hah! These men, I think, had a work! The weak thing, weaker than a child, becomes strong one day, if it be a true thing. Puritanism was only despicable, laughable then; but nobody can manage to laugh at it now. Puritanism has got weapons and sinews; it has fire-arms, war-navies; it has cunning in its ten fingers, strength in its right arm; it can steer ships, fell forests, remove mountains; — it is one of the strongest things under this sun at present!

In the history of Scotland, too, I can find properly but one epoch: we may say, it contains nothing of world-interest at all but this Reformation by Knox. A poor barren country, full of continual broils, dissensions, massacrings; a people in the last state of rudeness and destitution, little better perhaps than Ireland at this day. Hungry fierce barons, not so much as able to form any arrangement with each other *how to divide* what they fleeced from these poor drudges; but obliged, as the Columbian Republics are at this day, to make of every alteration a revolution; no way of changing a ministry but by hanging the old ministers on gib-

[1] Neal (London, 1755), i. 490. (Carlyle's note.)

bets : this is a historical spectacle of no very singular significance! 'Bravery' enough, I doubt not; fierce fighting in abundance : but not braver or fiercer than that of their old Scandinavian Sea-king ancestors; *whose* exploits we have not found worth dwelling on! It is a country as yet without a soul : nothing developed in it but what is rude, external, semi-animal. And now at the Reformation, the internal life is kindled, as it were, under the ribs of this outward material death.[1] A cause, the noblest of causes, kindles itself, like a beacon set on high ; high as Heaven, yet attainable from Earth; — whereby the meanest man becomes not a Citizen only, but a Member of Christ's visible Church ; a veritable Hero, if he prove a true man!

Well ; this is what I mean by a whole ' nation of heroes;' a *believing* nation. There needs not a great soul to make a hero; there needs a god-created soul which will be true to its origin ; that will be a great soul! The like has been seen, we find. The like will be again seen, under wider forms than the Presbyterian : there can be no lasting good done till then. — Impossible! say some. Possible ? Has it not *been*, in this world, as a practised fact ? Did Hero-worship fail in Knox's case ? Or are we made of other clay now ? Did the Westminster Confession of Faith [2] add some new property to the soul of man ? God made the soul of man. He did not doom any soul of man to live as a Hypothesis and Hearsay, in a world filled with such, and with the fatal work and fruit of such ! —

---

[1] Strains that might create a soul
Under the ribs of death.   *Comus*, 561, 562.
[2] The Presbyterian creed, promulgated by the Puritans in 1646.

But to return : This that Knox did for his Nation,
I say, we may really call a resurrection as from death.
It was not a smooth business ; but it was welcome
surely, and cheap at that price, had it been far rougher.
On the whole, cheap at any price ; — as life is.
The people began to *live:* they needed first of all to
do that, at what cost and costs soever. Scotch Literature and Thought, Scotch Industry ; James Watt,[1]
David Hume,[2] Walter Scott, Robert Burns: I find
Knox and the Reformation acting in the heart's core
of every one of these persons and phenomena ; I find
that without the Reformation they would not have
been. Or what of Scotland? The Puritanism of Scotland became that of England, of New England. A
tumult in the High Church of Edinburgh[3] spread into
a universal battle and struggle over all these realms ;
— there came out, after fifty-years struggling, what we
all call the '*Glorious* Revolution,'[4] a *Habeas-Corpus*[5]
Act, Free Parliaments, and much else ! — Alas, is it
not too true what we said, That many men in the van
do always, like Russian soldiers march into the ditch
of Schweidnitz, and fill it up with their dead bodies,

[1] Of steam-engine fame (1736–1819).

[2] Philosopher and historian (1711–1776).

[3] St. Giles's, July 23, 1637, when Jenny Geddes, so tradition
reports, threw her folding stool at the officiating bishop in
protest against the introduction of the Anglican order of service.

[4] Of 1688, in opposition to the tyranny and Roman Catholicism
of James II ; resulting in the establishment of a purer constitutional government, and the accession to the throne of William of
Orange and Mary (James's daughter). Compare p. 205, n. 2.

[5] "Thou shalt have the body," of a person, confined on any
charge, brought before a magistrate, to examine whether he is
lawfully deprived of his liberty.

that the rear may pass-over them dry-shod, and gain the honour? How many earnest rugged Cromwells, Knoxes, poor Peasant Covenanters,[1] wrestling, battling for very life, in rough miry places, have to struggle, and suffer, and fall, greatly censured, *bemired*, — before a beautiful Revolution of Eighty-eight can step-over them in official pumps and silk-stockings,[2] with universal three-times-three!

It seems to me hard measure that this Scottish man, now after three-hundred years, should have to plead like a culprit before the world; intrinsically for having been, in such way as it was then possible to be, the bravest of all Scotchmen! Had he been a poor Half-and-half, he could have crouched into the corner, like so many others; Scotland had not been delivered; and Knox had been without blame. He is the one Scotchman to whom, of all others, his country and the world owe a debt. He has to plead that Scotland would forgive him for having been worth to it any million ' unblamable' Scotchmen that need no forgiveness! He bared his breast to the battle; had to row in French galleys,[3] wander forlorn in exile,[4] in clouds and storms;

[1] Signers or adherents to the *National Covenant* (1638), an agreement to oppose the introduction of the Anglican ritual in Scotch churches.

[2] Formal court dress: — " It may seem almost an abuse of terms to call a proceeding, conducted with so much deliberation, with so much sobriety, and with such minute attention to proscriptive etiquette, by the terrible name of Revolution." Macaulay, *History of England*, Chap. x, near end.

[3] See p. 207, n. 2.

[4] The persecutions of Queen Mary of England caused him to make the Continent his headquarters from 1554 to 1559. Compare p. 164, n. 5.

was censured, shot-at through his windows; had a right sore fighting life : if this world were his place of recompense, he had made but a bad venture of it. I cannot apologise for Knox. To him it is very indifferent, these two-hundred-and-fifty years or more, what men say of him. But we, having got above all those details of his battle, and living now in clearness on the fruits of his victory, we, for our own sake, ought to look through the rumours and controversies enveloping the man, into the man himself.

For one thing, I will remark that this post of Prophet to his Nation was not of his seeking ; Knox had lived forty years [1] quietly obscure, before he became conspicuous. He was the son of poor parents; had got a college education; [2] become a Priest; adopted the Reformation, and seemed well content to guide his own steps by the light of it, nowise unduly intruding it on others. He had lived as Tutor in gentlemen's families ; preaching when any body of persons wished to hear his doctrine : resolute he to walk by the truth, and speak the truth when called to do it : not ambitious of more ; not fancying himself capable of more. In this entirely obscure way he had reached the age of forty; was with the small body of Reformers who were standing siege in St. Andrew's Castle, — when one day in their chapel, the Preacher after finishing his exhortation to these fighters in the forlorn hope, said suddenly, That there ought to be other speakers, that all men who had a priest's heart and gift in them ought now to speak ; — which gifts and heart one of their own num-

[1] He was born in 1505.
[2] At the University of Glasgow, but took no degree.

ber, John Knox the name of him, had : Had he not ?
said the Preacher, appealing to all the audience : what
then is *his* duty ? The people answered affirmatively ;
it was a criminal forsaking of his post, if such a man
held the word that was in him silent. Poor Knox was
obliged to stand-up ; he attempted to reply ; he could
say no word ; — burst into a flood of tears, and ran
out. It is worth remembering, that scene. He was in
grievous trouble for some days. He felt what a small
faculty was his for this great work. He felt what a
baptism he was called to be baptised withal.[1] He ' burst
into tears.'

Our primary characteristic of a Hero, that he is sincere, applies emphatically to Knox. It is not denied
anywhere that this, whatever might be his other qualities or faults, is among the truest of men. With a
singular instinct he holds to the truth and fact ; the
truth alone is there for him, the rest a mere shadow
and deceptive nonentity. However feeble, forlorn the
reality may seem, on that and that only *can* he take
his stand. In the Galleys of the River Loire, whither
Knox and the others, after their Castle of St. Andrew's was taken, had been sent as Galley-slaves, [2] —
some officer or priest, one day, presented them an Image
of the Virgin Mother, requiring that they, the blasphemous heretics, should do it reverence. Mother ?
Mother of God ? said Knox, when the turn came to
him : This is no Mother of God : this is ' a *pented*

[1] But I have a baptism to be baptized with ; and how am I
straitened till it be accomplished ! Luke xii, 50.
[2] On charge of being concerned in the assassination of Cardinal Beatoun, Knox was in the galleys two years.

bredd,' — a piece of wood, I tell you, with paint on it! She is fitter for swimming, I think, than for being worshipped, added Knox; and flung the thing into the river. It was not very cheap jesting there: but come of it what might, this thing to Knox was and must continue nothing other than the real truth ; it was a *pented bredd ;* worship it he would not.

He told his fellow-prisoners, in this darkest time, to be of courage ; the Cause they had was the true one, and must and would prosper; the whole world could not put it down. Reality is of God's making; it is alone strong. How many *pented bredds*, pretending to be real, are fitter to swim than to be worshipped ! — This Knox cannot live but by fact : he clings to reality as the shipwrecked sailor to the cliff. He is an instance to us how a man, by sincerity itself, becomes heroic : it is the grand gift he has. We find in Knox a good honest intellectual talent, no transcendent one ; — a narrow, inconsiderable man, as compared with Luther : but in heartfelt instinctive adherence to truth, in *sincerity*, as we say, he has no superior ; nay, one might ask, What equal he has ? The heart of him is of the true Prophet cast. " He lies there," said the Earl of Morton [1] at his grave, " who never feared the face of man." He resembles, more than any of the moderns, an Old-Hebrew Prophet. The same inflexibility, intolerance, rigid narrow-looking adherence to God's truth, stern rebuke in the name of God to all that forsake truth : an Old-Hebrew Prophet in the guise of an Edinburgh Minister of the Sixteenth Century. We are to take him for that ; not require him to be other.

[1] Regent 1572–1577, executed 1581.

Knox's conduct to Queen Mary,[1] the harsh visits he used to make in her own palace, to reprove her there, have been much commented upon. Such cruelty, such coarseness fills us with indignation. On reading the actual narrative of the business, what Knox said, and what Knox meant, I must say one's tragic feeling is rather disappointed. They are not so coarse, these speeches; they seem to me about as fine as the circumstances would permit! Knox was not there to do the courtier; he came on another errand. Whoever, reading these colloquies of his with the Queen, thinks they are vulgar insolences of a plebeian priest to a delicate high lady, mistakes the purport and essence of them altogether. It was unfortunately not possible to be polite with the Queen of Scotland, unless one proved untrue to the Nation and Cause of Scotland. A man who did not wish to see the land of his birth made a hunting-field for intriguing ambitious Guises,[2] and the Cause of God trampled underfoot of Falsehoods, Formulas and the Devil's Cause, had no method of making himself agreeable! "Better that women weep," said Morton, "than that bearded men be forced to weep." Knox was the constitutional opposition-party in Scotland: the Nobles of the country, called by their station to take that post, were not found in it; Knox had to go, or no one. The hapless Queen; — but the still more hapless Country, if *she* were made happy! Mary herself was not without sharpness enough, among her other

[1] The beautiful, accomplished, and altogether inscrutable Mary Stuart, Queen of Scots. Born 1542, beheaded 1587; of Roman Catholic faith, and of French-bred gayety of manner.

[2] The mother of the Queen was a daughter of the French ducal house of Guise.

qualities: "Who are you," said she once, "that presume to school the nobles and sovereign of this realm?" — "Madam, a subject born within the same," answered he. Reasonably answered! If the 'subject' have truth to speak, it is not the 'subject's' footing that will fail him here. —

We blame Knox for his intolerance. Well, surely it is good that each of us be as tolerant as possible. Yet, at bottom, after all the talk there is and has been about it, what is tolerance? Tolerance has to tolerate the *un*essential; and to see well what that is. Tolerance has to be noble, measured, just in its very wrath, when it can tolerate no longer. But, on the whole, we are not altogether here to tolerate! We are here to resist, to control and vanquish withal. We do not 'tolerate' Falsehoods, Thieveries, Iniquities, when they fasten on us; we say to them, Thou art false, thou art not tolerable! We are here to extinguish Falsehoods, and put an end to them, in some wise way! I will not quarrel so much with the way; the doing of the thing is our great concern. In this sense Knox was, full surely, intolerant.

A man sent to row in French Galleys, and suchlike, for teaching the Truth in his own land, cannot always be in the mildest humour! I am not prepared to say that Knox had a soft temper; nor do I know that he had what we call an ill temper. An ill nature he decidedly had not. Kind honest affections dwelt in the much-enduring, hard-worn, ever-battling man. That he *could* rebuke Queens, and had such weight among those proud turbulent Nobles, proud enough whatever else they were; and could maintain to the end a kind

of virtual Presidency and Sovereignty in that wild
realm, he who was only ' a subject born within the
same : ' this of itself will prove to us that he was
found, close at hand, to be no mean acrid man; but
at heart a healthful, strong, sagacious man. Such
alone can bear rule in that kind. They blame him
for pulling-down cathedrals, and so forth, as if he
were a seditious rioting demagogue : precisely the
reverse is seen to be the fact, in regard to cathedrals
and the rest of it, if we examine ! Knox wanted no
pulling-down of stone edifices ; he wanted leprosy and
darkness to be thrown out of the lives of men. Tumult was not his element ; it was the tragic feature of
his life that he was forced to dwell so much in that.
Every such man is the born enemy of Disorder ; hates
to be in it : but what then ? Smooth Falsehood is not
Order ; it is the general sumtotal of *Dis*order. Order is
Truth, — each thing standing on the basis that belongs
to it : Order and Falsehood cannot subsist together.

Withal, unexpectedly enough, this Knox has a vein
of drollery in him ; which I like much, in combination
with his other qualities. He has a true eye for the
ridiculous. His *History*, with its rough earnestness, is
curiously enlivened with this. When the two Prelates,
entering Glasgow Cathedral, quarrel about precedence ;
march rapidly up, take to hustling one another, twitch-
ing one another's rochets,[1] and at last flourishing their
crosiers[2] like quarter-staves, it is a great sight[3] for
him everyway ! Not mockery, scorn, bitterness alone ;
though there is enough of that too. But a true, loving,

[1] A vestment worn usually by bishops.
[2] A bishop's staff.   [3] He calls it " a merry game."

illuminating laugh mounts-up over the earnest visage ;
not a loud laugh ; you would say, a laugh in the *eyes*
most of all. An honest-hearted, brotherly man ; brother
to the high, brother also to the low ; sincere in his sympathy with both. He had his pipe [1] of Bordeaux too,
we find, in that old Edinburgh house of his ; a cheery
social man, with faces that loved him ! They go far
wrong who think this Knox was a gloomy, spasmodic,
shrieking fanatic. Not at all : he is one of the solidest
of men. Practical, cautious-hopeful, patient ; a most
shrewd, observing, quietly discerning man. In fact, he
has very much the type of character we assign to the
Scotch at present : a certain sardonic taciturnity is in
him ; insight enough ; and a stouter heart than he himself knows of. He has the power of holding his peace
over many things which do not vitally concern him, —
" They? what are they?" But the thing which does
vitally concern him, that thing he will speak of ; and
in a tone the whole world shall be made to hear : all
the more emphatic for his long silence.

This Prophet of the Scotch is to me no hateful man !
— He had a sore fight of an existence ; wrestling with
Popes and Principalities ; in defeat, contention, life-
long struggle ; rowing as a galley-slave, wandering as
an exile. A sore fight : but he won it. " Have you
hope ? " they asked him in his last moment, when he
could no longer speak. He lifted his finger, ' pointed
upwards with his finger,' and so died.[2] Honour to
him ! His works have not died. The letter of his work
dies, as of all men's ; but the spirit of it never.

[1] A measure of wine, — one hundred gallons and upwards.
[2] 1572.

One word more as to the letter of Knox's work.
The unforgivable offence in him is, that he wished to
set-up Priests over the head of Kings. In other words,
he strove to make the Government of Scotland a *Theocracy*. This indeed is properly the sum of his offences,
the essential sin ; for which what pardon can there be ?
It is most true, he did, at bottom, consciously or unconsciously, mean a Theocracy, or Government of God.
He did mean that Kings and Prime Ministers, and all
manner of persons, in public or private, diplomatising
or whatever else they might be doing, should walk
according to the Gospel of Christ, and understand that
this was their Law, supreme over all laws. He hoped
once to see such a thing realised ; and the Petition,
Thy Kingdom come, no longer an empty word. He
was sore grieved when he saw greedy worldly Barons
clutch hold of the Church's property ; when he ex-
postulated that it was not secular property, that it
was spiritual property, and should be turned to *true*
churchly uses, education, schools, worship ; — and the
Regent Murray [1] had to answer, with a shrug of the
shoulders, " It is a devout imagination ! " This was
Knox's scheme of right and truth ; this he zealously
endeavoured after, to realise it. If we think his scheme
of truth was too narrow, was not true, we may rejoice
that he could not realise it ; that it remained after
two centuries of effort, unrealisable, and is a ' devout
imagination ' still. But how shall we blame *him* for
struggling to realise it ? Theocracy, Government of
God, is precisely the thing to be struggled for ! All

[1] Half-brother of Mary, leader of the Protestant party, Regent from 1567, murdered 1570.

Prophets, zealous Priests, are there for that purpose. Hildebrand [1] wished a Theocracy; Cromwell wished it, fought for it; Mahomet attained it. Nay, is it not what all zealous men, whether called Priests, Prophets, or whatsoever else called, do essentially wish, and must wish? That right and truth, or God's Law, reign supreme among men, this is the Heavenly Ideal (well named in Knox's time, and namable in all times, a revealed ' Will of God ') towards which the Reformer will insist that all be more and more approximated. All true Reformers, as I said, are by the nature of them Priests, and strive for a Theocracy.

How far such Ideals can ever be introduced into Practice, and at what point our impatience with their non-introduction ought to begin, is always a question. I think we may say safely, Let them introduce themselves as far as they can contrive to do it! If they are the true faith of men, all men ought to be more or less impatient always where they are not found introduced. There will never be wanting Regent-Murrays enough to shrug their shoulders, and say, " A devout imagination ! " We will praise the Hero-Priest rather, who does what is in *him* to bring them in ; and wears-out, in toil, calumny, contradiction, a noble life, to make a God's Kingdom of this Earth. The Earth will not become too godlike !

[1] Gregory VII, Pope 1073–1085 ; stoutly defended the supremacy of the Church against the power of the Emperor, Henry IV

LECTURE V

[Tuesday, 19th May 1840.]

HERO-GODS, Prophets, Poets, Priests are forms of
Heroism that belong to the old ages, make their appearance in the remotest times; some of them have
ceased to be possible long since, and cannot any more
show themselves in this world. The Hero as *Man of
Letters*, again, of which class we are to speak today,
is altogether a product of these new ages; and so long
as the wondrous art of *Writing*, or of Ready-writing
which we call *Printing*, subsists, he may be expected
to continue, as one of the main forms of Heroism for
all future ages. He is, in various respects, a very
singular phenomenon.

He is new, I say; he has hardly lasted above a
century in the world yet. Never, till about a hundred
years ago, was there seen any figure of a Great Soul
living apart in that anomalous manner; endeavouring
to speak-forth the inspiration that was in him by
Printed Books, and find place and subsistence by
what the world would please to give him for doing
that. Much had been sold and bought, and left to
make its own bargain in the marketplace; but the
inspired wisdom of a Heroic Soul never till then, in
that naked manner. He, with his copy-rights and

copy-wrongs, in his squalid garret, in his rusty coat; ruling (for this is what he does), from his grave, after death, whole nations and generations who would, or would not, give him bread while living, — is a rather curious spectacle! Few shapes of Heroism can be more unexpected.

Alas, the Hero from of old has had to cramp himself into strange shapes: the world knows not well at any time what to do with him, so foreign is his aspect in the world! It seemed absurd to us, that men, in their rude admiration, should take some wise great Odin for a god, and worship him as such; some wise great Mahomet for one god-inspired, and religiously follow his Law for twelve centuries; but that a wise great Johnson, a Burns, a Rousseau, should be taken for some idle nondescript, extant in the world to amuse idleness, and have a few coins and applauses thrown him, that he might live thereby; *this* perhaps, as before hinted, will one day seem a still absurder phasis of things! — Meanwhile, since it is the spiritual always that determines the material, this same Man-of-Letters Hero must be regarded as our most important modern person. He, such as he may be, is the soul of all. What he teaches, the whole world will do and make. The world's manner of dealing with him is the most significant feature of the world's general position. Looking well at his life, we may get a glance, as deep as is readily possible for us, into the life of those singular centuries which have produced him, in which we ourselves live and work.

There are genuine Men of Letters, and not genuine; as in every kind there is a genuine and a spurious.

If *Hero* be taken to mean genuine, then I say the
Hero as Man of Letters will be found discharging a
function for us which is ever honourable, ever the
highest; and was once well known to be the highest.
He is uttering-forth, in such way as he has, the inspired soul of him; all that a man, in any case, can
do. I say *inspired;* for what we call 'originality,'
'sincerity,' 'genius,' the heroic quality we have no good
name for, signifies that. The Hero is he who lives in
the inward sphere of things, in the True, Divine and
Eternal, which exists always, unseen to most, under
the Temporary, Trivial: his being is in that; he declares that abroad, by act or speech as it may be, in
declaring himself abroad. His life, as we said before,
is a piece of the everlasting heart of Nature herself: all
men's life is, — but the weak many know not the fact,
and are untrue to it, in most times; the strong few
are strong, heroic, perennial, because it cannot be
hidden from them. The Man of Letters, like every
Hero, is there to proclaim this in such sort as he can.
Intrinsically it is the same function which the old
generations named a man Prophet, Priest, Divinity for
doing; which all manner of Heroes, by speech or by
act, are sent into the world to do.

Fichte [1] the German Philosopher delivered, some
forty years ago at Erlangen,[2] a highly remarkable
Course of Lectures on this subject: '*Ueber das
Wesen des Gelehrten*, On the Nature of the Literary
Man.' Fichte, in conformity with the Transcendental
Philosophy, of which he was a distinguished teacher,

[1] 1762–1848.
[2] University town in Bavaria.

declares first : That all things which we see or work
with in this Earth, especially we ourselves and all
persons, are as a kind of vesture or sensuous Appearance: that under all there lies, as the essence of them,
what he calls the ' Divine Idea of the World ; ' this is
the Reality which ' lies at the bottom of all Appearance.'
To the mass of men no such Divine Idea is recognisable in the world; they live merely, says Fichte, among
the superficialities, practicalities and shows of the
world, not dreaming that there is anything divine
under them. But the Man of Letters is sent hither
specially that he may discern for himself, and make
manifest to us, this same Divine Idea: in every new
generation it will manifest itself in a new dialect; and
he is there for the purpose of doing that. Such is
Fichte's phraseology ; with which we need not quarrel.
It is his way of naming what I here, by other words,
am striving imperfectly to name ; what there is at
present no name for : The unspeakable Divine Significance, full of splendour, of wonder and terror, that
lies in the being of every man, of every thing, — the
Presence of the God who made every man, and thing.
Mahomet taught this in his dialect ; Odin in his : it
is the thing which all thinking hearts, in one dialect
or another, are here to teach.

Fichte calls the Man of Letters, therefore, a Prophet,
or as he prefers to phrase it, a Priest, continually
unfolding the Godlike to men : Men of Letters are a
perpetual Priesthood, from age to age, teaching all
men that a God is still present in their life ; that all
' Appearance,' whatsoever we see in the world, is but
as a vesture for the ' Divine Idea of the World,' for

'that which lies at the bottom of Appearance.' In the
true Literary Man there is thus ever, acknowledged or
not by the world, a sacredness : he is the light of the
world ; the world's Priest; — guiding it, like a sacred
Pillar of Fire, in its dark pilgrimage through the waste
of Time.[1] Fichte discriminates with sharp zeal the *true*
Literary Man, what we here call the *Hero* as Man of
Letters, from multitudes of false unheroic. Whoever
lives not wholly in this Divine Idea, or living partially
in it, struggles not, as for the one good, to live wholly
in it, — he is, let him live where else he like, in what
pomps and prosperities he like, no Literary Man ; he
is, says Fichte, a 'Bungler, *Stümper*.' Or at best, if
he belong to the prosaic provinces, he may be a ' Hod-
man ; ' Fichte even calls him elsewhere a ' Nonentity,'
and has in short no mercy for him, no wish that *he*
should continue happy among us ! This is Fichte's
notion of the Man of Letters. It means, in its own
form, precisely what we here mean.

In this point of view, I consider that, for the last
hundred years, by far the notablest of all Literary Men
is Fichte's countryman, Goethe. To that man too, in
a strange way, there was given what we may call a life
in the Divine Idea of the World ; vision of the inward
divine mystery : and strangely, out of his Books, the
world rises imaged once more as godlike, the work-
manship and temple of a God. Illuminated all, not
in fierce impure fire-splendour as of Mahomet, but in
mild celestial radiance ; — really a Prophecy in these

[1] And the Lord went before them by day in a pillar of a cloud,
to lead them the way ; and by night in a pillar of fire, to give
them light. Exod. xiii, 21.

most unprophetic times; to my mind, by far the greatest, though one of the quietest, among all the great things that have come to pass in them. Our chosen specimen of the Hero as Literary Man would be this Goethe.[1] And it were a very pleasant plan for me here to discourse of his heroism : for I consider him to be a true Hero; heroic in what he said and did, and perhaps still more in what he did not say and did not do ; to me a noble spectacle : a great heroic ancient man, speaking and keeping silence as an ancient Hero, in the guise of a most modern, high-bred, high-cultivated Man of Letters! We have had no such spectacle; no man capable of affording such, for the last hundred-and-fifty years.

But at present, such is the general state of knowledge about Goethe, it were worse than useless to attempt speaking of him in this case. Speak as I might, Goethe, to the great majority of you, would remain problematic, vague ; no impression but a false one could be realised. Him we must leave to future times. Johnson, Burns, Rousseau, three great figures from a prior time, from a far inferior state of circumstances, will suit us better here. Three men of the Eighteenth Century ; the conditions of their life far more resemble what those of ours still are in England, than what Goethe's in Germany were. Alas, these men did not conquer like him; they fought bravely, and fell. They were not heroic bringers of the light, but heroic seekers of it. They lived under galling conditions ; struggling as under mountains of impedi-

---

[1] Johann Wolfgang von Goethe, 1749–1832. *The Correspondence between Goethe and Carlyle* was published in 1887.

ment, and could not unfold themselves into clearness, or victorious interpretation of that ' Divine Idea.' It is rather the *Tombs* of three Literary Heroes that I have to show you. There are the monumental heaps, under which three spiritual giants lie buried. Very mournful, but also great and full of interest for us. We will linger by them for a while.

Complaint is often made, in these times, of what we call the disorganised condition of society : how ill many arranged forces of society fulfil their work ; how many powerful forces are seen working in a wasteful, chaotic, altogether unarranged manner. It is too just a complaint, as we all know. But perhaps if we look at this of Books and the Writers of Books, we shall find here, as it were, the summary of all other disorganisation ; — a sort of *heart*, from which, and to which, all other confusion circulates in the world ! Considering what Book-writers do in the world, and what the world does with Book-writers, I should say, It is the most anomalous thing the world at present has to show. — We should get into a sea far beyond sounding, did we attempt to give account of this : but we must glance at it for the sake of our subject. The worst element in the life of these three Literary Heroes was, that they found their business and position such a chaos. On the beaten road there is tolerable travelling ; but it is sore work, and many have to perish, fashioning a path through the impassable !

Our pious Fathers, feeling well what importance lay in the speaking of man to men, founded churches, made endowments, regulations ; everywhere in the

civilised world there is a Pulpit, environed with all
manner of complex dignified appurtenances and furtherances, that therefrom a man with the tongue may,
to best advantage, address his fellow-men. They felt
that this was the most important thing ; that without
this there was no good thing. It is a right pious work,
that of theirs ; beautiful to behold! But now with
the art of Writing, with the art of Printing, a total
change has come over that business. The Writer of a
Book, is not he a Preacher preaching not to this parish or that, on this day or that, but to all men in all
times and places ? Surely it is of the last importance
that *he* do his work right, whoever do it wrong ; —
that the *eye* report not falsely, for then all the other
members are astray ! Well; how he may do his work,
whether he do it right or wrong, or do it at all, is a
point which no man in the world has taken the pains
to think of. To a certain shopkeeper, trying to get
some money for his books, if lucky, he is of some importance ; to no other man of any. Whence he came,
whither he is bound, by what ways he arrived, by
what he might be furthered on his course, no one
asks. He is an accident in society. He wanders like
a wild Ishmaelite,[1] in a world of which he is as
the spiritual light, either the guidance or the mis-
guidance !

Certainly the Art of Writing is the most miraculous of all things man has devised. Odin's *Runes* were
the first form of the work of a Hero; *Books*, written

[1] And he will be a wild man ; his hand will be against every
man, and every man's hand against him (said of Ishmael);
Gen. xvi, 12. See p. 68, n. 3.

words, are still miraculous *Runes*, the latest form! In Books lies the *soul* of the whole Past Time; the articulate audible voice of the Past, when the body and material substance of it has altogether vanished like a dream. Mighty fleets and armies, harbours and arsenals, vast cities, high-domed, many-engined, — they are precious, great: but what do they become? Agamemnon, the many Agamemnons, Pericleses, and their Greece; all is gone now to some ruined fragments, dumb mournful wrecks and blocks: but the Books of Greece! There Greece, to every thinker, still very literally lives; can be called-up again into life. No magic *Rune* is stranger than a Book. All that Mankind has done, thought, gained or been: it is lying as in magic preservation in the pages of Books. They are the chosen possession of men.

Do not Books still accomplish *miracles*, as *Runes* were fabled to do? They persuade men. Not the wretchedest circulating-library novel, which foolish girls thumb and con in remote villages, but will help to regulate the actual practical weddings and households of those foolish girls. So 'Celia' felt, so 'Clifford' acted: the foolish Theorem of Life, stamped into those young brains, comes out as a solid Practice one day. Consider whether any *Rune* in the wildest imagination of Mythologist ever did such wonders as, on the actual firm Earth, some Books have done! What built St. Paul's Cathedral? Look at the heart of the matter, it was that divine Hebrew BOOK, — the word partly of the man Moses, an outlaw tending his Midianitish herds, four-thousand years ago, in the wilderness of Sinai! It is the strangest of things, yet nothing is truer. With the art of Writing, of which Printing is a simple, an inevitable and comparatively insignificant corollary, the true reign of miracles for mankind commenced. It related, with a wondrous new contiguity and perpetual closeness, the Past and Distant with the Present in time and place; all times and all places with this our actual Here and Now. All things were altered for men ; all modes of important work of men: teaching, preaching, governing, and all else.

To look at Teaching, for instance. Universities are a notable, respectable product of the modern ages. Their existence too is modified, to the very basis of it, by the existence of Books. Universities arose while there were yet no Books procurable ; while a man, for a single Book, had to give an estate of land. That, in those circumstances, when a man had some knowledge to communicate, he should do it by gathering the learners round him, face to face, was a necessity for him. If you wanted to know what Abelard [1] knew, you must go and listen to Abelard. Thousands, as many as thirty-thousand, went to hear Abelard and that metaphysical theology of his. And now for any other teacher who had also something of his own to teach, there was a great convenience opened : so many thousands eager to learn were already assembled yonder ; of all places the best place for him was that. For any third teacher it was better still ; and grew ever the better, the more teachers there came. It only needed now that the King took notice of this new

[1] French philosopher, theologian, and teacher (1079–1142) ; most famous as the lover of Héloïse. See Pope's Eloïsa to Abelard.

phenomenon; combined or agglomerated the various schools into one school; gave it edifices, privileges, encouragements, and named it *Universitas*, or School of all Sciences : the University of Paris, in its essential characters, was there. The model of all subsequent Universities; which down even to these days, for six centuries now, have gone on to found themselves. Such, I conceive, was the origin of Universities.

It is clear, however, that with this simple circumstance, facility of getting Books, the whole conditions of the business from top to bottom were changed. Once invent Printing, you metamorphosed all Universities, or superseded them! The Teacher needed not now to gather men personally round him, that he might *speak* to them what he knew : print it in a Book, and all learners far and wide, for a trifle, had it each at his own fireside, much more effectually to learn it ! — Doubtless there is still peculiar virtue in Speech ; even writers of Books may still, in some circumstances, find it convenient to speak also, — witness our present meeting here ! There is, one would say, and must ever remain while man has a tongue, a distinct province for Speech as well as for Writing and Printing. In regard to all things this must remain ; to Universities among others. But the limits of the two have nowhere yet been pointed out, ascertained ; much less put in practice : the University which would completely take-in that great new fact, of the existence of Printed Books, and stand on a clear footing for the Nineteenth Century as the Paris one did for the Thirteenth, has not yet come into existence. If we think of it, all that a University or final highest

School can do for us, is still but what the first School
began doing, — teach us to *read*. We learn to *read*,
in various languages, in various sciences; we learn
the alphabet and letters of all manner of Books. But
the place where we are to get knowledge, even theo-
retic knowledge, is the Books themselves! It depends
on what we read, after all manner of Professors have
lone their best for us. The true University of these
days is a Collection of Books.

But to the Church itself, as I hinted already, all is
changed, in its preaching, in its working, by the introduction of Books. The Church is the working recognised Union of our Priests or Prophets, of those who
by wise teaching guide the souls of men. While there
was no Writing, even while there was no Easy-writing
or *Printing*, the preaching of the voice was the natural sole method of performing this. But now with
Books! — He that can write a true Book, to persuade
England, is not he the Bishop and Archbishop, the
Primate of England and of All England? I many a
time say, the writers of Newspapers, Pamphlets, Poems,
Books, these *are* the real working effective Church
of a modern country. Nay not only our preaching,
but even our worship, is not it too accomplished by
means of Printed Books? The noble sentiment which
a gifted soul has clothed for us in melodious words,
which brings melody into our hearts, — is not this
essentially, if we will understand it, of the nature of
worship? There are many, in all countries, who, in
this confused time, have no other method of worship.
He who, in any way, shows us better than we knew
before that a lily of the fields[1] is beautiful, does he

[1] See p. 112 n. 1.

not show it us as an effluence of the Fountain of all Beauty; as the *handwriting*, made visible there, of the great Maker of the Universe? He has sung for us, made us sing with him, a little verse of a sacred Psalm. Essentially so. How much more he who sings, who says, or in any way brings home to our heart the noble doings, feelings, darings and endurances of a brother man! He has verily touched our hearts as with a live coal *from the altar*.[1] Perhaps there is no worship more authentic.

Literature, so far as it is Literature, is an 'apocalypse of Nature,' a revealing of the 'open secret.' It may well enough be named, in Fichte's style, a 'continuous revelation' of the Godlike in the Terrestrial and Common. The Godlike does ever, in very truth, endure there; is brought out, now in this dialect, now in that, with various degrees of clearness: all true gifted Singers and Speakers are, consciously or unconsciously, doing so. The dark stormful indignation of a Byron,[2] so wayward and perverse, may have touches of it; nay the withered mockery of a French sceptic,[3] — his mockery of the False, a love and worship of the True. How much more the sphere-harmony of a Shakspeare, of a Goethe; the cathedral-music of a Milton! They are something too, those humble genuine lark-notes of a Burns, — skylark, starting from the humble furrow, far overhead into the blue depths, and singing to us so genuinely there! For all true singing is of the

---

[1] Then flew one of the seraphims unto me, having a live coal in his hand, which he had taken with the tongs from off the altar: and he laid it upon my mouth, . . . Isaiah vi, 6, 7.

[2] 1788-1824. See add. note.   [3] Voltaire. See p. 20, n. 2.

nature of worship; as indeed all true *working* may be said to be, — whereof such *singing* is but the record, and fit melodious representation, to us. Fragments of a real 'Church Liturgy' and 'Body of Homilies,' strangely disguised from the common eye, are to be found weltering in that huge froth-ocean of Printed Speech we loosely call Literature! Books are our Church too.

Or turning now to the Government of men. Witenagemote,[1] old Parliament, was a great thing. The affairs of the nation were there deliberated and decided; what we were to *do* as a nation. But does not, though the name Parliament subsists, the parliamentary debate go on now, everywhere and at all times, in a far more comprehensive way, *out* of Parliament altogether? Burke said there were Three Estates[2] in Parliament; but, in the Reporters' Gallery yonder, there sat a *Fourth Estate* more important far than they all. It is not a figure of speech, or a witty saying; it is a literal fact, — very momentous to us in these times. Literature is our Parliament too. Printing, which comes necessarily out of Writing, I say often, is equivalent to Democracy: invent Writing, Democracy is inevitable. Writing brings Printing; brings universal every-day extempore Printing, as we see at present. Whoever can speak, speaking now to the whole nation, becomes a power, a branch of government, with inalienable weight in law-making, in all acts of authority. It matters not what rank he has,

[1] " Assembly of counselors," the supreme parliamentary body of the nation in Anglo-Saxon times.

[2] Clergy, Nobles, and Commons.

what revenues or garnitures: the requisite thing is, that he have a tongue which others will listen to; this and nothing more is requisite. The nation is governed by all that has tongue in the nation: Democracy is virtually *there*. Add only, that whatsoever power exists will have itself, by and by, organised; working secretly under bandages, obscurations, obstructions, it will never rest till it get to work free, unencumbered, visible to all. Democracy virtually extant will insist on becoming palpably extant. —

On all sides, are we not driven to the conclusion that, of the things which man can do or make here below, by far the most momentous, wonderful and worthy are the things we call Books! Those poor bits of rag-paper with black ink on them; — from the Daily Newspaper to the sacred Hebrew BOOK, what have they not done, what are they not doing! — For indeed, whatever be the outward form of the thing (bits of paper, as we say, and black ink), is it not verily, at bottom, the highest act of man's faculty that produces a Book? It is the *Thought* of man; the true thauma-turgic[1] virtue; by which man works all things what-soever. All that he does, and brings to pass, is the vesture of a Thought. This London City, with all its houses, palaces, steamengines, cathedrals, and huge immeasurable traffic and tumult, what is it but a Thought, but millions of Thoughts made into One; — a huge immeasurable Spirit of a THOUGHT, embodied in brick, in iron, smoke, dust, Palaces, Parliaments, Hackney Coaches, Katherine Docks, and the rest of it! Not a brick was made but some man had to *think*

[1] Wonder- or miracle-working.

of the making of that brick. — The thing we called
' bits of paper with traces of black ink,' is the *purest*
embodiment a Thought of man can have. No wonder
it is, in all ways, the activest and noblest.

All this, of the importance and supreme importance
of the Man of Letters in modern Society, and how the
Press is to such a degree superseding the Pulpit, the
Senate, the *Senatus Academicus* and much else, has
been admitted for a good while; and recognised often
enough, in late times, with a sort of sentimental
triumph and wonderment. It seems to me, the Sentimental by and by will have to give place to the Practical. If Men of Letters *are* so incalculably influential,
actually performing such work for us from age to
age, and even from day to day, then I think we may
conclude that Men of Letters will not always wander
like unrecognised unregulated Ishmaelites among us !
Whatsoever thing, as I said above, has virtual unnoticed power will cast-off its wrappages, bandages, and
step-forth one day with palpably articulated, universally
visible power. That one man wear the clothes, and
take the wages, of a function which is done by quite
another: there can be no profit in this; this is not
right, it is wrong. And yet, alas, the *making* of it
right, — what a business, for long times to come !
Sure enough, this that we call Organisation of the
Literary Guild is still a great way off, encumbered
with all manner of complexities. If you asked me
what were the best possible organisation for the
Men of Letters in modern society; the arrangement
of furtherance and regulation, grounded the most
accurately on the actual facts of their position and

of the world's position, — I should beg to say that
the problem far exceeded my faculty! It is not one
man's faculty; it is that of many successive men
turned earnestly upon it, that will bring-out even an
approximate solution. What the best arrangement
were, none of us could say. But if you ask, Which
is the worst? I answer: This which we now have,
that Chaos should sit umpire[1] in it; this is the worst.
To the best, or any good one, there is yet a long
way.

One remark I must not omit, That royal or parliamentary grants of money are by no means the chief
thing wanted! To give our Men of Letters stipends,
endowments and all furtherance of cash, will do little
towards the business. On the whole, one is weary of
hearing about the omnipotence of money. I will say
rather that, for a genuine man, it is no evil to be
poor; that there ought to be Literary Men poor, — to
show whether they are genuine or not! Mendicant
Orders, bodies of good men doomed to *beg*, were instituted in the Christian Church; a most natural and
even necessary development of the spirit of Christianity. It was itself founded on Poverty, on Sorrow,
Contradiction, Crucifixion, every species of worldly
Distress and Degradation. We may say, that he who
has not known those things, and learned from them
the priceless lessons they have to teach, has missed a
good opportunity of schooling. To beg, and go bare-

---

[1] Chaos umpire sits,
And by decision more imbroils the fray
By which he reigns.
　　　　　　　Paradise Lost, II, 907–909.

foot, in coarse woollen cloak with a rope round your loins, and be despised of all the world, was no beautiful business;—nor an honourable one in any eye, till the nobleness of those who did so had made it honoured of some!

Begging is not in our course at the present time: but for the rest of it, who will say that a Johnson is not perhaps the better for being poor? It is needful for him, at all rates, to know that outward profit, that success of any kind is *not* the goal he has to aim at. Pride, vanity, ill-conditioned egoism of all sorts, are bred in his heart, as in every heart; need, above all, to be cast-out of his heart, — to be, with whatever pangs, torn-out of it, cast-forth from it, as a thing worthless. Byron, born rich and noble, made-out even less than Burns, poor and plebeian. Who knows but, in that same 'best possible organisation' as yet far off, Poverty may still enter as an important element? What if our Men of Letters, men setting-up to be Spiritual Heroes, were still *then*, as they now are, a kind of 'involuntary monastic order;' bound still to this same ugly Poverty, — till they had tried what was in it too, till they had learned to make it too do for them! Money, in truth, can do much, but it cannot do all. We must know the province of it, and confine it there; and even spurn it back, when it wishes to get farther.

Besides, were the money-furtherances, the proper season for them, the fit assigner of them, all settled, — how is the Burns to be recognised that merits these? He must pass through the ordeal, and prove himself. *This* ordeal; this wild welter of a chaos which is called Literary Life: this too is a kind of ordeal! There is clear truth in the idea that a struggle from the lower classes of society, towards the upper regions and rewards of society, must ever continue. Strong men are born there, who ought to stand elsewhere than there. The manifold, inextricably complex, universal struggle of these constitutes and must constitute, what is called the progress of society. For Men of Letters, as for all other sorts of men. How to regulate that struggle? There is the whole question. To leave it as it is, at the mercy of blind Chance; a whirl of distracted atoms, one cancelling the other; one of the thousand arriving saved, nine-hundred-and-ninety-nine lost by the way; your royal Johnson languishing inactive in garrets, or harnessed to the yoke of Printer Cave;[1] your Burns dying broken-hearted as a Gauger; your Rousseau driven into mad exasperation, kindling French Revolutions by his paradoxes: this, as we said, is clearly enough the *worst* regulation. The *best*, alas, is far from us!

And yet there can be no doubt but it is coming; advancing on us, as yet hidden in the bosom of centuries: this is a prophecy one can risk. For so soon as men get to discern the importance of a thing, they do infallibly set about arranging it, facilitating, forwarding it; and rest not till, in some approximate degree, they have accomplished that. I say, of all Priesthoods, Aristocracies, Governing Classes at present extant in the world, there is no class comparable for importance to that Priesthood of the Writers of Books. This is a

[1] Founder of *The Gentleman's Magazine* (1731), to which Johnson for a time contributed.

fact which he who runs may read,—and draw in-
ferences from. "Literature will take care of itself,"
answered Mr. Pitt,[1] when applied-to for some help
for Burns. "Yes," adds Mr. Southey,[2] "it will take
care of itself; *and of you too*, if you do not look to
it!"

The result to individual Men of Letters is not the
momentous one; they are but individuals, an infinitesimal fraction of the great body; they can struggle
on, and live or else die, as they have been wont.
But it deeply concerns the whole society, whether it
will set its *light* on high places, to walk thereby;
or trample it under foot, and scatter it in all ways
of wild waste (not without conflagration), as hereto-
fore! Light is the one thing wanted for the world.
Put wisdom in the head of the world, the world will fight
its battle victoriously, and be the best world man can
make it. I call this anomaly of a disorganic Literary
Class the heart of all other anomalies, at once product
and parent; some good arrangement for that would
be as the *punctum saliens* of a new vitality and just
arrangement for all. Already, in some European
countries, in France, in Prussia, one traces some
beginning of an arrangement for the Literary Class;
indicating the gradual possibility of such. I believe
that it is possible; that it will have to be possible.

By far the most interesting fact I hear about the
Chinese is one on which we cannot arrive at clearness,
but which excites endless curiosity even in the dim

[1] William Pitt, the Younger (1759–1806), several times Prime
Minister.

[2] English poet (laureate) and prose-writer (1774–1843).

state : this namely, that they do attempt to make their
Men of Letters their Governors ! [1] It would be rash
to say, one understood how this was done, or with what
degree of success it was done. All such things must
be very *un*successful ; yet a small degree of success is
precious ; the very attempt how precious ! There does
seem to be, all over China, a more or less active search
everywhere to discover the men of talent that grow
up in the young generation. Schools there are for every
one : a foolish sort of training, yet still a sort. The
youths who distinguish themselves in the lower school
are promoted into favourable stations in the higher,
that they may still more distinguish themselves, — forward and forward : it appears to be out of these that
the Official Persons, and incipient Governors, are taken.
These are they whom they *try* first whether they can
govern or not. And surely with the best hope : for they
are the men that have already shown intellect. Try
them : they have not governed or administered as yet ;
perhaps they cannot ; but there is no doubt they *have*
some Understanding, — without which no man can !
Neither is Understanding a *tool*, as we are too apt to
figure ; ' it is a *hand* which can handle any tool.' Try
these men : they are of all others the best worth trying. — Surely there is no kind of government, constitution, revolution, social apparatus or arrangement,
that I know of in this world, so promising to one's
scientific curiosity as this. The man of intellect at the
top of affairs : this is the aim of all constitutions and

[1] The Emperor appoints the officers of the government from
the Literati, who receive their degrees by competitive examination, and constitute the highest social class.

revolutions, if they have any aim. <u>For the man of true intellect, as I assert and believe always, is the noblehearted man withal, the true, just, humane and valiant man.</u> Get *him* for governor, all is got; fail to get him, though you had Constitutions plentiful as blackberries,[1] and a Parliament in every village, there is nothing yet got! —

These things look strange, truly; and are not such as we commonly speculate upon. But we are fallen into strange times; these things will require to be speculated upon; to be rendered practicable, to be in some way put in practice. These, and many others. On all hands of us, there is the announcement, audible enough, that the old Empire of Routine has ended; that to say a thing has long been, is no reason for its continuing to be. The things which have been are fallen into decay, are fallen into incompetence; large masses of mankind, in every society of our Europe, are no longer capable of living at all by the things which have been. When millions of men can no longer by their utmost exertion gain food for themselves, and ' the third man for thirty-six weeks each year is short of third-rate potatoes,' the things which have been must decidedly prepare to alter themselves! — I will now quit this of the organisation of Men of Letters.

Alas, the evil that pressed heaviest on those Literary Heroes of ours was not the want of organisation for Men of Letters, but a far deeper one; out of

---

[1] Give you a reason on compulsion! if reasons were as plentiful as blackberries, I would give no man a reason upon compulsion, I. *I Hen. IV*, II, iv, **264 ff.**

which, indeed, this and so many other evils for the
Literary Man, and for all men, had, as from their
fountain, taken rise. That our Hero as Man of Letters had to travel without highway, companionless,
through an inorganic chaos, — and to leave his own
life and faculty lying there, as a partial contribution
towards *pushing* some highway through it: this, had
not his faculty itself been so perverted and paralysed,
he might have put-up with, might have considered to
be but the common lot of Heroes. His fatal misery
was the *spiritual paralysis*, so we may name it, of
the Age in which his life lay; whereby his life too, do
what he might, was half-paralysed! The Eighteenth
was a *Sceptical* Century; in which little word there
is a whole Pandora's [1] Box of miseries. Scepticism
means not intellectual Doubt alone, but moral Doubt;
all sorts of *in*fidelity, insincerity, spiritual paralysis.
Perhaps, in few centuries that one could specify since
the world began, was a life of Heroism more difficult
for a man. That was not an age of Faith, — an age
of Heroes! The very possibility of Heroism had been,
as it were, formally abnegated in the minds of all.
Heroism was gone forever; Triviality, Formulism
and Commonplace were come forever. The 'age of
miracles' had been, or perhaps had not been; but
it was not any longer. An effete world; wherein
Wonder, Greatness, Godhood could not now dwell; —
in one word, a godless world!

[1] In Greek mythology, the first woman on earth. To her the
gods gave a box containing all human blessings; but curiosity
led her to open the box, and all the blessings flew away except
hope. According to another version the box was full of miseries,
which Pandora let loose on the world.

How mean, dwarfish are their ways of thinking, in this time, — compared not with the Christian Shakspeares and Miltons, but with the old Pagan Skalds, with any species of believing men! The living TREE Igdrasil, with the melodious prophetic waving of its world-wide boughs, deep-rooted as Hela, has died-out into the clanking of a World-MACHINE. 'Tree' and 'Machine:' contrast these two things. I, for my share, declare the world to be no machine! I say that it does *not* go by wheel-and-pinion 'motives,' self-interests, checks, balances; that there is something far other in it than the clank of spinning-jennies, and parliamentary majorities; and, on the whole, that it is not a machine at all! — The old Norse Heathen had a truer notion of God's-world than these poor Machine-Sceptics: the old Heathen Norse were *sincere* men. But for these poor Sceptics there was no sincerity, no truth. Half-truth and hearsay was called truth. Truth, for most men, meant plausibility; to be measured by the number of votes you could get. They had lost any notion that sincerity was possible, or of what sincerity was. How many Plausibilities asking, with unaffected surprise and the air of offended virtue, What! am not I sincere? Spiritual Paralysis, I say, nothing left but a Mechanical life, was the characteristic of that century. For the common man, unless happily he stood *below* his century and belonged to another prior one, it was impossible to be a Believer, a Hero; he lay buried, unconscious, under these baleful influences. To the strongest man, only with infinite struggle and confusion was it possible to work himself half-loose; and lead as it were, in an enchanted, most tragical way, a spiritual death-in-life, and be a Half-Hero!

Scepticism is the name we give to all this; as the chief symptom, as the chief origin of all this. Concerning which so much were to be said! It would take many Discourses, not a small fraction of one Discourse, to state what one feels about that Eighteenth Century and its ways. As indeed this, and the like of this, which we now call Scepticism, is precisely the black malady and life-foe, against which all teaching and discoursing since man's life began has directed itself: the battle of Belief against Unbelief is the never-ending battle! Neither is it in the way of crimination that one would wish to speak. Scepticism, for that century, we must consider as the decay of old ways of believing, the preparation afar off for new better and wider ways, — an inevitable thing. We will not blame men for it; we will lament their hard fate. We will understand that destruction of old *forms* is not destruction of everlasting *substances;* that Scepticism, as sorrowful and hateful as we see it, is not an end but a beginning.

The other day speaking, without prior purpose that way, of Bentham's theory of man and man's life, I chanced to call it a more beggarly one than Mahomet's. I am bound to say, now when it is once uttered, that such is my deliberate opinion. Not that one would mean offence against the man Jeremy Bentham, or those who respect and believe him. Bentham himself, and even the creed of Bentham, seems to me comparatively worthy of praise. It is a determinate *being* what all the world, in a cowardly half-and-half manner, was tending to be. Let us have the crisis; we shall either have death or the cure. I call this gross, steam-engine Utilitarianism an approach towards new Faith. It was a laying-down of cant; a saying to oneself: " Well then, this world is a dead iron machine, the god of it Gravitation and selfish Hunger ; let us see what, by checking and balancing, and good adjustment of tooth and pinion, can be made of it!" Benthamism has something complete, manful, in such fearless committal of itself to what it finds true ; you may call it Heroic, though a Heroism with its *eyes* put out! It is the culminating point, and fearless ultimatum, of what lay in the half-and-half state, pervading man's whole existence in that Eighteenth Century. It seems to me, all deniers of Godhood, and all lip-believers of it, are bound to be Benthamites, if they have courage and honesty. Benthamism is an *eyeless* Heroism : the Human Species, like a hapless blinded Samson grinding in the Philistine Mill, clasps convulsively the pillars of its Mill ; brings huge ruin down, but ultimately deliverance withal. Of Bentham I meant to say no harm.

But this I do say, and would wish all men to know and lay to heart, that he who discerns nothing but Mechanism in the Universe has in the fatalest way missed the secret of the Universe altogether. That all Godhood should vanish out of men's conception of this Universe seems to me precisely the most brutal error, — I will not disparage Heathenism by calling it a Heathen error, — that men could fall into. It is not true ; it is false at the very heart of it. A man who thinks so will think *wrong* about all things in the world; this original sin will vitiate all other conclusions he can form. One might call it the most lamentable of Delusions, — not forgetting Witchcraft itself! Witchcraft worshipped at least a living Devil; but this worships a dead iron Devil; no God, not even a Devil! — Whatsoever is noble, divine, inspired, drops thereby out of life. There remains everywhere in life a despicable *caput-mortuum;* the mechanical hull, all soul fled out of it. How can a man act heroically? The 'Doctrine of Motives' will teach him that it is, under more or less disguise, nothing but a wretched love of Pleasure, fear of Pain; that Hunger, of applause, of cash, of whatsoever victual it may be, is the ultimate fact of man's life. Atheism, in brief; — which does indeed frightfully punish itself. The man, I say, is become spiritually a paralytic man; this godlike Universe a dead mechanical steamengine, all working by motives, checks, balances, and I know not what; wherein, as in the detestable belly of some Phalaris'- [1] Bull of his own contriving, he the poor Phalaris sits miserably dying!

Belief I define to be the healthy act of a man's mind. It is a mysterious indescribable process, that of getting to believe; — indescribable, as all vital acts are. We have our mind given us, not that it may cavil and argue, but that it may see into something, give us clear belief and understanding about something, whereon we are then to proceed to act. Doubt, truly, is not itself a crime. Certainly we do not rush out,

---

[1] A Sicilian tyrant, sixth century, B. C. The brazen bull devised for roasting his enemies was first tried on its inventor, Perillus (not on Phalaris, as in the text).

clutch-up the first thing we find, and straightway believe that! All manner of doubt, inquiry, σκέψις as it
is named, about all manner of objects, dwells in every
reasonable mind. It is the mystic working of the mind,
on the object it is *getting* to know and believe. Belief
comes out of all this, above ground, like the tree from
its hidden *roots*. But now if, even on common things,
we require that a man keep his doubts *silent*, and not
babble of them till they in some measure become affirma-
tions or denials; how much more in regard to the highest things, impossible to speak-of in words at all! That
a man parade his doubt, and get to imagine that debating and logic (which means at best only the manner of *telling* us your thought, your belief or disbelief,
about a thing) is the triumph and true work of what
intellect he has: alas, this is as if you should *overturn*
the tree, and instead of green boughs, leaves and fruits,
show us ugly taloned roots turned-up into the air, —
and no growth, only death and misery going-on!

For the Scepticism, as I said, is not intellectual only;
it is moral also; a chronic atrophy and disease of the
whole soul. A man lives by believing something; not
by debating and arguing about many things. A sad
case for him when all that he can manage to believe
is something he can button in his pocket, and with one
or the other organ eat and digest! Lower than that
he will not get. We call those ages in which he gets
so low the mournfulest, sickest and meanest of all ages.
The world's heart is palsied, sick: how can any limb
of it be whole? Genuine Acting ceases in all departments of the world's work; dextrous Similitude of Acting begins. The world's wages are pocketed, the world's

work is not done. Heroes have gone-out; Quacks have
come-in. Accordingly, what Century, since the end of
the Roman world, which also was a time of scepticism,
simulacra and universal decadence, so abounds with
Quacks as that Eighteenth? Consider them, with their
tumid sentimental vapouring about virtue, benevolence,
— the wretched Quack-squadron, Cagliostro[1] at the
head of them! Few men were without quackery; they
had got to consider it a necessary ingredient and amal-
gam for truth. Chatham,[2] our brave Chatham himself, comes down to the House, all wrapt and ban-
daged; he 'has crawled out in great bodily suffering,'
and so on; — *forgets*, says Walpole, that he is acting
the sick man; in the fire of debate, snatches his arm
from the sling, and oratorically swings and brandishes
it! Chatham himself lives the strangest mimetic life,
half-hero, half-quack, all along. For indeed the world
is full of dupes; and you have to gain the *world's* suffrage! How the duties of the world will be done in
that case, what quantities of error, which means failure, which means sorrow and misery, to some and to
many, will gradually accumulate in all provinces of the
world's business, we need not compute.

It seems to me, you lay your finger here on the
heart of the world's maladies, when you call it a Sceptical World. An insincere world; a godless untruth
of a world! It is out of this, as I consider, that the

[1] See p. 61, n. 2.
[2] The elder Pitt (1708–1778), " the great Commoner." A few
days before his death he delivered a fiery speech in denunciation
of the peace with France and the recognition of the United
States, and fainted as he finished.

whole tribe of social pestilences, French Revolutions,
Chartisms,[1] and what not, have derived their being,
— their chief necessity to be. This must alter. Till
this alter, nothing can beneficially alter. My one hope
of the world, my inexpugnable consolation in looking
at the miseries of the world, is that this is altering. Here and there one does now find a man who
knows, as of old, that this world is a Truth, and no
Plausibility and Falsity; that he himself is alive, not
dead or paralytic; and that the world is alive, instinct
with Godhood, beautiful and awful, even as in the
beginning of days! One man once knowing this, many
men, all men, must by and by come to know it. It
lies there clear, for whosoever will take the *spectacles*
off his eyes and honestly look, to know! For such a
man the Unbelieving Century, with its unblessed Products, is already past; a new century is already come.
The old unblessed Products and Performances, as
solid as they look, are Phantasms, preparing speedily
to vanish. To this and the other noisy, very great-
looking Simulacrum with the whole world huzzahing
at its heels, he can say, composedly stepping aside:
Thou art not *true ;* thou art not extant, only semblant;
go thy way! — Yes, hollow Formulism, gross Benthamism, and other unheroic atheistic Insincerity is
visibly and even rapidly declining. An unbelieving
Eighteenth Century is but an exception, — such as now
and then occurs. I prophesy that the world will once

[1] Chartism ; a radical reform movement (1838–1848) named
from the " People's Charter," demanding certain changes in the
parliamentary system. Carlyle's *Essay on Chartism* (1839) is one
of the best known and most vigorous of his shorter works.

more become *sincere;* a believing world; with *many*
Heroes in it, a heroic world ! It will then be a victorious world; never till then.

Or indeed what of the world and its victories ? Men
speak too much about the world. Each one of us here,
let the world go how it will, and be victorious or not
victorious, has he not a Life of his own to lead ? One
Life ; a little gleam of Time between two Eternities ;
no second chance to us for evermore ! It were well for
us to live not as fools and simulacra, but as wise and
realities. The world's being saved will not save us ;
nor the world's being lost destroy us. We should look
to ourselves : there is great merit here in the ' duty of
staying at home ' ! And, on the whole, to say truth, I
never heard of ' worlds ' being ' saved ' in any other
way. That mania of saving worlds is itself a piece of
the Eighteenth Century with its windy sentimentalism.
Let us not follow it too far. For the saving of the
world I will trust confidently to the Maker of the
world ; and look a little to my own saving, which I
am more competent to ! — In brief, for the world's
sake, and for our own, we will rejoice greatly that
Scepticism, Insincerity, Mechanical Atheism, with all
their poison-dews, are going, and as good as gone. —

Now it was under such conditions, in those times of
Johnson, [1] that our Men of Letters had to live. Times
in which there was properly no truth in life. Old
truths had fallen nigh dumb ; the new lay yet hidden,
not trying to speak. That Man's Life here below was
a Sincerity and Fact, and would forever continue such,
no new intimation, in that dusk of the world, had yet

[1] 1709-1784.

dawned. No intimation; not even any French Revolution, — which we define to be a Truth once more,
though a Truth clad in hellfire! How different was
the Luther's pilgrimage, with its assured goal, from
the Johnson's, girt with mere traditions, suppositions,
grown now incredible, unintelligible! Mahomet's Formulas were of 'wood waxed and oiled,' and could be
burnt out of one's way: poor Johnson's were far more
difficult to burn. — The strong man will ever find
work, which means difficulty, pain, to the full measure
of his strength. But to make-out a victory, in those
circumstances of our poor Hero as Man of Letters, was
perhaps more difficult than in any. Not obstruction,
disorganisation, Bookseller Osborne [1] and Fourpence-
halfpenny a day; not this alone; but the light of his
own soul was taken from him. No landmark on the
Earth; and, alas, what is that to having no loadstar in
the Heaven! We need not wonder that none of those
Three men rose to victory. That they fought truly is
the highest praise. With a mournful sympathy we
will contemplate, if not three living victorious Heroes,
as I said, the Tombs of three fallen Heroes! They
fell for us too; making a way for us. There are the
mountains which they hurled abroad in their confused
War of the Giants; under which, their strength and
life spent, they now lie buried.

I have already written of these three Literary
Heroes, expressly or incidentally; what I suppose is
known to most of you; what need not be spoken or

[1] He employed Johnson in cataloguing a library (1742) and
was knocked down by Johnson for insolent behavior.

written a second time. They concern us here as the singular *Prophets* of that singular age; for such they virtually were; and the aspect they and their world exhibit, under this point of view, might lead us into reflections enough! I call them, all three, Genuine Men more or less; faithfully, for most part unconsciously, struggling, to be genuine, and plant themselves on the everlasting truth of things. This to a degree that eminently distinguishes them from the poor artificial mass of their contemporaries; and renders them worthy to be considered as Speakers, in some measure, of the everlasting truth, as Prophets in that age of theirs. By Nature herself a noble necessity was laid on them to be so. They were men of such magnitude that they could not live on unrealities, — clouds, froth and all inanity gave-way under them: there was no footing for them but on firm earth; no rest or regular motion for them, if they got not footing there. To a certain extent, they were Sons of Nature once more in an age of Artifice; once more, Original Men.

As for Johnson, I have always considered him to be, by nature, one of our great English souls. A strong and noble man; so much left undeveloped in him to the last: in a kindlier element what might he not have been, — Poet, Priest, sovereign Ruler! On the whole, a man must not complain of his 'element,' of his 'time,' or the like; it is thriftless work doing so. His time is bad: well then, he is there to make it better! — Johnson's youth was poor, isolated, hopeless, very miserable. Indeed, it does not seem possible that, in any the favourablest outward circumstances, Johnson's life could have been other than a painful one.

The world might have had more of profitable *work*
out of him, or less ; but his *effort* against the world's
work could never have been a light one. Nature,
in return for his nobleness had said to him, Live
in an element of diseased sorrow. Nay, perhaps the
sorrow and the nobleness were intimately and even
inseparably connected with each other. At all events,
poor Johnson had to go about girt with continual
hypochondria, physical and spiritual pain. Like a
Hercules with the burning Nessus'-shirt[1] on him, which
shoots-in on him dull incurable misery : the Nessus'-
shirt not to be stript-off, which is his own natural skin !
In this manner *he* had to live. Figure him there, with
his scrofulous diseases, with his great greedy heart, and
unspeakable chaos of thoughts ; stalking mournful
as a stranger in this Earth ; eagerly devouring what
spiritual thing he could come at : school-languages and
other merely grammatical stuff, if there were nothing
better ! The largest soul that was in all England ;
and provision made for it of ' fourpence-half-penny
a day.' Yet a giant invincible soul ; a true man's.
One remembers always that story of the shoes at
Oxford :[2] the rough, seamy-faced, rawboned College
Servitor stalking about, in winter-season, with his shoes
worn-out ; how the charitable Gentleman Commoner
secretly places a new pair at his door ; and the rawboned Servitor, lifting them, looking at them near,

[1] A robe dipped in the poisoned blood of the Centaur Nessus,
which, causing great pain, was torn off, stripping off the flesh
with it.

[2] Johnson was intermittently resident at Oxford for three
years, beginning in 1728. See the story of the shoes, under the
year 1729 in Boswell's *Life of Johnson*.

SAMUEL JOHNSON

From the painting by Sir Joshua Reynolds

with his dim eyes, with what thoughts, — pitches
them out of window! Wet feet, mud, frost, hunger or
what you will; but not beggary: we cannot stand
beggary! Rude stubborn self-help here; a whole world
of squalor, rudeness, confused misery and want, yet of
nobleness and manfulness withal. It is a type of the
man's life, this pitching-away of the shoes. An original
man; — not a secondhand, borrowing or begging man.
Let us stand on our own basis, at any rate! On such
shoes as we ourselves can get. On frost and mud, if
you will, but honestly on that; — on the reality and
substance which Nature gives *us*, not on the semblance,
on the thing she has given another than us! —

And yet with all this rugged pride of manhood and
self-help, was there ever soul more tenderly affectionate, loyally submissive to what was really higher than
he? Great souls are always loyally submissive, rever-
ent to what is over them; only small mean souls are
otherwise. I could not find a better proof of what I
said the other day, That the sincere man was by
nature the obedient man; that only in a World of
Heroes was there loyal Obedience to the Heroic. The
essence of *originality* is not that it be *new:* Johnson
believed altogether in the old; he found the old
opinions credible for him, fit for him; and in a right
heroic manner lived under them. He is well worth
study in regard to that. For we are to say that Johnson was far other than a mere man of words and
formulas; he was a man of truths and facts. He stood
by the old formulas; the happier was it for him that
he could so stand: but in all formulas that *he* could
stand by, there needed to be a most genuine sub-

stance. Very curious how, in that poor Paper-age,
so barren, artificial, thick-quilted with Pedantries,
Hearsays, the great Fact of this Universe glared in,
forever wonderful, indubitable, unspeakable, divine-
infernal, upon this man too! How he harmonised his
Formulas with it, how he managed at all under such
circumstances : that is a thing worth seeing. A thing
‘ to be looked at with reverence, with pity, with awe.’ [1]
That Church of St. Clement Danes,[2] where Johnson
still *worshipped* in the era of Voltaire, is to me a
venerable place.

It was in virtue of his *sincerity*, of his speaking
still in some sort from the heart of Nature, though in
current artificial dialect, that Johnson was a Prophet. Are not all dialects ‘artificial’? Artificial things
are not all false ; — nay every true Product of Nature
will infallibly *shape* itself ; we may say all artificial
things are, at the starting of them, *true*. What we
call ‘ Formulas ’ are not in their origin bad ; they are
indispensably good. Formula is *method*, habitude ;
found wherever man is found. Formulas fashion themselves as Paths do, as beaten Highways, leading towards some sacred or high object, whither many men
are bent. Consider it. One man, full of heartfelt
earnest impulse, finds-out a way of doing somewhat, —
were it of uttering his soul’s reverence for the Highest, were it but of fitly saluting his fellow-man. An
inventor was needed to do that, a *poet ;* he has articu-

[1] Quotation from Carlyle himself, *Essay on Boswell’s Life of
Johnson.*
[2] In The Strand, London ; still one of the “sights” of the
city for Johnson’s sake.

lated the dim-struggling thought that dwelt in his own and many hearts. This is his way of doing that; these are his footsteps, the beginning of a 'Path.' And now see: the second man travels naturally in the footsteps of his foregoer, it is the *easiest* method. In the footsteps of his foregoer; yet with improvements, with changes where such seem good; at all events with enlargements, the Path ever *widening* itself as more travel it; — till at last there is a broad Highway whereon the whole world may travel and drive. While there remains a City or Shrine, or any Reality to drive to, at the farther end, the Highway shall be right welcome! When the City is gone, we will forsake the Highway. In this manner all Institutions, Practices, Regulated Things in the world have come into existence, and gone out of existence. Formulas all begin by being *full* of substance; you may call them the *skin*, the articulation into shape, into limbs and skin, of a substance that is already there: *they* had not been there otherwise. Idols, as we said, are not idolatrous till they become doubtful, empty for the worshipper's heart. Much as we talk against Formulas, I hope no one of us is ignorant withal of the high significance of *true* Formulas; that they were, and will ever be, the indispensablest furniture of our habitation in this world. ——

Mark, too, how little Johnson boasts of his 'sincerity.' He has no suspicion of his being particularly sincere, — of his being particularly anything! A hard-struggling, weary-hearted man, or 'scholar' as he calls himself, trying hard to get some honest livelihood in the world, not to starve, but to live — without stealing! A noble unconsciousness is in him. He does not 'engrave *Truth* on his watch-seal;' no, but he stands by truth, speaks by it, works and lives by it. Thus it ever is. Think of it once more. The man whom Nature has appointed to do great things is, first of all, furnished with that openness to Nature which renders him incapable of being *in*sincere! To his large, open, deep-feeling heart Nature is a Fact: all hearsay is hearsay; the unspeakable greatness of this Mystery of Life, let him acknowledge it or not, nay even though he seem to forget it or deny it, is ever present to *him*, — fearful and wonderful, on this hand and on that. He has a basis of sincerity; unrecognised, because never questioned or capable of question. Mirabeau, Mahomet, Cromwell, Napoleon: all the Great Men I ever heard-of have this as the primary material of them. Innumerable commonplace men are debating, are talking everywhere their commonplace doctrines, which they have learned by logic, by rote, at secondhand: to that kind of man all this is still nothing. He must have truth; truth which *he* feels to be true. How shall he stand otherwise? His whole soul, at all moments, in all ways, tells him that there is no standing. He is under the noble necessity of being true. Johnson's way of thinking about this world is not mine, any more than Mahomet's was: but I recognise the everlasting element of heart-*sincerity* in both; and see with pleasure how neither of them remains ineffectual. Neither of them is as *chaff* sown; in both of them is something which the seed-field will *grow*.

Johnson was a Prophet to his people; preached a

Gospel to them, — as all like him always do. The highest Gospel he preached we may describe as a kind of Moral Prudence: 'in a world where much is to be done, and little is to be known,' see how you will *do* it! A thing well worth preaching. 'A world where much is to be done, and little is to be known:' do not sink yourselves in boundless bottomless abysses of Doubt, of wretched god-forgetting Unbelief; — you were miserable then, powerless, mad: how could you *do* or work at all? Such Gospel Johnson preached and taught; — coupled, theoretically and practically, with this other great Gospel, 'Clear your mind of Cant!' Have no trade with Cant: stand on the cold mud in the frosty weather, but let it be in your own *real* torn shoes: 'that will be better for you,' as Mahomet says! I call this, I call these two things *joined together*, a great Gospel, the greatest perhaps that was possible at that time.

Johnson's Writings, which once had such currency and celebrity, are now as it were disowned by the young generation. It is not wonderful; Johnson's opinions are fast becoming obsolete: but his style of thinking and of living, we may hope, will never become obsolete. I find in Johnson's Books the indisputablest traces of a great intellect and great heart; — ever welcome, under what obstructions and perversions soever. They are *sincere* words, those of his; he means things by them. A wondrous buckram style, — the best he could get to then; a measured grandiloquence, stepping or rather stalking along in a very solemn way, grown obsolete now; sometimes a tumid *size* of phraseology not in proportion to the contents

of it : all this you will put-up with. For the phraseology, tumid or not, has always *something within it.*
So many beautiful styles and books, with *nothing*
in them ; — a man is a *male*factor to the world who
writes such ! *They* are the avoidable kind ! — Had
Johnson left nothing but his *Dictionary*, one might
have traced there a great intellect, a genuine man.
Looking to its clearness of definition, its general solid-
ity, honesty, insight and successful method, it may be
called the best of all Dictionaries. There is in it a
kind of architectural nobleness ; it stands there like a
great solid square-built edifice, finished, symmetrically
complete : you judge that a true Builder did it.

One word, in spite of our haste, must be granted
to poor Bozzy.[1] He passes for a mean, inflated, glut-
tonous creature ; and was so in many senses. Yet the
fact of his reverence for Johnson will ever remain
noteworthy. The foolish conceited Scotch Laird, the
most conceited man of his time, approaching in such
awestruck attitude the great dusty irascible Pedagogue
in his mean garret there : it is a genuine reverence for
Excellence ; a *worship* for Heroes, at a time when
neither Heroes nor worship were surmised to exist.
Heroes, it would seem, exist always, and a certain worship of them ! We will also take the liberty to deny
altogether that of the witty Frenchman, that no man is
a hero to his valet-de-chambre.[2] Or if so, it is not the
Hero's blame, but the Valet's : that his soul, namely, is

---

[1] James Boswell (1740–1795); introduced to Johnson in 1763;
published his *Life of Johnson*, 1791.

[2] Attributed to a bewildering number of French wits, both
men and women.

a mean *valet*-soul! He expects his Hero to advance in royal stage-trappings, with measured step, trains borne behind him, trumpets sounding before him. It should stand rather, No man can be a *Grand-Monarque* to his valet-de-chambre. Strip your Louis Quatorze [1] of his king-gear, and there *is* left nothing but a poor forked radish with a head fantastically carved; [2] — admirable to no valet. The Valet does not know a Hero when he sees him! Alas, no: it requires a kind of *Hero* to do that; — and one of the world's wants, in *this* as in other senses, is for most part want of such.

On the whole, shall we not say, that Boswell's admiration was well bestowed; that he could have found no soul in all England so worthy of bending down before? Shall we not say, of this great mournful Johnson too, that he guided his difficult confused existence wisely; led it *well*, like a right-valiant man? That waste chaos of Authorship by trade; that waste chaos of Scepticism in religion and politics, in life-theory and life-practice; in his poverty, in his dust and dimness, with the sick body and the rusty coat: he made it do for him, like a brave man. Not wholly without a loadstar in the Eternal; he had still a loadstar, as the brave all need to have: with his eye set on that, he would change his course for nothing in these confused vortices of the lower sea of Time. 'To the Spirit of Lies, bearing death and hunger, he would in no wise strike his flag.' Brave old Samuel: *ultimus Romanorum!*

[1] Louis XIV (b. 1635, king 1643–1715), the most magnificent of French monarchs.

[2] A phrase of Falstaff's in description of Justice Shallow. *II Hen. IV*, III, ii, last speech.

Of Rousseau[1] and his Heroism I cannot say so
much. He is not what I call a strong man. A morbid,
excitable, spasmodic man; at best, intense rather than
strong. He had not 'the talent of Silence,' an invaluable talent; which few Frenchmen, or indeed men of
any sort in these times, excel in! The suffering man
ought really 'to consume his own smoke;' there is no
good in emitting *smoke* till you have made it into *fire*,
— which, in the metaphorical sense too, all smoke is
capable of becoming! Rousseau has not depth or
width, not calm force for difficulty; the first characteristic of true greatness. A fundamental mistake to call
vehemence and rigidity strength! A man is not strong
who takes convulsion-fits; though six men cannot
hold him then. He that can walk under the heaviest
weight without staggering, he is the strong man. We
need forever, especially in these loud-shrieking days,
to remind ourselves of that. A man who cannot *hold
his peace*, till the time come for speaking and acting,
is no right man.

Poor Rousseau's face is to me expressive of him.
A high but narrow contracted intensity in it: bony
brows; deep, strait-set eyes, in which there is something bewildered-looking, — bewildered, peering with
lynx-eagerness. A face full of misery, even ignoble
misery, and also of the antagonism against that; something mean, plebeian there, redeemed only by *intensity:* the face of what is called a Fanatic, — a sadly
contracted Hero! We name him here because, with
all his drawbacks, and they are many, he has the first
and chief characteristic of a Hero: he is heartily *in*

[1] 1712–1778.

earnest. In earnest, if ever man was ; as none of these
French Philosophes were. Nay, one would say, of an
earnestness too great for his otherwise sensitive, rather
feeble nature ; and which indeed in the end drove him
into the strangest incoherences, almost delirations.
There had come, at last, to be a kind of madness in
him : his Ideas *possessed* him like demons ; hurried
him so about, drove him over steep places ! —

The fault and misery of Rousseau was what we easily
name by a single word, *Egoism ;* which is indeed the
source and summary of all faults and miseries whatsoever. He had not perfected himself into victory
over mere Desire ; a mean Hunger, in many sorts, was
still the motive principle of him. I am afraid he was
a very vain man ; hungry for the praises of men. You
remember Genlis's experience of him. She took Jean
Jacques to the Theatre ; he bargaining for a strict
incognito, — "*He* would not be seen there for the
world ! " The curtain did happen nevertheless to be
drawn aside : the Pit recognised Jean Jacques, but
took no great notice of him ! He expressed the bit-
terest indignation ; gloomed all evening, spake no
other than surly words. The glib Countess remained
entirely convinced that his anger was not at being seen,
but at not being applauded when seen. How the whole
nature of the man is poisoned ; nothing but suspicion,
self-isolation, fierce moody ways ! He could not live
with anybody. A man of some rank from the country,
who visited him often, and used to sit with him, expressing all reverence and affection for him, comes one
day ; finds Jean Jacques full of the sourest unintelligible humour. " Monsieur," said Jean Jacques, with

flaming eyes, "I know why you come here. You come to see what a poor life I lead; how little is in my poor pot that is boiling there. Well, look into the pot! There is half a pound of meat, one carrot and three onions; that is all: go and tell the whole world that, if you like, Monsieur!" — A man of this sort was far gone. The whole world got itself supplied with anecdotes, for light laughter, for a certain theatrical interest, from these perversions and contortions of poor Jean Jacques. Alas, to him they were not laughing or theatrical; too real to him! The contortions of a dying gladiator: the crowded amphitheatre looks-on with entertainment; but the gladiator is in agonies and dying.

And yet this Rousseau, as we say, with his passionate appeals to Mothers, with his *Contrat-social*,[1] with his celebrations of Nature, even of savage life in Nature, did once more touch upon Reality, struggle towards Reality; was doing the function of a Prophet to his Time. As *he* could, and as the Time could! Strangely through all that defacement, degradation and almost madness, there is in the inmost heart of poor Rousseau a spark of real heavenly fire. Once more, out of the element of that withered mocking Philosophism, Scepticism and Persiflage, there has arisen in this man the ineradicable feeling and knowledge that this Life of ours is *true;* not a Scepticism, Theorem, or Persiflage, but a Fact, an awful Reality.

[1] A treatise on government, advocating the direct sovereignty of the people as the only natural and ideal government. The drafters of the American Declaration of Independence were largely and directly indebted to Rousseau.

Nature had made that revelation to him ; had ordered him to speak it out. He got it spoken out ; if not well and clearly, then ill and dimly, — as clearly as he could. Nay what are all errors and perversities of his, even those stealings of ribbons,[1] aimless confused miseries and vagabondisms, if we will interpret them kindly, but the blinkard dazzlement and staggerings to and fro of a man sent on an errand he is too weak for, by a path he cannot yet find? Men are led by strange ways. One should have tolerance for a man, hope of him ; leave him to try yet what he will do. While life lasts, hope lasts for every man.

Of Rousseau's literary talents, greatly celebrated still among his countrymen, I do not say much. His Books,[2] like himself, are what I call unhealthy ; not the good sort of Books. There is a sensuality in Rousseau. Combined with such an intellectual gift as his, it makes pictures of a certain gorgeous attractiveness : but they are not genuinely poetical. Not white sunlight : something *operatic ;* a kind of rosepink, artificial bedizenment. It is frequent, or rather it is universal, among the French since his time. Madame de Stael[3] has something of it ; St. Pierre ;[4] and down

[1] At the death of Mme. de Vercellis, in whose household he was an attendant, Rousseau, provoked thereto by his chagrin at not being mentioned in her will, stole a piece of ribbon of slight value. On being found in possession of it he declared that a young girl of the household had given it to him. His remorse at having brought baseless suspicion on her fills the closing paragraphs of his *Confessions,* I.

[2] His most famous book, *Confessions,* appeared in 1782, after his death.

[3] 1766–1817.

[4] 1737–1814 ; author of *Paul and Virginia.*

onwards to the present astonishing convulsionary ' Literature of Desperation,' it is everywhere abundant. That same *rosepink* is not the right hue. Look at a Shakspeare, at a Goethe, even at a Walter Scott! He who has once seen into this, has seen the difference of the True from the Sham-True, and will discriminate them ever afterwards.

We had to observe in Johnson how much good a Prophet, under all disadvantages and disorganisations, can accomplish for the world. In Rousseau we are called to look rather at the fearful amount of evil which, under such disorganisation, may accompany the good. Historically it is a most pregnant spectacle, that of Rousseau. Banished into Paris garrets, in the gloomy company of his own Thoughts and Necessities there ; driven from post to pillar ;[1] fretted, exasperated till the heart of him went mad, he had grown to feel deeply that the world was not his friend nor the world's law.[2] It was expedient, if anyway possible, that such a man should *not* have been set in flat hostility with the world. He could be cooped into garrets, laughed at as a maniac, left to starve, like a wild-beast

---

[1] The storm of protest provoked by *Émile* (1762) caused him to leave Paris. He was driven in turn from various towns in Switzerland and France. For a while he was living in England, then wandering about France, and finally back to Paris again.

[2] Famine is in thy cheeks,
Need and oppression starveth in thine eyes,
Contempt and beggary hangs upon thy back ;
The world is not thy friend nor the world's law.
                              Romeo and Juliet, V, i, 69–72.
It was an unsuccessful attempt to get justice against an influential aristocrat that first stirred Rousseau against the order of things in France.

in his cage ; — but he could not be hindered from setting the world on fire. The French Revolution found
its Evangelist in Rousseau. His semi-delirious [1] speculations on the miseries of civilised life, the preferability of the savage to the civilised, and suchlike,
helped well to produce a whole delirium in France
generally. True, you may well ask, What could the
world, the governors of the world do with such a
man ? Difficult to say what the governors of the world
could do with him ! What he could do with them is
unhappily clear enough, — *guillotine* a great many
of them ! Enough now of Rousseau.

It was a curious phenomenon, in the withered, unbelieving, secondhand Eighteenth Century, that of a
Hero starting up, among the artificial pasteboard figures and productions, in the guise of a Robert Burns.
Like a little well in the rocky desert places, — like a
sudden splendour of Heaven in the artificial Vauxhall !
People knew not what to make of it. They took it
for a piece of the Vauxhall fire-work ; alas, it *let*
itself be so taken, though struggling half-blindly, as
in bitterness of death, against that ! Perhaps no man
had such a false reception from his fellow-men. Once
more a very wasteful life-drama was enacted under
the sun.

The tragedy of Burns's life is known to all of you.
Surely we may say, if discrepancy between place held
and place merited constitute perverseness of lot for
a man, no lot could be more perverse than Burns's.
Among those secondhand acting-figures, *mimes* for

[1] Literally so.

most part, of the Eighteenth Century, once more a
giant Original Man ; one of those men who reach down
to the perennial Deeps, who take rank with the Heroic
among men : and he was born[1] in a poor Ayrshire
hut. The largest soul of all the British lands came
among us in the shape of a hard-handed Scottish
Peasant.

His Father, a poor toiling man, tried various things;
did not succeed in any; was involved in continual
difficulties. The Steward, Factor as the Scotch call
him, used to send letters and threatenings, Burns says,
'which threw us all into tears.' The brave, hard-
toiling, hard-suffering Father, his brave heroine of a
wife ; and those children, of whom Robert was one!
In this Earth, so wide otherwise, no shelter for *them*.
The letters 'threw us all into tears :' figure it. The
brave Father, I say always ; — a *silent* Hero and Poet;
without whom the son had never been a speaking one!
Burns's Schoolmaster came afterwards to London,
learnt what good society was ; but declares that in no
meeting of men did he ever enjoy better discourse than
at the hearth of this peasant. And his poor 'seven
acres of nursery-ground,' — not that, nor the miserable
patch of clay-farm, nor anything he tried to get a
living by, would prosper with him ; he had a sore un-
equal battle all his days. But he stood to it valiantly ;
a wise, faithful, unconquerable man ; — swallowing
down how many sore sufferings daily into silence ;
fighting like an unseen Hero, — nobody publishing
newspaper paragraphs about his nobleness ; voting
pieces of plate to him! However, he was not lost:

[1] 1759.

nothing is lost. Robert is there; the outcome of him, — and indeed of many generations of such as him.

This Burns appeared under every disadvantage : uninstructed, poor, born only to hard manual toil; and writing, when it came to that, in a rustic special dialect, known only to a small province of the country he lived in. Had he written, even what he did write, in the general language of England, I doubt not he had already become universally recognised as being, or capable to be, one of our greatest men. That he should have tempted so many to penetrate through the rough husk of that dialect of his, is proof that there lay something far from common within it. He has gained a certain recognition, and is continuing to do so over all quarters of our wide Saxon world : wheresoever a Saxon dialect is spoken, it begins to be understood, by personal inspection of this and the other, that one of the most considerable Saxon men of the Eighteenth century was an Ayrshire Peasant named Robert Burns. Yes, I will say, here too was a piece of the right Saxon stuff : strong as the Harz-rock, rooted in the depths of the world ; — rock, yet with wells of living softness in it ! A wild impetuous whirlwind of passion and faculty slumbered quiet there ; such heavenly *melody* dwelling in the heart of it. A noble rough genuineness; homely, rustic, honest; true simplicity of strength; with its lightning-fire, with its soft dewy pity ; — like the old Norse Thor, the Peasant-god ! —

Burns's Brother Gilbert, a man of much sense and worth, has told me that Robert, in his young days, in spite of their hardship, was usually the gayest of

speech ; a fellow of infinite frolic, laughter, sense and
heart ; far pleasanter to hear there, stript cutting
peats in the bog, or suchlike, than he ever afterwards
knew him. I can well believe it. This basis of mirth
(*fond gaillard*,' as old Marquis Mirabeau calls it),
a primal-element of sunshine and joyfulness, coupled
with his other deep and earnest qualities, is one of
the most attractive characteristics of Burns. A large
fund of Hope dwells in him ; spite of his tragical history, he is not a mourning man. He shakes his sorrows
gallantly aside ; bounds forth victorious over them. It
is as the lion shaking ' dew-drops from his mane ; ' [1] as
the swift-bounding horse, that *laughs* at the shaking
of the spear. — But indeed, Hope, Mirth, of the sort
like Burns's, are they not the outcome properly of
warm generous affection, — such as is the beginning of
all to every man ?

You would think it strange if I called Burns the
most gifted British soul we had in all that century of
his : and yet I believe the day is coming when there
will be little danger in saying so. His writings, all
that he *did* under such obstructions, are only a poor
fragment of him. Professor Stewart [2] remarked very
justly, what indeed is true of all Poets good for much,
that his poetry was not any particular faculty ; but
the general result of a naturally vigorous original mind
expressing itself in that way. Burns's gifts, expressed

[1] Cupid

Shall from your neck unloose his amorous fold,
And, like a dew-drop from the lion's mane,
Be shook to air.   *Troilus and Cressida*, III, iii, 222–225.

[2] Of Edinburgh University. He entertained the poet in his
house, and is speaking here from personal acquaintance.

in conversation, are the theme of all that ever heard
him. All kinds of gifts: from the gracefulest utterances of courtesy, to the highest fire of passionate
speech; loud floods of mirth, soft wailings of affection,
laconic emphasis, clear piercing insight; all was in
him. Witty duchesses celebrate him as a man whose
speech 'led them off their feet.' This is beautiful:
but still more beautiful that which Mr. Lockhart [1] has
recorded, which I have more than once alluded to,
How the waiters and ostlers at inns would get out of
bed, and come crowding to hear this man speak!
Waiters and ostlers: — they too were men, and here
was a man! I have heard much about his speech;
but one of the best things I ever heard of it was, last
year, from a venerable gentleman long familiar with
him. That it was speech distinguished by always
having something in it. " He spoke rather little than
much," this old man told me; " sat rather silent in
those early days, as in the company of persons above
him; and always when he did speak, it was to throw
new light on the matter." I know not why any one
should ever speak otherwise! — But if we look at his
general force of soul, his healthy *robustness* everyway,
the rugged downrightness, penetration, generous valour and manfulness that was in him, — where shall
we readily find a better-gifted man?

Among the great men of the Eighteenth Century,
I sometimes feel as if Burns might be found to resemble Mirabeau more than any other. They differ widely
in vesture; yet look at them intrinsically. There is

[1] Son-in-law of Scott, biographer of Scott and Burns (1794–
1854).

the same burly thick-necked strength of body as of soul ; — built, in both cases, on what the old Marquis calls a *fond gaillard.* By nature, by course of breeding, indeed by nation, Mirabeau has much more of bluster ; a noisy, forward, unresting man. But the characteristic of Mirabeau too is veracity and sense, power of true *insight*, superiority of vision. The thing that he says is worth remembering. It is a flash of insight into some object or other : so do both these men speak. The same raging passions ; capable too in both of manifesting themselves as the tenderest noble affections. Wit, wild laughter, energy, directness, sincerity : these were in both. The types of the two men are not dissimilar. Burns too could have governed, debated in National Assemblies ; politicised, as few could. Alas, the courage which had to exhibit itself in capture of smuggling schooners in the Solway Frith ; in keeping *silence* over so much, where no good speech, but only inarticulate rage was possible : this might have bellowed forth Ushers de Brézé [1] and the like ; and made itself visible to all men, in managing of kingdoms, in ruling of great ever-memorable epochs ! But they said to him reprovingly, his Official Superiors said, and wrote : ' You are to work, not think.' Of your *thinking*-faculty, the greatest in this land, we have no need ; you are to gauge beer [2] there ; for that only are *you* wanted. Very notable ; — and worth mentioning, though we know what is to be said and answered ! As if Thought, Power of Thinking, were

[1] See Carlyle's *French Revolution*, I, v, ii.

[2] Beginning 1788, at a salary of £70. An incautious expression of his political sentiments almost cost him his appointment.

not, at all times, in all places and situations of the world, precisely the thing that *was* wanted. The fatal man, is he not always the *un*thinking man, the man who cannot think and *see;* but only grope, and hallucinate, and *mis*see the nature of the thing he works with? He missees it, mis*takes* it as we say; takes it for one thing, and it *is* another thing, — and leaves him standing like a Futility there! He is the fatal man; unutterably fatal, put in the high places of men. — " Why complain of this?" say some: " Strength is mournfully denied its arena; that was true from of old." Doubtless; and the worse for the *arena*, answer I! *Complaining* profits little; stating of the truth may profit. That a Europe, with its French Revolution just breaking out, finds no need of a Burns except for gauging beer, — is a thing I, for one, cannot *rejoice* at! —

Once more we have to say here, that the chief quality of Burns is the *sincerity* of him. So in his Poetry, so in his Life. The Song he sings is not of fantasticalities; it is of a thing felt, really there; the prime merit of this, as of all in him, and of his Life generally, is truth. The Life of Burns is what we may call a great tragic sincerity. A sort of savage sincerity, — not cruel, far from that; but wild, wrestling naked with the truth of things. In that sense, there is something of the savage in all great men.

Hero-worship, — Odin, Burns? Well; these Men of Letters too were not without a kind of Hero-worship: but what a strange condition has that got into now! The waiters and ostlers of Scotch inns, prying about the door, eager to catch any word that fell from Burns,

were doing unconscious reverence to the Heroic.
Johnson had his Boswell for worshipper. Rousseau
had worshippers enough; princes calling on him in
his mean garret; the great, the beautiful doing reverence to the poor moonstruck man. For himself a most
portentous contradiction; the two ends of his life not
to be brought into harmony. He sits at the tables of
grandees; and has to copy music for his own living.
He cannot even get his music copied: "By dint of
dining out," says he, "I run the risk of dying by
starvation at home." For his worshippers too a most
questionable thing! If doing Hero-worship well or
badly be the test of vital wellbeing or illbeing to a
generation, can we say that *these* generations are very
first-rate?— And yet our heroic Men of Letters do
teach, govern, are kings, priests, or what you like to
call them; intrinsically there is no preventing it by
any means whatever. The world *has* to obey him who
thinks and sees in the world. The world can alter the
manner of that; can either have it as blessed continuous summer sunshine, or as unblessed black thunder
and tornado, — with unspeakable difference of profit
for the world! The manner of it is very alterable; the
matter and fact of it is not alterable by any power
under the sky. Light; or, failing that, lightning: the
world can take its choice. Not whether we call an
Odin god, prophet, priest, or what we call him; but
whether we believe the word he tells us: there it all
lies. If it be a true word, we shall have to believe it;
believing it, we shall have to do it. What *name* or
welcome we give him or it, is a point that concerns
ourselves mainly. *It,* the new Truth, new deeper

revealing of the Secret of this Universe, is verily of
the nature of a message from on high ; and must and
will have itself obeyed. —

My last remark is on that notablest phasis of Burns's
history, — his visit to Edinburgh. Often it seems to
me as if his demeanour there were the highest proof
he gave of what a fund of worth and genuine manhood
was in him. If we think of it, few heavier burdens
could be laid on the strength of a man. So sudden ; all
common *Lionism*, which ruins innumerable men, was
as nothing to this. It is as if Napoleon had been made
a King of, not gradually, but at once from the Artillery Lieutenancy in the Regiment La Fère.[1] Burns,
still only in his twenty-seventh year, is no longer even
a ploughman ; he is flying to the West Indies to escape disgrace and a jail. This month he is a ruined
peasant, his wages seven pounds a year, and these gone
from him : next month he is in the blaze of rank and
beauty, handing down jewelled Duchesses to dinner ;[2]
the cynosure[3] of all eyes ! Adversity is sometimes hard
upon a man ; but for one man who can stand pros-

---

[1] See p. 334, n. 1.

[2] In July, 1786, he published a volume of poems to raise money
for his passage to Jamaica, where he intended to turn slave-driver.
The volume won him the instant and enthusiastic recognition of
the intellectual and social aristocracy of Edinburgh, whither he
went in November. A new edition of his poems brought him
about £500.

[3] "Dog's Tail," the name of the constellation containing the
polar star ; hence any object of conspicuous attention.

> Where perhaps some Beauty lies,
> The Cynosure of neighbouring eyes.
>
> *L'Allegro*, 79, 80.

perity, there are a hundred that will stand adversity. I admire much the way in which Burns met all this. Perhaps no man one could point out, was ever so sorely tried, and so little forgot himself. Tranquil, unastonished ; not abashed, not inflated, neither awkwardness nor affectation : he feels that *he* there is the man Robert Burns ; that the ' rank is but the guinea-stamp ; '[1] that the celebrity is but the candle-light, which will show *what* man, not in the least make him a better or other man ! Alas, it may readily, unless he look to it, make him a *worse* man ; a wretched inflated windbag, — inflated till he *burst*, and become a *dead* lion ; for whom, as some one has said, ' there is no resurrection of the body ; ' worse than a living dog ! — Burns is admirable here.

And yet, alas, as I have observed elsewhere, these Lion-hunters were the ruin and death of Burns. It was they that rendered it impossible for him to live ! They gathered round him in his Farm ; hindered his industry ; no place was remote enough from them. He could not get his Lionism forgotten, honestly as he was disposed to do so. He falls into discontents, into miseries, faults ; the world getting ever more desolate for him ; health, character, peace of mind, all gone ; — solitary enough now. It is tragical to think of ! These men came but to *see* him ; it was out of no sympathy with him, nor no hatred to him. They came to get a little amusement : they got their amusement ; — and the Hero's life went for it !

---

[1] The rank is but the guinea's stamp,
The man 's the gowd for a' that.
Burns's *For a' That and a' That.*

Richter says, in the Island of Sumatra there is a kind of 'Light-chafers,' large Fire-flies, which people stick upon spits, and illuminate the ways with at night. Persons of condition can thus travel with a pleasant radiance, which they much admire. Great honour to the Fire-flies! But — ! —

LECTURE VI

THE HERO AS KING. CROMWELL, NAPOLEON :
MODERN REVOLUTIONISM

[Friday, 22d May 1840.]

We come now to the last form of Heroism; that which
we call Kingship. The Commander over Men ; he to
whose will our wills are to be subordinated, and loyally
surrender themselves, and find their welfare in doing
so, may be reckoned the most important of Great Men.
He is practically the summary for us of *all* the various
figures of Heroism ; Priest, Teacher, whatsoever of
earthly or of spiritual dignity we can fancy to reside
in a man, embodies itself here, to *command* over us,
to furnish us with constant practical teaching, to tell
us for the day and hour what we are to *do*. He is
called *Rex*, Regulator, *Roi :* our own name is still
better ; King, *Könning*, which means *Can*-ning, Able-
man.

Numerous considerations, pointing towards deep,
questionable, and indeed unfathomable regions, present themselves here : on the most of which we must
resolutely for the present forbear to speak at all. As
Burke said that perhaps fair *Trial by Jury* was the
soul of Government, and that all legislation, administration, parliamentary debating, and the rest of it,
went on, in 'order to bring twelve impartial men into
a jury-box ;' — so, by much stronger reason, may I say

here, that the finding of your *Ableman* and getting
him invested with the *symbols of ability*, with dignity,
worship (*worth*-ship), royalty, kinghood, or whatever
we call it, so that *he* may actually have room to guide
according to his faculty of doing it, — is the business,
well or ill accomplished, of all social procedure whatsoever in this world! Hustings-speeches,[1] Parliamentary motions, Reform Bills,[2] French Revolutions, all
mean at heart this; or else nothing. Find in any
country the Ablest Man that exists there; raise *him*
to the supreme place, and loyally reverence him: you
have a perfect government for that country; no ballot-
box, parliamentary eloquence, voting, constitution-
building, or other machinery whatsoever can improve
it a whit. It is in the perfect state; an ideal country.
The Ablest Man; he means also the truest-hearted,
justest, the Noblest Man: what he *tells us to do* must
be precisely the wisest, fittest, that we could anywhere
or anyhow learn; — the thing which it will in all ways
behove us, with right loyal thankfulness, and nothing
doubting, to do! Our *doing* and life were then, so
far as government could regulate it, well regulated;
that were the ideal of constitutions.

Alas, we know very well that Ideals can never be
completely embodied in practice. Ideals must ever lie
a very great way off; and we will right thankfully
content ourselves with any not intolerable approxima-
tion thereto! Let no man, as Schiller[3] says, too quer-

[1] See p. 145, n. 3.

[2] Most notably that of 1832 for the correction of abuses in
the parliamentary system.

[3] 1759-1805; German poet and dramatist, friend of Goethe.

ulously 'measure by a scale of perfection the meagre
product of reality' in this poor world of ours. We
will esteem him no wise man; we will esteem him a
sickly, discontented, foolish man. And yet, on the
other hand, it is never to be forgotten that Ideals do
exist; that if they be not approximated to at all, the
whole matter goes to wreck! Infallibly. No bricklayer builds a wall *perfectly* perpendicular, mathemat-
ically this is not possible; a certain degree of perpen-
dicularity suffices him; and he, like a good bricklayer,
who must have done with his job, leaves it so. And
yet if he sway *too much* from the perpendicular;
above all, if he throw plummet and level quite away
from him, and pile brick on brick heedless, just as it
comes to hand — ! Such bricklayer, I think, is in a
bad way. *He* has forgotten himself: but the Law of
Gravitation does not forget to act on him; he and his
wall rush-down into confused welter of ruin! —

This is the history of all rebellions, French Revolutions, social explosions in ancient or modern times.
You have put the too *Un*able Man at the head of affairs! The too ignoble, unvaliant, fatuous man. You
have forgotten that there is any rule, or natural necessity whatever, of putting the Able Man there. Brick
must lie on brick as it may and can. Unable Simulacrum of Ability, *quack*, in a word, must adjust himself with quack, in all manner of administration of
human things; — which accordingly lie unadministered,
fermenting into unmeasured masses of failure, of indigent misery: in the outward, and in the inward or
spiritual, miserable millions stretch-out the hand for
their due supply, and it is not there. The 'law of

gravitation' acts; Nature's laws do none of them
forget to act. The miserable millions burst-forth into
Sansculottism,[1] or some other sort of madness: bricks
and bricklayer lie as a fatal chaos! —

Much sorry stuff, written some hundred years ago or
more, about the 'Divine right of Kings,' moulders un-
read now in the Public Libraries of this country. Far
be it from us to disturb the calm process by which it
is disappearing harmlessly from the earth, in those re-
positories! At the same time, not to let the immense
rubbish go without leaving us, as it ought, some soul
of it behind — I will say that it did mean something;
something true, which it is important for us and all
men to keep in mind. To assert that in whatever man
you chose to lay hold of (by this or the other plan of
clutching at him); and clapt a round piece of metal
on the head of, and called King, —there straightway
came to reside a divine virtue, so that *he* became a
kind of god, and a Divinity inspired him with faculty
and right to rule over you to all lengths: this, — what
can we do with this but leave it to rot silently in the
Public Libraries? But I will say withal, and that is
vhat these Divine-right men meant, That in Kings,
and in all human Authorities, and relations that men
god-created can form among each other, there is verily

[1] The "ism" of those "without breeches," *i. e.* the Parisian
mob in the time of the French Revolution. *Culottes* were the
knee breeches of court dress. "It is in these places, in these
months, that the epithet *Sansculotte* first gets applied to indigent
Patriotism; . . . Destitute-of-Breeches: a mournful Destitution; which however, if Twenty millions share it, may become
more effective than most Possessions!" Carlyle's *French Revolution*, II, III, iv.

either a Divine Right or else a Diabolic Wrong; one
or the other of these two! For it is false altogether,
what the last Sceptical Century taught us, that this
world is a steamengine. There is a God in this world;
and a God's-sanction, or else the violation of such,
does look-out from all ruling and obedience, from all
moral acts of men. There is no act more moral between men than that of rule and obedience. Woe to
him that claims obedience when it is not due; woe to
him that refuses it when it is! God's law is in that, I
say, however the Parchment-laws may run: there is a
Divine Right [1] or else a Diabolic Wrong at the heart
of every claim that one man makes upon another.

It can do none of us harm to reflect on this: in all
the relations of life it will concern us; in Loyalty and
Royalty, the highest of these. I esteem the modern
error, That all goes by self-interest and the checking
and balancing of greedy knaveries, and that, in short,
there is nothing divine whatever in the association of
men, a still more despicable error, natural as it is to an
unbelieving century, than that of a 'divine right' in
people *called* Kings. I say, Find me the true *Kön-
ning*, King or Able-man, and he *has* a divine right over
me. That we knew in some tolerable measure how to
find him, and that all men were ready to acknowledge
his divine right when found: this is precisely the healing which a sick world is everywhere, in these ages,
seeking after! The true King, as guide of the practical, has ever something of the Pontiff in him, — guide
of the spiritual, from which all practice has its rise.
This too is a true saying, That the *King* is head of the

[1] Compare p. 2 : " the divine relation," etc.

Church. — But we will leave the Polemic stuff of a dead century to lie quiet on its bookshelves.

Certainly it is a fearful business, that of having your Able-man to *seek*, and not knowing in what manner to proceed about it! That is the world's sad predicament in these times of ours. They are times of revolution, and have long been. The bricklayer with his bricks, no longer heedful of plummet or the law of gravitation, have toppled, tumbled, and it all welters as we see! But the beginning of it was not the French Revolution; that is rather the *end*, we can hope. It were truer to say, the *beginning* was three centuries further back: in the Reformation of Luther.[1] That the thing which still called itself Christian Church had become a Falsehood, and brazenly went about pretending to pardon men's sins for metallic coined money, and to do much else which in the everlasting truth of Nature it did *not* now do : here lay the vital malady. The inward being wrong, all outward went ever more and more wrong. Belief died away; all was Doubt, Disbelief. The builder *cast away* his plummet; said to himself, " What is gravitation ? Brick lies on brick there ! " Alas, does it not still sound strange to many of us, the assertion that there *is* a God's-truth in the business of god-created men ; that all is not a kind of grimace, an 'expediency,' diplomacy, one knows not what ! —

From that first necessary assertion of Luther's, " You, self-styled *Papa*,[2] you are no Father in God at

---

[1] Compare p. 173, end.

[2] The original form and meaning of " pope."

all ; you are — a Chimera,[1] whom I know not how to
name in polite language ! " — from that onwards to the
shout [2] which rose round Camille Desmoulins in the
Palais-Royal, " *Aux armes !* " when the people had
burst-up against *all* manner of Chimeras, — I find a
natural historical sequence. That shout too, so frightful, half-infernal, was a great matter. Once more the
voice of awakened nations ; — starting confusedly, as
out of nightmare, as out of death-sleep, into some dim
feeling that Life was real ; that God's-world was not
an expediency and diplomacy ! Infernal ; — yes, since
they would not have it otherwise. Infernal, since not
celestial or terrestrial ! Hollowness, insincerity *has* to
cease ; sincerity of some sort has to begin. Cost what
it may, reigns of terror, horrors of French Revolution or what else, we have to return to truth. Here is
a Truth, as I said: a Truth clad in hellfire, since they
would not but have it so ! —

A common theory among considerable parties of
men in England and elsewhere used to be, that the
French Nation had, in those days, as it were gone
mad ; that the French Revolution was a general act
of insanity, a temporary conversion of France and
large sections of the world into a kind of Bedlam.[3]
The Event had risen and raged ; but was a madness
and nonentity, — gone now happily into the region of

---

[1] See p. 18, n. 1.

[2] " To arms ! " from the crowd in the garden of the Palais
Royal, addressed from a café table by Desmoulins, a journalist,
July 12, 1789. The French Revolution began then : the Bastille
fell two days later. (See *French Revolution*, I, v, iv.)

[3] A corrupted pronunciation of " Bethlehem," — the Hospital
(for lunatics) of St. Mary of Bethlebem, London, founded 1246.

Dreams and the Picturesque! — To such comfortable philosophers, the Three Days of July 1830 [1] must have been a surprising phenomenon. Here is the French Nation risen again, in musketry and death-struggle, out shooting and being shot, to make that same mad French Revolution good! The sons and grandsons of those men, it would seem, persist in the enterprise: they do not disown it; they will have it made good; will have themselves shot, if it be not made good! To philosophers who had made-up their life-system on that ' madness' quietus, no phenomenon could be more alarming. Poor Niebuhr,[2] they say, the Prussian Professor and Historian, fell broken-hearted in consequence; sickened, if we can believe it, and died of the Three Days! It was surely not a very heroic death; — little better than Racine's,[3] dying because Louis Fourteenth looked sternly on him once. The world had stood some considerable shocks, in its time; might have been expected to survive the Three Days too, and be found turning on its axis after even them! The Three Days told all mortals that the old French Revolution, mad as it might look, was not a transitory ebullition of Bedlam, but a genuine product of this Earth where we all live; that it was verily a Fact, and that the world in general would do well everywhere to regard it as such.

Truly, without the French Revolution, one would

[1] Overthrowing Charles X and his arbitrary and incapable government: Louis Philippe became " the Citizen King " by the will of the people.

[2] 1776–1831.

[3] One of the greatest French tragic poets (1639–1699); called Louis XIV's " toy."

not know what to make of an age like this at all. We will hail the French Revolution, as shipwrecked mariners might the sternest rock, in a world otherwise all of baseless sea and waves. A true Apocalypse, though a terrible one, to this false withered artificial time; testifying once more that Nature is *preter*natural; if not divine, then diabolic; that Semblance is not Reality; that it has to become Reality, or the world will take-fire under it, — burn *it* into what it is, namely Nothing! Plausibility has ended; empty Routine has ended; much has ended. This, as with a Trump of Doom, has been proclaimed to all men. They are the wisest who will learn it soonest. Long confused generations before it be learned; peace impossible till it be! The earnest man, surrounded, as ever, with a world of inconsistencies, can await patiently, patiently strive to do *his* work, in the midst of that. Sentence of Death is written down in Heaven against all that; sentence of Death is now proclaimed on the Earth against it: this he with his eyes may see. And surely, I should say, considering the other side of the matter, what enormous difficulties lie there, and how fast, fearfully fast, in all countries, the inexorable demand for solution of them is pressing on, — he may easily find other work to do than labouring in the Sansculottic province at this time of day !

To me, in these circumstances, that of 'Hero-worship' becomes a fact inexpressibly precious; the most solacing fact one sees in the world at present. There is an everlasting hope in it for the management of the world. Had all traditions, arrangements, creeds, societies that men ever instituted, sunk away, this would remain.

The certainty of Heroes being sent us; our faculty, our necessity, to reverence Heroes when sent: it shines like a polestar through smoke-clouds, dust-clouds, and all manner of down-rushing and conflagration.

Hero-worship would have sounded very strange to those workers and fighters in the French Revolution. Not reverence for Great Men; not any hope or belief, or even wish, that Great Men could again appear in the world! Nature, turned into a ' Machine,' was as if effete now: could not any longer produce Great Men: — I can tell her, she may give-up the trade altogether, then; we cannot do without Great Men! — But neither have I any quarrel with that of ' Liberty and Equality;' with the faith that, wise great men being impossible, a level immensity of foolish small men would suffice. It was a natural faith then and there. " Liberty and Equality; no Authority needed any longer. Hero-worship, reverence for *such* Authorities, has proved false, is itself a falsehood; no more of it! We have had such *forgeries*, we will now trust nothing. So many base plated coins passing in the market, the belief has now become common that no gold any longer exists, — and even that we can do very well without gold! " I find this, among other things, that universal cry of Liberty and Equality; and find in it very natural, as matters then stood.

And yet surely it is but the *transition* from false to true. Considered as the whole truth, it is false altogether; — the product of entire sceptical blindness, as yet only *struggling* to see. Hero-worship exists forever, and everywhere: not Loyalty alone; it extends from divine adoration down to the lowest practical regions of life. 'Bending before men,' if it is not to be a mere empty grimace, better dispensed with than practised, is Hero-worship, — a recognition that there does dwell in that presence of our brother something divine; that every created man, as Novalis said, is a 'revelation in the Flesh.' They were Poets too, that devised all those graceful courtesies which make life noble! Courtesy is not a falsehood or grimace; it need not be such. And Loyalty, religious Worship itself, are still possible; nay still inevitable.

May we not say, moreover, while so many of our late Heroes have worked rather as revolutionary men, that nevertheless every Great Man, every genuine man, is by the nature of him a son of Order, not of Disorder? It is a tragical position for a true man to work in revolutions. He seems an anarchist; and indeed a painful element of anarchy does encumber him at every step, — him to whose whole soul anarchy is hostile, hateful. His mission is Order; every man's is. He is here to make what was disorderly, chaotic, into a thing ruled, regular. He is the missionary of Order. Is not all work of man in this world a *making of Order?* The carpenter finds rough trees; shapes them, constrains them into square fitness, into purpose and use. We are all born enemies of Disorder: it is tragical for us all to be concerned in image-breaking and down-pulling; for the Great Man, *more* a man than we, it is doubly tragical.

Thus too all human things, maddest French Sans-culottisms, do and must work towards Order. I say, there is not a *man* in them, raging in the thickest of the madness, but is impelled withal, at all moments, towards Order. His very life means that; Disorder is dissolution, death. No chaos but it seeks a *centre* to revolve round. While man is man, some Cromwell or Napoleon is the necessary finish of a Sansculottism. — Curious: in those days when Hero-worship was the most incredible thing to every one, how it does come-out nevertheless, and assert itself practically, in a way which all have to credit. Divine *right*, take it on the great scale, is found to mean divine *might* withal! While old false Formulas are getting trampled every-where into destruction, new genuine Substances unex-pectedly unfold themselves indestructible. In rebel-lious ages, when Kingship itself seems dead and abolished, Cromwell, Napoleon step-forth again as Kings. The history of these men is what we have now to look at, as our last phasis of Heroism. The old ages are brought back to us; the manner in which Kings were made, and Kingship itself first took rise, is again exhibited in the history of these Two.

We have had many civil-wars in England ; wars of Red and White Roses,[1] wars of Simon de Montfort;[2] wars enough, which are not very memorable. But that war of the Puritans has a significance which belongs to no one of the others. Trusting to your can-dour, which will suggest on the other side what I have not room to say, I will call it a section once more of that great universal war which alone makes-up the true History of the World, — the war of Belief against

[1] Between the houses of Lancaster (red) and York (white), 1450–1485.

[2] About 1208–1265 ; leader of insurgent barons against Henry III.

Unbelief! The struggle of men intent on the real essence of things, against men intent on the semblances and forms of things. The Puritans, to many, seem mere savage Iconoclasts,[1] fierce destroyers of Forms; but it were more just to call them haters of *untrue* Forms. I hope we know how to respect Laud [2] and his King as well as them. Poor Laud seems to me to have been weak and ill-starred, not dishonest; an unfortunate Pedant rather than anything worse. His 'Dreams' and superstitions, at which they laugh so, have an affectionate, lovable kind of character. He is like a College-Tutor, whose whole world is forms, College-rules; whose notion is that these are the life and safety of the world. He is placed suddenly, with that unalterable luckless notion of his, at the head not of a College but of a Nation, to regulate the most complex deep-reaching interests of men. He thinks they ought to go by the old decent regulations; nay that their salvation will lie in extending and improving these. Like a weak man, he drives with spasmodic vehemence towards his purpose; cramps himself to it, heeding no voice of prudence, no cry of pity : He will have his College-rules obeyed by his Collegians; that first; and till that, nothing. He is an ill-starred Pedant, as I said. He would have it the world was a College of that kind, and the world *was not* that. Alas, was not his doom stern enough? Whatever wrongs he did, were they not all frightfully avenged on him?

[1] Image-breakers.
[2] 1573–1645 ; Archbishop of Canterbury, — a chief object of Puritan hostility. Laud and his king (Charles I, 1600–1649) were both beheaded.

It is meritorious to insist on forms; Religion and all else naturally clothes itself in forms. Everywhere the *formed* world is the only habitable one. The naked formlessness of Puritanism is not the thing I praise in the Puritans; it is the thing I pity, — praising only the spirit which had rendered that inevitable! All substances clothe themselves in forms: but there are suitable true forms, and then there are untrue unsuitable. As the briefest definition, one might say, Forms which *grow* round a substance, if we rightly understand that, will correspond to the real nature and purport of it, will be true, good; forms which are consciously *put* round a substance, bad. I invite you to reflect on this. It distinguishes true from false in Ceremonial Form, earnest solemnity from empty pageant, in all human things.

There must be a veracity, a natural spontaneity in forms. In the commonest meeting of men, a person making, what we call, 'set speeches,' is not he an offence? In the mere drawing-room, whatsoever courtesies you see to be grimaces, prompted by no spontaneous reality within, are a thing you wish to get away from. But suppose now it were some matter of vital concernment, some transcendent matter (as Divine Worship is), about which your whole soul, struck dumb with its excess of feeling, knew not how to *form* itself into utterance at all, and preferred formless silence to any utterance there possible, — what should we say of a man coming forward to represent or utter it for you in the way of upholsterer-mummery? Such a man, — let him depart swiftly, if he love himself! You have lost your only son; are

mute, struck down, without even tears: an importunate
man importunately offers to celebrate Funeral Games
for him in the manner of the Greeks! Such mummery
is not only not to be accepted, — it is hateful, unen-
durable. It is what the old Prophets called ' Idolatry,'
worshipping of hollow *shows;* what all earnest men do
and will reject. We can partly understand what those
poor Puritans meant. Laud dedicating that St. Cath-
erine Creed's Church,[1] in the manner we have it described; with his multiplied ceremonial bowings, gestic-
ulations, exclamations: surely it is rather the rigorous
formal *Pedant*, intent on his ' College-rules,' than the
earnest Prophet, intent on the essence of the matter.

Puritanism found *such* forms insupportable; trampled on such forms ; — we have to excuse it for saying,
No form at all rather than such! It stood preaching
in its bare pulpit, with nothing but the Bible in its
hand. Nay, a man preaching from his earnest *soul*
into the earnest *souls* of men : is not this virtually the
essence of all Churches whatsoever? The nakedest,
savagest reality, I say, is preferable to any semblance,
however dignified. Besides, it will clothe itself with
due semblance by and by, if it be real. No fear of
that; actually no fear at all. Given the living *man*,
there will be found *clothes* for him; he will find himself clothes. But the suit-of-clothes pretending that *it*
is both clothes and man — ! — We cannot ' fight
the French ' by three-hundred-thousand red uniforms;
there must be *men* in the inside of them! Semblance,
I assert, must actually *not* divorce itself from Reality.

[1] In London, January, 1631, thereby giving fresh offense to
the Puritans.

If Semblance do, — why then there must be men found
to rebel against Semblance, for it has become a lie!
These two Antagonisms at war here, in the case of
Laud and the Puritans, are as old nearly as the world.
They went to fierce battle over England in that age;
and fought-out their confused controversy to a certain
length, with many results for all of us.

In the age which directly followed that of the Puritans, their cause or themselves were little likely to
have justice done them. Charles Second[1] and his
Rochesters were not the kind of men you would set to
judge what the worth or meaning of such men might
have been. That there could be any faith or truth in
the life of a man, was what these poor Rochesters, and
the age they ushered-in, had forgotten. Puritanism
was hung on gibbets, — like the bones of the leading
Puritans. Its work nevertheless went on accomplish-
ing itself. All true work of a man, hang the author
of it on what gibbet you like, must and will accomplish itself. We have our *Habeas-Corpus*, our free
Representation of the People; acknowledgment, wide
as the world, that all men are, or else must, shall, and
will become, what we call *free* men; — men with their
life grounded on reality and justice, not on tradition,
which has become unjust and a chimera! This in part,
and much besides this,[2] was the work of the Puritans.

[1] 1630–1685; "restored" 1660. Rochester was one of the
most corrupt favorites of his corrupt court; also a skillful versi-
fier.

[2] "Slowly but steadily it introduced its own seriousness and
purity into English society, English literature, English politics.
The whole history of English progress since the Restoration, on its

And indeed, as these things became gradually manifest, the character of the Puritans began to clear itself. Their memories were, one after another, taken
down from the gibbet; nay a certain portion of them
are now, in these days, as good as canonised. Eliot,[1]
Hampden,[1] Pym,[1] nay Ludlow,[2] Hutchinson,[1] Vane[3]
himself, are admitted to be a kind of Heroes ; political Conscript Fathers,[4] to whom in no small degree
we owe what makes us a free England : it would not be
safe for anybody to designate these men as wicked now.
Few Puritans of note but find their apologists somewhere, and have a certain reverence paid them by earnest men. One Puritan, I think, and almost he alone,
our poor Cromwell, seems to hang yet on the gibbet,
and find no hearty apologist anywhere. Him neither
saint nor sinner will acquit of great wickedness. A
man of ability, infinite talent, courage, and so forth :
but he betrayed the Cause. Selfish ambition, dishonesty, duplicity; a fierce, coarse, hypocritical *Tartufe* ;[5]
turning all that noble Struggle for constitutional
Liberty into a sorry farce played for his own benefit :
this and worse is the character they give of Cromwell.
And then there come contrasts with Washington and
others; above all, with these noble Pyms and Hampdens, whose noble work he stole for himself, and
ruined into a futility and deformity.

moral and spiritual sides, has been the history of Puritanism."
J. R. Green, *Short History of the English People*, III, 1285 (N. Y.
1894).

[1] See later notes.
[2] One of the Regicides, 1617(?)–1692 ; died in exile.
[3] The Younger, born 1612, beheaded 1662.
[4] Title of the Senators of ancient Rome.
[5] Hero of Molière's comedy of same name, 1667.

This view of Cromwell seems to me the not unnatural product of a century like the Eighteenth. As we said of the Valet, so of the Sceptic : He does not know a Hero when he sees him! The Valet expected purple mantles, gilt sceptres, bodyguards and flourishes of trumpets: the Sceptic of the Eighteenth century looks for regulated respectable Formulas, ' Principles,' or what else he may call them ; a style of speech and conduct which has got to seem ' respectable,' which can plead for itself in a handsome articulate manner, and gain the suffrages of an enlightened sceptical Eighteenth century ! It is, at bottom, the same thing that both the Valet and he expect: the garnitures of some *acknowledged* royalty, which *then* they will acknowledge ! The King coming to them in the rugged *un*-formulistic state shall be no King.

For my own share, far be it from me to say or insinuate a word of disparagement against such characters as Hampden, Eliot, Pym; whom I believe to have been right worthy and useful men. I have read diligently what books and documents about them I could come at ; — with the honestest wish to admire, to love and worship them like Heroes ; but I am sorry to say, if the real truth must be told, with very indifferent success ! At bottom, I found that it would not do. They are very noble men, these ; step along in their stately way, with their measured euphemisms, philosophies, parliamentary eloquences, Ship-moneys,[1] *Mon*-

---

[1] An obsolete tax which Charles I sought to revive by way of raising money independently of Parliament. Hampden (1594–1643) led the resistance against its payment in 1637, and as a result was for a time imprisoned.

archies of Man; [1] a most constitutional, unblamable,
dignified set of men. But the heart remains cold
before them; the fancy alone endeavours to get-up
some worship of them. What man's heart does, in
reality, break-forth into any fire of brotherly love for
these men? They are become dreadfully dull men!
One breaks-down often enough in the constitutional
eloquence of the admirable Pym,[2] with his ' seventhly
and lastly.' You find that it may be the admirablest
thing in the world, but that it is heavy, — heavy as
lead, barren as brick-clay; that, in a word, for you
there is little or nothing now surviving there! One
leaves all these Nobilities standing in their niches of
honour: the rugged outcast Cromwell, he is the man
of them all in whom one still finds human stuff. The
great savage *Baresark:* [3] he could write no euphemistic
Monarchy of Man; did not speak, did not work with
glib regularity; had no straight story to tell for himself anywhere. But he stood bare, not cased in euphemistic coat-of-mail; he grappled like a giant, face to
face, heart to heart, with the naked truth of things!
That, after all, is the sort of man for one. I plead
guilty to valuing such a man beyond all other sorts of
men. Smooth-shaven Respectabilities not a few one
finds, that are not good for much. Small thanks to a

---

[1] Eliot, imprisoned in the Tower of London on charge of con-
spiracy against the King, wrote the *Monarchy of Man* (1630). He
refused to win his freedom by acknowledging himself wrong in
his conduct towards the King, and died in the Tower, 1632.

[2] 1584–1643.

[3] " Bare shirt " (*i. e.* without armor), from the supposed (mistaken) etymology of " berserk " (a wild Norse warrior) which
means a shirt or coat of bear skin.

man for keeping his hands clean, who would not touch the work but with gloves on!

Neither, on the whole, does this constitutional tolerance of the Eighteenth century for the other happier Puritans seen to be a very great matter. One might say, it is but a piece of Formulism and Scepticism, like the rest. They tell us, It was a sorrowful thing to consider that the foundation of our English Liberties should have been laid by 'Superstition.' These Puritans came forward with Calvinistic incredible Creeds, Anti-Laudisms, Westminster Confessions; demanding, chiefly of all, that they should have liberty to *worship* in their own way. Liberty to *tax* themselves: that was the thing they should have demanded! It was Superstition, Fanaticism, disgraceful ignorance of Constitutional Philosophy to insist on the other thing!—Liberty to *tax* oneself? Not to pay-out money from your pocket except on reason shown? No century, I think, but a rather barren one would have fixed on that as the first right of man! I should say, on the contrary, A just man will generally have better cause than *money* in what shape soever, before deciding to revolt against his Government. Ours is a most confused world; in which a good man will be thankful to see any kind of Government maintain itself in a not insupportable manner: and here in England, to this hour, if he is not ready to pay a great many taxes which *he* can see very small reason in, it will not go well with him, I think! He must try some other climate than this. Taxgatherer? Money? He will say: "Take my money, since you *can*, and it is so desirable to you; take it,—and take

yourself away with it; and leave me alone to my
work here. *I* am still here; can still work, after all
the money you have taken from me!" But if they
come to him, and say, " Acknowledge a Lie; pretend
to say you are worshipping God, when you are not
doing it: believe not the thing that *you* find true, but
the thing that I find, or pretend to find true!" He
will answer: "No; by God's help, no! You may
take my purse; but I cannot have my moral Self
annihilated. The purse is any Highwayman's who
might meet me with a loaded pistol: but the Self is
mine and God my Maker's; it is not yours; and I
will resist you to the death, and revolt against you,
and, on the whole, front all manner of extremities,
accusations and confusions, in defence of that!" —

Really, it seems to me the one reason which could
justify revolting, this of the Puritans. It has been the
soul of all just revolts among men. Not *Hunger* alone
produced even the French Revolution; no, but the
feeling of the insupportable all-pervading *Falsehood*
which had now embodied itself in Hunger, in universal
material Scarcity and Nonentity, and thereby become
indisputably false in the eyes of all! We will leave
the Eighteenth century with its ' liberty to tax itself.'
We will not astonish ourselves that the meaning of
such men as the Puritans remained dim to it. To men
who believe in no reality at all, how shall a *real* human
soul, the intensest of all realities, as it were the voice
of this world's Maker still speaking to *us*, — be intelligible? What it cannot reduce into constitutional doctrines relative to ' taxing,' or other the like material
interest, gross, palpable to the sense, such a century

will needs reject as an amorphous heap of rubbish. Hampdens, Pyms and Ship-money will be the theme of much constitutional eloquence, striving to be fervid; — which will glitter, if not as fire does, then as *ice* does: and the irreducible Cromwell will remain a chaotic mass of 'madness,' 'hypocrisy,' and much else.

From of old, I will confess, this theory of Cromwell's falsity has been incredible to me. Nay I cannot believe the like, of any Great Man whatever. Multitudes of Great Men figure in History as false selfish men; but if we will consider it, they are but *figures* for us, unintelligible shadows; we do not see into them as men that could have existed at all. A superficial unbelieving generation only, with no eye but for the surfaces and semblances of things, could form such notions of Great Men. Can a great soul be possible without a *conscience* in it, the essence of all *real* souls, great or small? — No, we cannot figure Cromwell as a Falsity and Fatuity; the longer I study him and his career, I believe this the less. Why should we? There is no evidence of it. Is it not strange that, after all the mountains of calumny this man has been subject to, after being represented as the very prince of liars, who never, or hardly ever, spoke truth, but always some cunning counterfeit of truth, there should not yet have been one falsehood clearly brought home to him? A prince of liars, and no lie spoken by him. Not one that I could yet get sight of. It is like Pococke asking Grotius, Where is your *proof* of Mahomet's Pigeon? No proof! — Let us leave all these calumnious chimeras, as chimeras ought to be left.

They are not portraits of the man ; they are distracted phantasms of him, the joint product of hatred and darkness.

Looking at the man's life with our own eyes, it seems to me, a very different hypothesis suggests itself. What little we know of his earlier obscure years, distorted as it has come down to us, does it not all betoken an earnest, affectionate, sincere kind of man? His nervous melancholic temperament indicates rather a seriousness *too* deep for him. Of those stories of 'Spectres;' of the white Spectre in broad daylight, predicting that he should be King of England, we are not bound to believe much ; — probably no more than of the other black Spectre, or Devil in person, to whom the Officer *saw* him sell himself before Worcester Fight ! [1] But the mournful, over-sensitive, hypochondriac humour of Oliver, in his young years, is otherwise indisputably known. The Huntingdon [2] Physician told Sir Philip Warwick himself, He had often been sent for at midnight ; Mr. Cromwell was full of hypochondria, thought himself near dying, and " had fancies about the Towncross." These things are significant. Such an excitable deep-feeling nature, in that rugged stubborn strength of his, is not the symptom of falsehood ; it is the symptom and promise of quite other than falsehood !

The young Oliver is sent to study Law ; falls, or is said to have fallen, for a little period, into some of

---

[1] September 3, 1651; Cromwell defeated the Scotch Royalists led by Charles II.

[2] About forty-four to sixty miles north of London; Cromwell was born there, April 25, 1599. St. Ives and Ely, where he lived later, are not far off, toward the east.

the dissipations of youth; but if so, speedily repents, abandons all this: not much above twenty, he is married, settled as an altogether grave and quiet man. 'He pays-back what money he had won at gambling,' says the story; — he does not think any gain of that kind could be really *his*. It is very interesting, very natural, this 'conversion,' as they well name it; this awakening of a great true soul from the worldly slough, to see into the awful *truth* of things; — to see that Time and its shows all rested on Eternity, and this poor Earth of ours was the threshold either of Heaven or of Hell! Oliver's life at St. Ives and Ely, as a sober industrious Farmer, is it not altogether as that of a true and devout man? He has renounced the world and its ways; *its* prizes are not the thing that can enrich him. He tills the earth; he reads his Bible; daily assembles his servants round him to worship God. He comforts persecuted ministers, is fond of preachers; nay can himself preach, — exhorts his neighbours to be wise, to redeem the time. In all this what 'hypocrisy,' 'ambition,' 'cant,' or other falsity? The man's hopes, I do believe, were fixed on the other Higher World; his aim to get well *thither*, by walking well through his humble course in *this* world. He courts no notice: what could notice here do for him? 'Ever in his great Taskmaster's eye.'[1]

It is striking, too, how he comes-out once into public view; he, since no other is willing to come: in resistance to a public grievance. I mean, in that mat-

[1] All is, if I have grace to use it so
As ever in my great Task-master's eye.
— Milton's sonnet, *On arriving at the age of twenty-three.*

ter of the Bedford Fens.[1] No one else will go to law
with Authority; therefore he will. That matter once
settled, he returns back into obscurity, to his Bible
and his Plough. 'Gain influence'? His influence is
the most legitimate; derived from personal knowledge
of him, as a just, religious, reasonable, and determined
man. In this way he has lived till past forty; old age
is now in view of him, and the earnest portal of Death
and Eternity; it was at this point that he suddenly
became 'ambitious'! I do not interpret his Parliamentary mission in that way!

His successes in Parliament, his successes through
the war, are honest successes of a brave man; who
has more resolution in the heart of him, more light in
the head of him than other men. His prayers to God;
his spoken thanks to the God of Victory, who had
preserved him safe, and carried him forward so far,
through the furious clash of a world all set in conflict,
through desperate-looking envelopments at Dunbar;[2]
through the death-hail of so many battles; mercy
after mercy; to the 'crowning mercy'[3] of Worcester
Fight: all this is good and genuine for a deep-hearted
Calvinistic Cromwell. Only to vain unbelieving Cavaliers, worshipping not God but their own 'lovelocks,'
frivolities and formalities, living quite apart from con-
templations of God, living *without* God in the world,
need it seem hypocritical.

Nor will his participation in the King's death

---

[1] The draining of the Fens in 1637.

[2] September 3, 1650; the account of this battle is one of the
most striking passages in Carlyle's *Cromwell*.

[3] Cromwell's own phrase.

involve him in condemnation with us. It is a stern
business killing of a King! But if you once go to war
with him, it lies *there;* this and all else lies there.
Once at war, you have made wager of battle with
him: it is he to die, or else you. Reconciliation is
problematic; may be possible, or, far more likely, is
impossible. It is now pretty generally admitted that
the Parliament, having vanquished Charles First, had
no way of making any tenable arrangement with him.
The large Presbyterian party, apprehensive now of the
Independents, were most anxious to do so; anxious
indeed as for their own existence; but it could not be.
The unhappy Charles, in those final Hampton-Court [1]
negotiations, shows himself as a man fatally incapable
of being dealt with. A man who, once for all, could
not and would not *understand* :—whose thought did
not in any measure represent to him the real fact of
the matter; nay worse, whose *word* did not at all
represent his thought. We may say this of him without cruelty, with deep pity rather : but it is true and
undeniable. Forsaken there of all but the *name* of
Kingship, he still, finding himself treated with outward
respect as a King, fancied that he might play-off
party against party, and smuggle himself into his old
power by deceiving both. Alas, they both *discovered*
that he was deceiving them. A man whose *word* will
not inform you at all what he means or will do, is not
a man you can bargain with. You must get out of
that man's way, or put him out of yours! The Pres-
byterians, in their despair, were still for believing

[1] A royal palace on the Thames, several miles above London,
whither Charles was brought in 1647.

Charles, though found false, unbelievable again and again. Not so Cromwell: "For all our fighting," says he, "we are to have a little bit of paper?" No!—

In fact, everywhere we have to note the decisive practical *eye* of this man; how he drives towards the practical and practicable; has a genuine insight into what *is* fact. Such an intellect, I maintain, does not belong to a false man: the false man sees false shows, plausibilities, expediencies: the true man is needed to discern even practical truth. Cromwell's advice about the Parliament's Army, early in the contest, How they were to dismiss their city-tapsters, flimsy riotous persons, and choose substantial yeomen, whose heart was in the work, to be soldiers for them: this is advice by a man who *saw*. Fact answers, if you see into Fact! Cromwell's *Ironsides* were the embodiment of this insight of his; men fearing God; and without any other fear. No more conclusively genuine set of fighters ever trod the soil of England, or of any other land.

Neither will we blame greatly that word of Cromwell's to them; which was so blamed: "If the King should meet me in battle, I would kill the King." Why not? These words were spoken to men who stood as before a Higher than Kings. They had set more than their own lives on the cast. The Parliament may call it, in official language, a fighting '*for* the King;' but we, for our share, cannot understand that. To us it is no dilettante work, no sleek officiality; it is sheer rough death and earnest. They have brought it to the calling-forth of *War;* horrid internecine fight, man grappling with man in fire-eyed rage,—the *infernal*

element in man called forth, to try it by that! *Do*
that therefore; since that is the thing to be done. —
The successes of Cromwell seem to me a very natural
thing! Since he was not shot in battle, they were an
inevitable thing. That such a man, with the eye to
see, with the heart to dare, should advance, from post
to post, from victory to victory, till the Huntingdon
Farmer became, by whatever name you might call
him, the acknowledged Strongest Man in England,
virtually the King of England, requires no magic to
explain it! —

Truly it is a sad thing for a people, as for a man,
to fall into Scepticism, into dilettantism, insincerity;
not to know a Sincerity when they see it. For this
world, and for all worlds, what curse is so fatal? The
heart lying dead, the eye cannot see. What intellect
remains is merely the *vulpine* intellect. That a true
King be sent them is of small use; they do not know
him when sent. They say scornfully, Is this your
King? The Hero wastes his heroic faculty in bootless
contradiction from the unworthy; and can accomplish
little. For himself he does accomplish a heroic life,
which is much, which is all; but for the world he
accomplishes comparatively nothing. The wild rude
Sincerity, direct from Nature, is not glib in answering
from the witness-box: in your small-debt *pie-powder*[1]
court, he is scouted as a counterfeit. The vulpine
intellect ' detects ' him. For being a man worth any

[1] From Fr. *pied* (foot) and *poudre* (dust), " dusty foot," *i. e.*,
peddler. An inferior court for the immediate trial of disputes
arising at fairs and other places where peddlers most do congre-
gate.

LIBRARY OF

Western Union College

LE MARS, IOWA

thousand men, the response your Knox, your Cromwell gets, is an argument for two centuries whether he was a man at all. God's greatest gift to this Earth is sneeringly flung away. The miraculous talisman is a paltry plated coin, not fit to pass in the shops as a common guinea.

Lamentable this! I say, this must be remedied. Till this be remedied in some measure, there is nothing remedied. 'Detect quacks'? Yes do, for Heaven's sake; but know withal the men that are to be trusted! Till we know that, what is all our knowledge; how shall we even so much as 'detect'? For the vulpine sharpness, which considers itself to be knowledge, and 'detects' in that fashion, is far mistaken. Dupes indeed are many: but, of all *dupes*, there is none so fatally situated as he who lives in undue terror of being duped. The world does exist; the world has truth in it, or it would not exist! First recognise what is true, we shall *then* discern what is false; and properly never till then.

'Know the men that are to be trusted:' alas, this is yet, in these days, very far from us. The sincere alone can recognise sincerity. Not a Hero only is needed, but a world fit for him; a world not of *Valets ;* — the Hero comes almost in vain to it otherwise! Yes, it is far from us: but it must come; thank God, it is visibly coming. Till it do come, what have we? Ballot-boxes, suffrages, French Revolutions: — if we are as Valets, and do not know the Hero when we see him, what good are all these? A heroic Cromwell comes; and for a hundred-and-fifty years he cannot have a vote from us. Why, the insincere, unbelieving

world is the *natural property* of the Quack, and of
the Father of quacks and quackeries! Misery, confusion, unveracity are alone possible there. By ballot-
boxes we alter the *figure* of our Quack; but the
substance of him continues. The Valet-World *has* to
be governed by the Sham-Hero, by the King merely
dressed in King-gear. It is his; he is its! In brief,
one of two things: We shall either learn to know a
Hero, a true Governor and Captain, somewhat better,
when we see him; or else go on to be forever governed
by the Unheroic;— had we ballot-boxes clattering at
every street-corner, there were no remedy in these.

Poor Cromwell, — great Cromwell! The inarticulate Prophet; Prophet who could not *speak*. Rude,
confused, struggling to utter himself, with his savage
depth, with his wild sincerity; and he looked so
strange, among the elegant Euphemisms,[1] dainty little
Falklands,[2] didactic Chillingworths,[3] diplomatic Clar-
endons![4] Consider him. An outer hull of chaotic
confusion, visions of the Devil, nervous dreams, almost semi-madness; and yet such a clear determinate
man's-energy working in the heart of that. A kind of
chaotic man. The ray as of pure starlight and fire,
working in such an element of boundless hypochondria, *un*formed black of darkness! And yet withal
this hypochondria, what was it but the very greatness

[1] The avoidance of calling things by their right names, for
the sake of greater pleasantness or delicacy or smoothness.
"Smoothshaven respectabilities" of speech.

[2] Statesman (*c.* 1610–1643); served in Royalist Army.

[3] Clergyman (1602–1644); served in Royalist Army.

[4] Royalist parliamentarian (1608–1674); wrote *History of the
Rebellion*.

of the man ? The depth and tenderness of his wild
affections : the quantity of *sympathy* he had with
things,— the quantity of insight he would yet get
into the heart of things, the mastery he would yet get
over things: this was his hypochondria. The man's
misery, as man's misery always does, came of his
greatness. Samuel Johnson too is that kind of man.
Sorrow-stricken, half-distracted ; the wild element of
mournful *black* enveloping him, — wide as the world.
It is the character of a prophetic man ; a man with
his whole soul *seeing*, and struggling to see.

On this ground, too, I explain to myself Cromwell's
reputed confusion of speech. To himself the internal
meaning was sun-clear; but the material with which
he was to clothe it in utterance was not there. He
had *lived* silent ; a great unnamed sea of Thought
round him all his days ; and in his way of life little
call to attempt *naming* or uttering that. With his
sharp power of vision, resolute power of action, I
doubt not he could have learned to write Books withal,
and speak fluently enough ;— he did harder things
than writing of Books. This kind of man is precisely
he who is fit for doing manfully all things you will
set him on doing. Intellect is not speaking and logi-
cising; it is seeing and ascertaining. Virtue, *Vir-tus*,
manhood, *hero*hood, is not fair-spoken immaculate regularity; it is first of all, what the Germans well
name it, *Tugend* (*Taugend*, *dow*-ing or *Dough*-tiness),
Courage and the Faculty to *do*. This basis of the
matter Cromwell had in him.

One understands moreover how, though he could
not speak in Parliament, he might *preach*, rhapsodic

preaching; above all, how he might be great in extempore prayer. These are the free outpouring utterances
of what is in the heart: method is not required in them;
warmth, depth, sincerity are all that is required. Cromwell's habit of prayer is a notable feature of him. All
his great enterprises were commenced with prayer. In
dark inextricable-looking difficulties, his Officers and
he used to assemble, and pray alternately, for hours,
for days, till some definite resolution rose among them,
some ' door of hope,' as they would name it, disclosed
itself. Consider that. In tears, in fervent prayers,
and cries to the great God, to have pity on them, to
make His light shine before them. They, armed Soldiers of Christ, as they felt themselves to be; a little
band of Christian Brothers, who had drawn the sword
against a great black devouring world not Christian,
but Mammonish, Devilish, — they cried to God in
their straits, in their extreme need, not to forsake the
Cause that was His. The light which now rose upon
them, — how could a human soul, by any means at
all, get better light? Was not the purpose so formed
like to be precisely the best, wisest, the one to be followed without hesitation any more? To them it was
as the shining of Heaven's own Splendour in the
waste-howling darkness; the Pillar of Fire by night,
that was to guide them on their desolate perilous way.
Was it not such? Can a man's soul, to this hour, get
guidance by any other method than intrinsically by
that same, — devout prostration of the earnest struggling soul before the Highest, the Giver of all Light;
be such *prayer* a spoken, articulate, or be it a voiceless, inarticulate one? There is no other method.

' Hypocrisy ' ? One begins to be weary of all that.
They who call it so, have no right to speak on such
matters. They never formed a purpose, what one can
call a purpose. They went about balancing expediencies, plausibilities ; gathering votes, advices ; they
never were alone with the *truth* of a thing at all. —
Cromwell's prayers were likely to be ' eloquent,' and
much more than that. His was the heart of a man
who *could* pray.

But indeed his actual Speeches, I apprehend, were
not nearly so ineloquent, incondite, as they look. We
find he was, what all speakers aim to be, an impressive
speaker, even in Parliament ; one who, from the first,
had weight. With that rude passionate voice of his,
he was always understood to *mean* something, and
men wished to know what. He disregarded eloquence,
nay despised and disliked it ; spoke always without
premeditation of the words he was to use. The Reporters, too, in those days seem to have been singu-
larly candid ; and to have given the Printer precisely
what they found on their own note-paper. And
withal, what a strange proof is it of Cromwell's being
the premeditative ever-calculating hypocrite, acting a
play before the world, That to the last he took no
more charge of his Speeches ! How came he not to
study his words a little, before flinging them out to
the public ? If the words were true words, they could
be left to shift for themselves.

But with regard to Cromwell's ' lying,' we will make
one remark. This, I suppose, or something like this,
to have been the nature of it. All parties found themselves deceived in him ; each party understood him to

be meaning *this*, heard him even say so, and behold he turns-out to have been meaning *that!* He was, cry they, the chief of liars. But now, intrinsically, is not all this the inevitable fortune, not of a false man in such times, but simply of a superior man? Such a man must have *reticences* in him. If he walk wearing his heart upon his sleeve for daws to peck at, his journey will not extend far! There is no use for any man's taking-up his abode in a house built of glass. A man always is to be himself the judge how much of his mind he will show to other men; even to those he would have work along with him. There are impertinent inquiries made: your rule is, to leave the inquirer *un*informed on that matter; not, if you can help it, *mis*informed, but precisely as dark as he was! This, could one hit the right phrase of response, is what the wise and faithful man would aim to answer in such a case.

Cromwell, no doubt of it, spoke often in the dialect of small subaltern parties; uttered to them a *part* of his mind. Each little party thought him all its own. Hence their rage, one and all, to find him not of their party, but of his own party! Was it his blame? At all seasons of his history he must have felt, among such people, how, if he explained to them the deeper insight he had, they must either have shuddered aghast at it, or believing it, their own little compact hypothesis must have gone wholly to wreck. They could not have worked in his province any more; nay perhaps they could not now have worked in their own province. It is the inevitable position of a great man among small men. Small men, most

active, useful, are to be seen everywhere, whose whole
activity depends on some conviction which to you is
palpably a limited one; imperfect, what we call an
error. But would it be a kindness always, is it a duty
always or often, to disturb them in that? Many a
man, doing loud work in the world, stands only on
some thin traditionality, conventionality; to him indubitable, to you incredible : break that beneath him,
he sinks to endless depths! "I might have my hand
full of truth," said Fontenelle,[1] "and open only my
little finger."

And if this be the fact even in matters of doctrine,
how much more in all departments of practice! He
that cannot withal *keep his mind to himself* cannot
practise any considerable thing whatever. And we call
it ' dissimulation,' all this? What would you think of
calling the general of an army a dissembler because
he did not tell every corporal and private soldier, who
pleased to put the question, what his thoughts were
about everything?— Cromwell, I should rather say,
managed all this in a manner we must admire for its
perfection. An endless vortex of such questioning
' corporals ' rolled confusedly round him through his
whole course; whom he did answer. It must have
been as a great true-seeing man that he managed this
too. Not one proved falsehood, as I said; not one!
Of what man that ever wound himself through such
a coil of things will you say so much?—

But in fact there are two errors, widely prevalent,
which pervert to the very basis our judgments formed

[1] French poet and prose-writer (1657-1757).

about such men as Cromwell; about their 'ambition,' 'falsity,' and suchlike. The first is what I might
call substituting the *goal* of their career for the course
and starting-point of it. The vulgar Historian of a
Cromwell fancies that he had determined on being
Protector of England, at the time when he was
ploughing the marsh lands of Cambridgeshire. His
career lay all mapped-out: a program of the whole
drama; which he then step by step dramatically
unfolded, with all manner of cunning, deceptive dra-
maturgy, as he went on, — the hollow, scheming
Ὑποκριτής, or Play-actor, that he was! This is a radical perversion; all but universal in such cases. And
think for an instant how different the fact is! How
much does one of *us* foresee of his own life? Short
way ahead of us it is all dim; an *un*wound skein of
possibilities, of apprehensions, attemptabilities, vague-
looming hopes. This Cromwell had *not* his life lying
all in that fashion of Program, which he needed then,
with that unfathomable cunning of his, only to enact
dramatically, scene after scene! Not so. We see it
so; but to him it was in no measure so. What absurdities would fall-away of themselves, were this one
undeniable fact kept honestly in view by History!
Historians indeed will tell you that they do keep it in
view;— but look whether such is practically the fact!
Vulgar History, as in this Cromwell's case, omits it
altogether; even the best kinds of History only remember it now and then. To remember it duly with
rigorous perfection, as in the fact it *stood*, requires
indeed a rare faculty; rare, nay impossible. A very
Shakspeare for faculty; or more than Shakspeare;

who could *enact* a brother man's biography, see with
the brother man's eyes at all points of his course what
things *he* saw ; in short, *know* his course and him, as
few ' Historians ' are like to do. Half or more of all
the thick-plied perversions which distort our image of
Cromwell, will disappear, if we honestly so much as
try to represent them so ; in sequence, as they *were ;*
not in the lump, as they are thrown-down before us.

But a second error, which I think the generality
commit, refers to this same 'ambition' itself. We exaggerate the ambition of Great Men ; we mistake what
the nature of it is. Great Men are not ambitious in
that sense ; he is a small poor man that is ambitious
so. Examine the man who lives in misery because he
does not shine above other men ; who goes about producing himself, pruriently anxious about his gifts and
claims ; struggling to force everybody, as it were begging everybody for God's sake, to acknowledge him a
great man, and set him over the heads of men ! Such
a creature is among the wretchedest sights seen under
this sun. A *great* man? A poor morbid prurient
empty man ; fitter for the ward of a hospital, than for
a throne among men. I advise you to keep-out of his
way. He cannot walk on quiet paths ; unless you will
look at him, wonder at him, write paragraphs about
him, he cannot live. It is the *emptiness* of the man,
not his greatness. Because there is nothing in himself,
he hungers and thirsts that you would find something
in him. In good truth, I believe no great man, not so
much as a genuine man who had health and real substance in him of whatever magnitude, was ever much
tormented in this way.

Your Cromwell, what good could it do him to be
'noticed' by noisy crowds of people? God his maker
already noticed him. He, Cromwell, was already there;
no notice would make *him* other than he already was.
Till his hair was grown gray; and Life from the down-
hill slope was all seen to be limited, not infinite but
finite, and all a measurable matter *how* it went, — he
had been content to plough the ground, and read his
Bible. He in his old days could not support it any
longer, without selling himself to Falsehood, that he
might ride in gilt carriages to Whitehall,[1] and have
clerks with bundles of papers haunting him, " Decide
this, decide that," which in utmost sorrow of heart no
man can perfectly decide ! What could gilt carriages
do for this man ? From of old, was there not in his
life a weight of meaning, a terror and a splendour
as of Heaven itself? His existence there as man
set him beyond need of gilding. Death, Judgment
and Eternity : these already lay as the background of
whatsoever he thought or did. All his life lay begirt
as in the sea of nameless Thoughts, which no speech
of a mortal could name. God's Word, as the Puritan
prophets of that time had read it : this was great, and
all else was little to him. To call such a man 'ambitious,' to figure him as the prurient windbag described
above, seems to me the poorest solecism. Such a man
will say: "Keep your gilt carriages and huzzaing mobs,
keep your red-tape clerks, your influentialities, your
important businesses. Leave me alone, leave me alone;
there is *too much of life* in me already!" Old Samuel

---

[1] Royal residence in London in the sixteenth and seventeenth
centuries.

Johnson, the greatest soul in England in his day, was not ambitious. ' Corsica Boswell ' [1] flaunted at public shows with printed ribbons round his hat; but the great old Samuel stayed at home. The world-wide soul wrapt-up in its thoughts, in its sorrows; — what would paradings, and ribbons in the hat, do for it?

Ah yes, I will say again: The great *silent* men! Looking round on the noisy inanity of the world, words with little meaning, actions with little worth, one loves to reflect on the great Empire of *Silence*. The noble silent men, scattered here and there, each in his department; silently thinking, silently working; whom no Morning Newspaper makes mention of! They are the salt of the Earth. A country that has none or few of these is in a bad way. Like a forest which had no *roots ;* which had all turned into leaves and boughs ; — which must soon wither and be no forest. Woe for us if we had nothing but what we can *show*, or speak. Silence, the great Empire of Silence: higher than the stars; deeper than the Kingdoms of Death! It alone is great; all else is small. — I hope we English will long maintain our *grand talent pour le silence*. Let others that cannot do without standing on barrelheads, to spout, and be seen of all the market-place, cultivate speech exclusively, — become a most green forest without roots! Solomon says, There is a time to speak; but also a time to keep silence.[2] Of some great silent Samuel, not urged to

[1] Bozzy earned the title by his enthusiasm for Corsica in her fight for independence from France in the 1760's.

[2] To every thing there is a season, and a time to every purpose under the heaven ; . . . A time to rend, and a time to sew; a time to keep silence, and a time to speak. Eccles. iii, 1, 7.

writing, as old Samuel Johnson says he was, by *want of money*, and nothing other, one might ask, "Why do not you too get up and speak; promulgate your system, found your sect?" "Truly," he will answer, "I am *continent* of my thought hitherto ; happily I have yet had the ability to keep it in me, no compulsion strong enough to speak it. My ' system ' is not for promulgation first of all ; it is for serving myself to live by. That is the great purpose of it to me. And then the ' honour '? Alas, yes ; — but as Cato said of the statue : So many statues in that Forum of yours, may it not be better if they ask, Where is Cato's[1] statue?"— —

But now, by way of counterpoise to this of Silence, let me say that there are two kinds of ambition ; one wholly blamable, the other laudable and inevitable. Nature has provided that the great silent Samuel shall not be silent too long. The selfish wish to shine over others, let it be accounted altogether poor and miserable. ' Seekest thou great things? seek them not : '[2] this is most true. And yet, I say, there is an irrepressible tendency in every man to develop himself according to the magnitude which Nature has made him of ; to speak-out, to act-out, what Nature has laid in him. This is proper, fit, inevitable ; nay it is a duty, and even the summary of duties for a man. The meaning of life here on earth might be defined as consisting in this : To unfold your *self*, to work what thing you have the faculty for. It is a necessity for the human

---

[1] The Elder, called "The Censor" (*c*. 234–149, B. C.); Roman statesman and author.

[2] And seekest thou great things for thyself ? seek them not. Jer. xlv, 5.

being, the first law of our existence. Coleridge beauti‧
fully remarks that the infant learns to *speak* by this
necessity it feels. — We will say therefore: To decide
about ambition, whether it is bad or not, you have two
things to take into view. Not the coveting of the
place alone, but the fitness of the man for the place
withal : that is the question. Perhaps the place was
his ; perhaps he had a natural right, and even obli‧
gation, to seek the place! Mirabeau's ambition to be
Prime Minister, how shall we blame it, if he were ' the
only man in France that could have done any good
there ' ? Hopefuler perhaps had he not so clearly *felt*
how much good he could do! But a poor Necker,[1]
who could do no good, and had even felt that he
could do none, yet sitting broken-hearted because they
had flung him out, and he was now quit of it, well
might Gibbon[2] mourn over him. — Nature, I say, has
provided amply that the silent great man shall strive
to speak withal; *too* amply, rather!

Fancy, for example, you had revealed to the brave
old Samuel Johnson, in his shrouded-up existence, that
it was possible for him to do priceless divine work for
his country and the whole world. That the perfect
Heavenly Law might be made Law on this Earth ;
that the prayer he prayed daily, ' Thy kingdom come,'
was at length to be fulfilled ! If you had convinced his
judgment of this ; that it was possible, practicable ; that
he the mournful silent Samuel was called to take a

---

[1] 1732-1804. It was his dismissal from control of the finances
of France that aroused Desmoulins. (See p. 278, n. 1.)

[2] 1737-1794; author of *The Decline and Fall of the Roman
Empire* (1776-1788).

part in it! Would not the whole soul of the man have flamed-up into a divine clearness, into noble utterance and determination to act; casting all sorrows and mis-givings under his feet, counting all affliction and con-tradiction small, — the whole dark element of his exist-ence blazing into articulate radiance of light and lightning? It were a true ambition this! And think now how it actually was with Cromwell. From of old, the sufferings of God's Church, true zealous Preachers of the truth flung into dungeons, whipt, set on pillories, their ears cropt-off, God's Gospel-cause trodden under foot of the unworthy : all this had lain heavy on his soul. Long years he had looked upon it, in silence, in prayer; seeing no remedy on Earth; trusting well that a remedy in Heaven's goodness would come, — that such a course was false, unjust, and could not last forever. And now behold the dawn of it; after twelve years silent waiting, all England stirs itself; there is to be once more a Parliament,[1] the Right will get a voice for itself: inexpressible well-grounded hope has come again into the Earth. Was not such a Parliament worth being a member of? Cromwell threw down his ploughs, and hastened thither.

He spoke there, — rugged bursts of earnestness, of a self-seen truth, where we get a glimpse of them. He worked there; he fought and strove, like a strong true

---

[1] In 1640. The Short Parliament sat for three weeks, in the spring. In the autumn the Long Parliament convened; being "purged" in 1648 of members inclining to treat with Charles, it received the name of "The Rump;" it was forcibly dissolved by Cromwell in 1653; restored in 1659, it was finally dissolved the next year.

giant of a man, through cannon-tumult and all else,—
on and on, till the Cause *triumphed*, its once so for-
midable enemies all swept from before it, and the dawn
of hope had become clear light of victory and certainty.
That *he* stood there as the strongest soul of England,
the undisputed Hero of all England,— what of this?
It was possible that the Law of Christ's Gospel could
now establish itself in the world! The Theocracy
which John Knox in his pulpit might dream of as a
'devout imagination,' this practical man, experienced
in the whole chaos of most rough practice, dared to
consider as capable of being *realised*. Those that were
highest in Christ's Church, the devoutest wisest men,
were to rule the land : in some considerable degree, it
might be so and should be so. Was it not *true*, God's
truth? And if *true*, was it not then the very thing to
do? The strongest practical intellect in England dared
to answer, Yes! This I call a noble true purpose; is
it not, in its own dialect, the noblest that could enter
into the heart of Statesman or man? For a Knox to
take it up was something; but for a Cromwell, with
his great sound sense and experience of what our world
was,— History, I think, shows it only this once in such
a degree. I account it the culminating point of Protestantism; the most heroic phasis that 'Faith in the
Bible' was appointed to exhibit here below. Fancy it:
that it were made manifest to one of us, how we could
make the Right supremely victorious over Wrong, and
all that we had longed and prayed for, as the highest
good to England and all lands, an attainable fact!

Well, I must say, the *vulpine* intellect, with its knowingness, its alertness and expertness in 'detecting

hypocrites, seems to me a rather sorry business. We have had but one such Statesman in England; one man, that I can get sight of, who ever had in the heart of him any such purpose at all. One man, in the course of fifteen-hundred years; and this was his welcome. He had adherents by the hundred or the ten; opponents by the million. Had England rallied all round him, — why, then, England might have been a *Christian* land! As it is, vulpine knowingness sits yet at its hopeless problem, ' Given a world of Knaves, to educe an Honesty from their united action; ' — how cumbrous a problem, you may see in Chancery [1] Law-Courts, and some other places! Till at length, by Heaven's just anger, but also by Heaven's great grace, the matter begins to stagnate; and this problem is becoming to all men a *palpably* hopeless one. —

But with regard to Cromwell and his purposes: Hume,[2] and a multitude following him, come upon me here with an admission that Cromwell *was* sincere at first; a sincere ' Fanatic ' at first, but gradually became a ' Hypocrite ' as things opened round him. This of the Fanatic-Hypocrite is Hume's theory of it; extensively applied since, — to Mahomet and many others. Think of it seriously, you will find something in it; not much, not all, very far from all. Sincere hero hearts do not sink in this miserable manner. The Sun flings-forth impurities, gets balefully incrusted with spots; but it does not quench itself, and become no Sun at all, but a mass of Darkness! I will venture

[1] The highest court of justice in Great Britain.
[2] In *History of England* (1654–1661). See p. 204, n. 2.

to say that such never befell a great deep Cromwell;
I think, never. Nature's own lion-hearted Son; An-
tæus-like,[1] his strength is got by *touching the Earth*,
his Mother; lift him up from the Earth, lift him up
into Hypocrisy, Inanity, his strength is gone. We will
not assert that Cromwell was an immaculate man; that
he fell into no faults, no insincerities among the rest
He was no dilettante professor of 'perfections,' 'immaculate conducts.' He was a rugged Orson,[2] rend-
ing his rough way through actual true *work*,— doubtless with many a *fall* therein. Insincerities, faults,
very many faults daily and hourly: it was too well
known to him; known to God and him! The Sun
was dimmed many a time; but the Sun had not himself grown a Dimness. Cromwell's last words, as he
lay waiting for death, are those of a Christian heroic
man. Broken prayers to God, that He would judge
him and this Cause, He since man could not, in justice
yet in pity. They are most touching words. He
breathed-out his wild great soul, its toils and sins all
ended now, into the presence of his Maker, in this
manner.

I, for one, will not call the man a Hypocrite! Hypocrite, mummer, the life of him a mere theatricality;
empty barren quack, hungry for the shouts of mobs?
The man had made obscurity do very well for him
till his head was gray; and now he *was*, there as he
stood recognised unblamed, the virtual King of Eng-

---

[1] Mythical Giant, son of Earth, who in wrestling received fresh
strength from every fall upon his mother.

[2] Carried off by a bear and brought up in rough forest savagery; his twin brother Valentine was brought up at court.

land. Cannot a man do without King's Coaches and
Cloaks? Is it such a blessedness to have clerks forever pestering you with bundles of papers in red tape?
A simple Diocletian [1] prefers planting of cabbages; a
George Washington, no very immeasurable man, does
the like. One would say, it is what any genuine man
could do; and would do. The instant his real work
were out in the matter of Kingship, — away with it!

Let us remark, meanwhile, how indispensable everywhere a *King* is, in all movements of men. It is strik-
ingly shown, in this very War, what becomes of men
when they cannot find a Chief Man, and their enemies
can. The Scotch Nation was all but unanimous in
Puritanism; zealous and of one mind about it, as in
this English end of the Island was always far from
being the case. But there was no great Cromwell
among them; poor tremulous, hesitating, diplomatic
Argyles [2] and suchlike: none of them had a heart true
enough for the truth, or durst commit himself to the
truth. They had no leader; and the scattered Cavalier party in that country had one: Montrose, [3] the
noblest of all the Cavaliers; an accomplished, gallant-
hearted, splendid man; what one may call the Hero-
Cavalier. Well, look at it; on the one hand subjects
without a King; on the other a King without subjects! The subjects without King can do nothing; the
subjectless King can do something. This Montrose,

[1] 245–313; he was Emperor of Rome, but abdicated and returned to his cabbages, — and philosophy.

[2] Marquis of Argyle, 1598–1661 (executed); utterly defeated
by Montrose in 1645. Character as stated by Carlyle.

[3] Marquis of Montrose, 1612–1650 (executed). See Scott's
Legend of Montrose.

with a handful of Irish or Highland savages, few of them so much as guns in their hands, dashes at the drilled Puritan armies like a wild whirlwind; sweeps them, time after time, some five times over, from the field before him. He was at one period, for a short while, master of all Scotland. One man; but he was a man : a million zealous men, but *without* the one; they against him were powerless! Perhaps of all the persons in that Puritan struggle, from first to last, the single indispensable one was verily Cromwell. To see and dare, and decide; to be a fixed pillar in the welter of uncertainty;— a King among them, whether they called him so or not.

Precisely here, however, lies the rub [1] for Cromwell. His other proceedings have all found advocates, and stand generally justified; but this dismissal of the Rump Parliament [2] and assumption of the Protectorship, is what no one can pardon him. He had fairly grown to be King in England; Chief Man of the victorious party in England : but it seems he could not do without the King's Cloak, and sold himself to perdition in order to get it. Let us see a little how this was.

England, Scotland, Ireland, all lying now subdued at the feet of the Puritan Parliament, the practical question arose, What was to be done with it? How will you govern these Nations, which Providence in a

[1] Obstacle, hindrance.

> To sleep : perchance to dream ; ay, there's the rub ;
> For in that sleep of death what dreams may come.
> *Hamlet,* iii, i, 65, 66.

[2] See p. 313, n. 1.

wondrous way has given-up to your disposal? Clearly
those hundred surviving members of the Long Parliament, who sit there as supreme authority, cannot continue forever to sit. What *is* to be done?— It was a
question which theoretical constitution-builders may
find easy to answer; but to Cromwell, looking there
into the real practical facts of it, there could be none
more complicated. He asked of the Parliament, What
it was they would decide upon? It was for the Parliament to say. Yet the Soldiers too, however contrary
to Formula, they who had purchased this victory with
their blood, it seemed to them that they also should
have something to say in it! We will not "For all our
fighting have nothing but a little piece of paper." We
understand that the Law of God's Gospel, to which
He through us has given the victory, shall establish
itself, or try to establish itself, in this land!

For three years, Cromwell says, this question had
been sounded in the ears of the Parliament. They
could make no answer; nothing but talk, talk. Perhaps it lies in the nature of parliamentary bodies;
perhaps no Parliament could in such case make any
answer but even that of talk, talk! Nevertheless the
question must and shall be answered. You sixty men
there, becoming fast odious, even despicable, to the
whole nation, whom the nation already calls Rump
Parliament, *you* cannot continue to sit there: who or
what then is to follow? 'Free Parliament,' right of
Election, Constitutional Formulas of one sort or the
other,— the thing is a hungry Fact coming on us,
which we must answer or be devoured by it! And who
are you that prate of Constitutional Formulas, rights

of Parliament? You have had to kill your King, to
make Pride's [1] Purges, to expel and banish by the law
of the stronger whosoever would not let your Cause
prosper: there are but fifty or three-score of you left
there, debating in these days. Tell us what we shall do;
not in the way of Formula, but of practicable Fact!

How they did finally answer, remains obscure to this
day. The diligent Godwin [2] himself admits that he cannot make it out. The likeliest is, that this poor Parliament still would not, and indeed could not dissolve
and disperse; that when it came to the point of actually dispersing, they again, for the tenth or twentieth
time, adjourned it, — and Cromwell's patience failed
him. But we will take the favourablest hypothesis ever
started for the Parliament; the favourablest, though I
believe it is not the true one, but too favourable.

According to this version: At the uttermost crisis,
when Cromwell and his Officers were met on the one
hand, and the fifty or sixty Rump Members on the
other, it was suddenly told Cromwell that the Rump in
its despair *was* answering in a very singular way; that
in their splenetic envious despair, to keep-out the Army
at least, these men were hurrying through the House a
kind of Reform Bill, — Parliament to be chosen by the
whole of England; equable electoral division into dis-
tricts; free suffrage, and the rest of it! A very questionable, or indeed for *them* an unquestionable thing.
Reform Bill, free suffrage of Englishmen? Why, the

[1] The colonel who carried out Commander-in-chief Fairfax's
orders for the "purging" of Parliament. See p. 313, n. 1.

[2] 1756–1831; author of *A History of the Commonwealth;* noted
for his radical views; father of Mary Shelley, the wife of the poet.

Royalists themselves, silenced indeed but not extermi-
nated, perhaps out*number* us; the great numerical majority of England was always indifferent to our Cause,
merely looked at it and submitted to it. It is in weight
and force, not by counting of heads, that we are the
majority! And now with your Formulas and Reform
Bills, the whole matter, sorely won by our swords, shall
again launch itself to sea; become a mere hope, and
likelihood, *small* even as a likelihood? And it is not
a likelihood: it is a certainty, which we have won, by
God's strength and our own right hands, and do now
hold *here*. Cromwell walked down to these refractory
Members; interrupted them in that rapid speed of their
Reform Bill; — ordered them to begone, and talk there
no more. — Can we not forgive him? Can we not understand him? John Milton, who looked on it all near at
hand,[1] could applaud him. The Reality had swept the
Formulas away before it. I fancy, most men who were
realities in England might see into the necessity of that.

The strong daring man, therefore, has set all manner of Formulas and logical superficialities against him;
has dared appeal to the genuine Fact of this England,
Whether it will support him or not? It is curious to
see how he struggles to govern in some constitutional
way; find some Parliament to support him; but cannot. His first Parliament, the one they call Barebones's
Parliament, is, so to speak, a *Convocation of the Notables.*[2] From all quarters of England the leading Min-

---

[1] And was in fact Latin Secretary of the Council of State under
Cromwell. See add. note.

[2] Council of prominent persons convoked by the King of France.
The last one, which Carlyle doubtless had in mind, was called

isters and chief Puritan Officials nominate the men most distinguished by religious reputation, influence and attachment to the true Cause: these are assembled to shape-out a plan. They sanctioned what was past; shaped as they could what was to come. They were scornfully called *Barebones's Parliament:* the man's name, it seems, was not *Barebones*, but Barbone,[1] — a good enough man. Nor was it a jest, their work; it was a most serious reality, — a trial on the part of these Puritan Notables how far the Law of Christ could become the Law of this England. There were men of sense among them, men of some quality; men of deep piety I suppose the most of them were. They failed, it seems, and broke-down, endeavouring to reform the Court of Chancery! They dissolved themselves, as incompetent; delivered-up their power again into the hands of the Lord General Cromwell, to do with it what he liked and could.

What *will* he do with it? The Lord General Cromwell, 'Commander-in-chief of all the Forces raised and to be raised;' he hereby sees himself, at this unexampled juncture, as it were the one available Authority left in England, nothing between England and utter Anarchy but him alone. Such is the undeniable Fact of his position and England's, there and then. What will he do with it? After deliberation, he decides that he will *accept* it; will formally, with public solemnity, say and vow before God and men, "Yes,

by Louis XVI the year before the outbreak of the French Revolution.

[1] Praisegod Barbone (variously spelled), a London leather merchant, was a member of the so-called "Little" Parliament of 1653, and lent it his memorable name.

the Fact is so, and I will do the best I can with it!"
Protectorship, Instrument of Government,[1] — these
are the external forms of the thing; worked out and
sanctioned as they could in the circumstances be, by
the Judges, by the leading Official people, 'Council of
Officers and Persons of interest in the Nation:' and
as for the thing itself, undeniably enough, at the pass
matters had now come to, there *was* no alternative but
Anarchy or that. Puritan England might accept it or
not; but Puritan England was, in real truth, saved
from suicide thereby! — I believe the Puritan People
did, in an inarticulate, grumbling, yet on the whole
grateful and real way, accept this anomalous act of
Oliver's; at least, he and they together made it good,
and always better to the last. But in their Parliamentary *articulate* way, they had their difficulties, and
never knew fully what to say to it! —

Oliver's second Parliament,[2] properly his *first* regular Parliament, chosen by the rule laid-down in the
Instrument of Government, did assemble, and worked;
— but got, before long, into bottomless questions as
to the Protector's *right*, as to 'usurpation,' and so
forth; and had at the earliest legal day to be dismissed.
Cromwell's concluding Speech to these men is a remarkable one. So likewise to his third Parliament,[3] in
similar rebuke for their pedantries and obstinacies.
Most rude, chaotic, all these Speeches are; but most
earnest-looking. You would say, it was a sincere helpless man; not used to *speak* the great inorganic

[1] A constitution drawn up by a council of Cromwell's officers.
[2] September, 1654; dismissed in the following January.
[3] September, 1656, to February, 1658.

thought of him, but to act it rather! A helplessness
of utterance, in such bursting fulness of meaning. He
talks much about 'births of Providence:' All these
changes, so many victories and events, were not fore-
thoughts, and theatrical contrivances of men, of *me* or
of men; it is blind blasphemers that will persist in
calling them so! He insists with a heavy sulphurous
wrathful emphasis on this. As he well might. As if a
Cromwell in that dark huge game he had been playing,
the world wholly thrown into chaos round him, had
foreseen it all, and played it all off like a precontrived
puppetshow by wood and wire! These things were
foreseen by no man, he says; no man could tell what
a day would bring forth: they were 'births of Providence,' God's finger guided us on, and we came at
last to clear height of victory, God's Cause triumphant
in these Nations; and you as a Parliament could
assemble together, and say in what manner all this
could be *organised*, reduced into rational feasibility
among the affairs of men. You were to help with your
wise counsel in doing that. " You have had such an
opportunity as no Parliament in England ever had."
Christ's Law, the Right and True, was to be in some
measure made the Law of this land. In place of that,
you have got into your idle pedantries, constitution-
alities, bottomless cavillings and questionings about
written laws for *my* coming here; — and would send
the whole matter in Chaos again, because I have no
Notary's parchment, but only God's voice from the
battle-whirlwind, for being President among you!
That opportunity is gone; and we know not when it
will return. You have had your constitutional Logic;

and Mammon's Law, not Christ's Law, rules yet in this land. " God be judge between you and me ! " These are his final words to them : Take you your constitution-formulas in your hand ; and I my *infor-*mal struggles, purposes, realities and acts; and "God be judge between you and me ! " —

We said above what shapeless, involved chaotic things the printed Speeches of Cromwell are. *Wil-fully* ambiguous, unintelligible, say the most : a hypo-crite shrouding himself in confused Jesuitic jargon! To me they do not seem so. I will say rather, they afforded the first glimpses I could ever get into the reality of this Cromwell, nay into the possibility of him. Try to believe that he means something, search lovingly what that may be : you will find a real *speech* lying imprisoned in these broken rude tortuous utter-ances ; a meaning in the great heart of this inarticu-late man! You will, for the first time, begin to see that he was a man ; not an enigmatic chimera, unintel-ligible to you, incredible to you. The Histories and Biographies written of this Cromwell, written in shal-low sceptical generations that could not know or con-ceive of a deep believing man, are far more *obscure* than Cromwell's Speeches. You look through them only into the infinite vague of Black and the Inane. ' Heats and jealousies,' says Lord Clarendon himself : ' heats and jealousies,' mere crabbed whims, theories and crotchets ; these induced slow sober quiet English-men to lay down their ploughs and work; and fly into red fury of confused war against the best-conditioned of Kings! *Try* if you can find that true. Scepticism writing about Belief may have great gifts; but it is really *ultra vires* there. It is Blindness laying-down the Laws of Optics. —

Cromwell's third Parliament split on the same rock as his second. Ever the constitutional Formula: How came *you* there? Show us some Notary parchment! Blind pedants: — " Why, surely the same power which makes you a Parliament, that, and something more, made me a Protector!" If my Protectorship is nothing, what in the name of wonder is your Parliamenteership, a reflex and creation of that? —

Parliaments having failed, there remained nothing but the way of Despotism. Military Dictators, each with his district, to *coerce* the Royalist and other gainsayers, to govern them, if not by act of Parliament, then by the sword. Formula shall *not* carry it, while the Reality is here! I will go on protecting oppressed Protestants abroad, appointing just judges, wise managers, at home, cherishing true Gospel ministers; doing the best I can to make England a Christian England, greater than old Rome, the Queen of Protestant Christianity; I, since you will not help me; I while God leaves me life! — Why did he not give it up; retire into obscurity again, since the Law would not acknowledge him? cry several. That is where they mistake. For him there was no giving of it up! Prime Ministers have governed countries, Pitt, Pombal,[1] Choiseul;[2] and their word was a law while it held: but this Prime Minister was one that *could not get resigned.* Let him once resign, Charles Stuart

---

[1] Portuguese statesman (1699–1782).
[2] French statesman (1719–1785).

and the Cavaliers [1] waited to kill him; to kill the Cause *and* him. Once embarked, there is no retreat, no return. This Prime Minister could *retire* no-whither except into his tomb.

One is sorry for Cromwell in his old days. His complaint is incessant of the heavy burden Providence has laid on him. Heavy; which he must bear till death. Old Colonel Hutchinson,[2] as his wife relates it, Hutchinson, his old battle-mate, coming to see him on some indispensable business, much against his will, — Cromwell 'follows him to the door,' in a most fraternal, domestic, conciliatory style; begs that he would be reconciled to him, his old brother in arms; says how much it grieves him to be misunderstood, deserted by true fellow-soldiers, dear to him from of old: the rigorous Hutchinson, cased in his Republican formula,[3] sullenly goes his way. — And the man's head now white; his strong arm growing weary with its long work! I think always too of his poor Mother, now very old, living in that Palace of his; a right brave woman; as indeed they lived all an honest God-fearing Household there: if she heard a shot go-off, she thought it was her son killed. He had to come to her at least once a day, that she might see with her own eyes that he was yet living. The poor old Mother! — — What had this man gained; what had he gained? He had a life of sore strife and toil, to his last day.[4]

[1] Partisans of Charles; the partisans of Puritanism were called Roundheads.

[2] 1616–1664; one of the Regicides.

[3] *I. e.*, having scruples against one-man rule.

[4] Cromwell, worn out under the strain, died of a fever, September 3, 1658, and was buried in Henry VII's Chapel in

Fame, ambition, place in History? His dead body was hung in chains; his 'place in History,' — place in History forsooth! — has been a place of ignominy, accusation, blackness and disgrace; and here, this day, who knows if it is not rash in me to be among the first that ever ventured to pronounce him not a knave and liar, but a genuinely honest man! Peace to him. Did he not, in spite of all, accomplish much for us? *We* walk smoothly over his great rough heroic life; step-over his body sunk in the ditch there. We need not *spurn* it, as we step on it! — Let the Hero rest. It was not to *men's* judgment that he appealed; nor have men judged him very well.

Precisely a century and a year after this of Puritanism had got itself hushed-up into decent composure, and its results made smooth, in 1688,[1] there broke-out a far deeper explosion, much more difficult to hush-up, known to all mortals, and like to be long known, by the name of French Revolution. It is properly the third and final act of Protestantism; the explosive confused return of mankind to Reality and Fact, now that they were perishing of Semblance and Sham. We call our English Puritanism the second act: "Well then, the Bible is true; let us go by the Bible!" "In Church," said Luther; "In Church and

Westminster Abbey, among the kings of England. His body was exhumed, January, 1661, and hanged on the gallows at Tyburn, the place of criminal execution. It was afterwards beheaded, and the head set upon a pole on top of Westminster Hall. See C. Collins, "What became of Cromwell?" in *Gentleman's Magazine*, 1881.

[1] See p. 204, n. 4; 205, n. 2.

State," said Cromwell, " let us go by what actually *is*
God's Truth." Men have to return to reality; they
cannot live on semblance. The French Revolution, or
third act, we may well call the final one; for lower
than that savage *Sansculottism* [1] men cannot go. They
stand there on the nakedest haggard Fact, undeniable
in all seasons and circumstances; and may and must
begin again confidently to build-up from that. The
French explosion, like the English one, got its King,
— who had no Notary parchment to show for himself.
We have still to glance for a moment at Napoleon,
our second modern King.

Napoleon does by no means seem to me so great a
man as Cromwell. His enormous victories which
reached over all Europe, while Cromwell abode mainly
in our little England, are but as the high *stilts* on
which the man is seen standing; the stature of the
man is not altered thereby. I find in him no such
sincerity as in Cromwell; only a far inferior sort.
No silent walking, through long years, with the Awful
Unnamable of this Universe; ' walking with God,' as
he called it; and faith and strength in that alone:
latent thought and valour, content to lie latent, then
burst out as in blaze of Heaven's lightning! Napoleon
lived in an age when God was no longer believed;
the meaning of all Silence, Latency, was thought to
be Nonentity: he had to begin not out of the Puritan
Bible, but out of poor Sceptical *Encyclopédies*.[2] This
was the length the man carried it. Meritorious to
get so far. His compact, prompt, everyway articulate

[1] See p. 275, n. 1.
[2] See p. 20, n. 2.

character is in itself perhaps small, compared with our great chaotic *in*articulate Cromwell's. Instead of 'dumb Prophet struggling to speak,' we have a portentous mixture of the Quack withal! Hume's notion of the Fanatic-Hypocrite, with such truth as it has, will apply much better to Napoleon than it did to Cromwell, to Mahomet or the like, — where indeed taken strictly it has hardly any truth at all. An element of blamable ambition shows itself, from the first, in this man; gets the victory over him at last, and involves him and his work in ruin.

'False as a bulletin' became a proverb in Napoleon's time. He makes what excuse he could for it: that it was necessary to mislead the enemy, to keep-up his own men's courage, and so forth. On the whole, there are no excuses. A man in no case has liberty to tell lies. It had been, in the long-run, *better* for Napoleon too if he had not told any. In fact, if a man have any purpose reaching beyond the hour and day, meant to be found extant *next* day, what good can it ever be to promulgate lies? The lies are found-out; ruinous penalty is exacted for them. No man will believe the liar next time even when he speaks truth, when it is of the last importance that he be believed. The old cry of wolf! — A Lie is *no*-thing; you cannot of nothing make something; you make *nothing* at last, and lose your labour into the bargain.

Yet Napoleon *had* a sincerity: we are to distinguish between what is superficial and what is fundamental in insincerity. Across these outer manœuverings and quackeries of his, which were many and most blamable, let us discern withal that the man had a

certain instinctive ineradicable feeling for reality;
and did base himself upon fact, so long as he had any
basis. He has an instinct of Nature better than his
culture was. His *savans*,[1] Bourrienne[2] tells us, in
that voyage to Egypt,[3] were one evening busily occupied arguing that there could be no God. They had
proved it, to their satisfaction, by all manner of logic.
Napoleon looking up into the stars, answers, " Very
ingenious, Messieurs : but *who made* all that ? " The
Atheistic logic runs-off from him like water ; the great
Fact stares him in the face : " Who made all that ? "
So too in Practice : he, as every man that can be
great, or have victory in this world, sees, through all
entanglements, the practical heart of the matter ;
drives straight towards that. When the steward of
his Tuileries[4] Palace was exhibiting the new upholstery, with praises, and demonstration how glorious it
was, and how cheap withal, Napoleon, making little
answer, asked for a pair of scissors, clipt one of the
gold tassels from a window-curtain, put it in his
pocket, and walked on. Some days afterwards, he
produced it at the right moment, to the horror of his
upholstery functionary ; it was not gold but tinsel!
In Saint Helena,[5] it is notable how he still, to his
last days, insists on the practical, the real. " Why

---

[1] Scholars, sages.

[2] 1769–1834. Author of *Mémoires ;* held various government
positions under Napoleon and under the restored Louis XVIII.

[3] 1798.

[4] " Tile-yards," the royal palace in Paris, destroyed by the
mob in 1871.

[5] Whither, after his defeat at Waterloo, June 18, 1815, he
was sent for the rest of his life.

talk and complain; above all, why quarrel with one another? There is no *result* in it; it comes to nothing that one can *do*. Say nothing, if one can do nothing!" He speaks often so, to his poor discontented followers; he is like a piece of silent strength in the middle of their morbid querulousness there.

And accordingly was there not what we can call a *faith* in him, genuine so far as it went? That this new enormous Democracy asserting itself here in the French Revolution is an insuppressible Fact, which the whole world, with its old forces and institutions, cannot put down; this was a true insight of his, and took his conscience and enthusiasm along with it, — a *faith*. And did he not interpret the dim purport of it well? ' *La carrière ouverte aux talens*,[1] The implements to him who can handle them: ' this actually is the truth, and even the whole truth; it includes whatever the French Revolution, or any Revolution, could mean. Napoleon, in his first period, was a true Democrat. And yet by the nature of him, fostered too by his military trade, he knew that Democracy, if it were a true thing at all, could not be an anarchy: the man had a heart-hatred for anarchy. On that Twentieth of June[2] (1792), Bourrienne and he sat in a coffee-house, as the mob rolled by: Napoleon expresses the deepest contempt for persons in authority that they do not restrain this rabble. On the Tenth of August[3]

[1] Literally : The career (race-course) open to the talents.

[2] The mob invaded the Tuileries, then occupied by Louis XVI.

[3] The revolutionary mob made a more violent armed assault on the palace, and massacred about 800 of the Swiss bodyguard of the King. The loyalty of the Swiss is commemorated by Thorwaldsen's Lion of Lucerne.

he wonders why there is no man to command these poor Swiss; they would conquer if there were. Such a faith in Democracy, yet hatred of anarchy, it is that carries Napoleon through all his great work. Through his brilliant Italian Campaigns,[1] onwards to the Peace of Leoben,[2] one would say, his inspiration is: 'Triumph to the French Revolution; assertion of it against these Austrian Simulacra that pretend to call it a Simulacrum!' Withal, however, he feels, and has a right to feel, how necessary a strong Authority is; how the Revolution cannot prosper or last without such. To bridle-in that great devouring, self-devouring French Revolution; to *tame* it, so that its intrinsic purpose can be made good, that it may become *organic*, and be able to live among other organisms and *formed* things, not as a wasting destruction alone: is not this still what he partly aimed at, as the true purport of his life; nay what he actually managed to do? Through Wagrams,[3] Austerlitzes;[4] triumph after triumph, — he triumphed so far. There was an eye to see in this man, a soul to dare and do. He rose naturally to be the King. All men saw that he *was* such. The common soldiers used to say on the march: "These babbling *Avocats*, up at Paris; all talk and no work! What wonder it runs all wrong? We shall have to go and put our *Petit Caporal* there!" They went,

[1] 1796–1797.

[2] In Austria, 1797, between Austria and the French Republic.

[3] Near Vienna, 1809.

[4] Seventy to eighty miles NNE of Vienna. One of Napoleon's most famous battles, in which he defeated a superior force of Austrians and Russians with a loss of *c.* 12,000 against 30,000. See p. 108.

and put him there ; they and France at large. Chief-
consulship, Emperorship, victory over Europe ; — till
the poor Lieutenant of *La Fère*,[1] not unnaturally,
might seem to himself the greatest of all men that
had been in the world for some ages.

But at this point, I think, the fatal charlatan-element got the upper hand. He apostatised from his old
faith in Facts, took to believing in Semblances ; strove
to connect himself with Austrian Dynasties,[2] Pope-
doms, with the old false Feudalities which he once saw
clearly to be false ; — considered that *he* would found
"his Dynasty" and so forth ; that the enormous French
Revolution meant only that ! The man was 'given-up
to strong delusion, that he should believe a lie ;'[3] a
fearful but most sure thing. He did not know true
from false now when he looked at them, — the fearful-
est penalty a man pays for yielding to untruth of heart.
Self and false ambition had now become his god : *self*-
deception once yielded to, *all* other deceptions follow
naturally more and more. What a paltry patchwork
of theatrical paper-mantles, tinsel and mummery, had
this man wrapt his own great reality in, thinking to
make it more real thereby ! His hollow Pope's-*Con-
cordat*,[4] pretending to be a re-establishment of Ca-

[1] A town in Aisne, northern France, which gives name to a
regiment of artillery. Napoleon was lieutenant in this regiment,
1785–1791.

[2] Napoleon divorced Josephine and married (1810) Maria
Louisa, daughter of the Emperor of Austria, who bore him a son,
" The King of Rome."

[3] And for this cause God shall send them strong delusion, that
they should believe a lie. 2 Thess. ii, 11.

[4] Between Napoleon and Pius VII, providing for mutual
official recognition, 1801.

OLIVER CROMWELL

From the painting by Robert Walker in the possession of the Earl of Sandwich,
Hinchingbrooke, England.
Probably painted soon after the beginning of the Civil War, when Cromwell
was about forty-four years old.

tholicism, felt by himself to be the method of extirpat-
ing it, "*la vaccine*[1] *de la religion:* " his ceremonial
Coronations, consecrations by the old Italian Chimera
in Notre-Dame,[2] — " wanting nothing to complete the
pomp of it," as Augereau[3] said, " nothing but the half-
million of men who had died to put an end to all that "!
Cromwell's Inauguration was by the Sword and Bible ;
what we must call a genuinely *true* one. Sword and
Bible were borne before him, without any chimera:
were not these the *real* emblems of Puritanism; its true
decoration and insignia ? It had used them both in a
very real manner, and pretended to stand by them now!
But this, poor Napoleon mistook : he believed too much
in the *Dupeability* of men; saw no fact deeper in man
than Hunger and this! He was mistaken. Like a
man that should build upon cloud; his house and he fall
down in confused wreck, and depart out of the world.

Alas, in all of us this charlatan-element exists ; and
might be developed, were the temptation strong enough.
' Lead us not into temptation '! But it is fatal, I say,
that it *be* developed. The thing into which it enters
as a cognisable ingredient is doomed to be altogether
transitory; and, however huge it may *look*, is in itself
small. Napoleon's working, accordingly, what was it
with all the noise it made ? A flash as of gunpowder
wide-spread ; a blazing-up as of dry heath. For an

[1] Vaccination to secure immunity from the disease of religion in future.

[2] Cathedral in Paris, where, December, 1804, Napoleon was
crowned Emperor in the presence of the Pope, summoned to Paris
for the purpose. The next spring he was crowned King of Italy
at Milan.

[3] One of Napoleon's generals (1757–1816).

hour the whole Universe seems wrapt in smoke and
flame ; but only for an hour. It goes out : the Universe
with its old mountains and streams, its stars above and
kind soil beneath, is still there.

The Duke of Weimar[1] told his friends always, To
be of courage; this Napoleonism was *unjust*, a falsehood, and could not last. It is true doctrine. The
heavier this Napoleon trampled on the world, holding
it tyrannously down, the fiercer would the world's re-
coil against him be, one day. Injustice pays itself with
frightful compound-interest. I am not sure but he had
better have lost his best park of artillery, or had his
best regiment drowned in the sea, than shot that poor
German Bookseller, Palm![2] It was a palpable tyran-
nous murderous injustice, which no man, let him paint
an inch thick, could make-out to be other. It burnt
deep into the hearts of men, it and the like of it ; suppressed fire flashed in the eyes of men, as they thought
of it, — waiting their day! Which day *came :* Germany rose round him. — What Napoleon *did* will in
the long-run amount to what he did *justly ;* what Nature with her laws will sanction. To what of reality
was in him ; to that and nothing more. The rest was
all smoke and waste. *La carrière ouverte aux talens :*
that great true Message, which has yet to articulate
and fulfil itself everywhere, he left in a most inarticulate state. He was a great *ébauche*,[3] a rude-draught

[1] Goethe's friend and patron. Goethe resided at Weimar for
more than fifty years; and he and Schiller are buried there.

[2] Of Nuremberg; condemned and shot (1806) by Napoleon's
orders for selling a pamphlet criticising Napoleon and his
troops.

[3] Rough preliminary sketch.

never completed ; as indeed what great man is other ? Left in *too* rude a state, alas !

His notions of the world, as he expresses them there at St. Helena, are almost tragical to consider. He seems to feel the most unaffected surprise that it has all gone so ; that he is flung-out on the rock here, and the World is still moving on its axis. France is great, and all-great ; and at bottom, he is France. England itself, he says, is by Nature only an appendage of France ; " another Isle of Oleron[1] to France." So it was *by Nature*, by Napoleon-Nature ; and yet look how in fact — HERE AM I ! He cannot understand it : inconceivable that the reality has not corresponded to his program of it ; that France was not all-great, that he was not France. ' Strong delusion,' that he should believe the thing to be which *is* not ! The compact, clear-seeing, decisive Italian nature of him, strong, genuine, which he once had, has enveloped itself, half-dissolved itself, in a turbid atmosphere of French fanfaronade. The world was not disposed to be trodden-down underfoot ; to be bound into masses, and built together, as *he* liked, for a pedestal to France and him : the world had quite other purposes in view ! Napoleon's aston-ishment is extreme. But alas, what help now ? He had gone that way of his ; and Nature also had gone her way. Having once parted with Reality, he tumbles helpless in Vacuity ; no rescue for him. He had to sink there, mournfully as man seldom did ; and break his great heart, and die,[2] — this poor Napoleon :

[1] Off the west coast of France, between the Loire and the Garonne.

[2] May 5, 1821.

a great implement too soon wasted, till it was useless: our last Great Man!

Our last, in a double sense. For here finally these wide roamings of ours through so many times and places, in search and study of Heroes, are to terminate. I am sorry for it: there was pleasure for me in this business, if also much pain. It is a great subject, and a most grave and wide one, this which, not to be too grave about it, I have named *Hero-worship.* It enters deeply, as I think, into the secret of Mankind's ways and vitalest interests in this world, and is well worth explaining at present. With six months, instead of six days, we might have done better. I promised to break-ground on it; I know not whether I have even managed to do that. I have had to tear it up in the rudest manner in order to get into it at all. Often enough, with these abrupt utterances thrown-out isolated, unexplained, has your tolerance been put to the trial. Tolerance, patient candour, all-hoping favour and kindness, which I will not speak of at present. The accomplished and distinguished, the beautiful, the wise, something of what is best in England, have listened patiently to my rude words. With many feelings, I heartily thank you all; and say, Good be with you all!

CARLYLE'S SUMMARY

LECTURE I

THE HERO AS DIVINITY. ODIN. PAGANISM : SCANDINAVIAN MYTHOLOGY

Heroes: Universal History consists essentially of their united Biographies. Religion not a man's church-creed, but his practical *belief* about himself and the Universe: Both with Men and Nations it is the One fact about them which creatively determines all the rest. Heathenism: Christianity: Modern Scepticism. The Hero as Divinity. Paganism a fact; not Quackery, nor Allegory: Not to be pretentiously 'explained;' to be looked at as old Thought, and with sympathy. (p. 1.) — Nature no more seems divine except to the Prophet or Poet, because men have ceased to *think:* To the Pagan Thinker, as to a child-man, all was either godlike or God. Canopus: Man. Hero-worship the basis of Religion, Loyalty, Society. A Hero not the 'creature of the time:' Hero-worship indestructible. Johnson: Voltaire. (9.) — Scandinavian Paganism the Religion of our Fathers. Iceland, the home of the Norse Poets, described. The *Edda*. The primary characteristic of Norse Paganism, the impersonation of the visible workings of Nature. Jötuns and the Gods. Fire: Frost : Thunder : The Sun : Sea-Tempest. Mythus of the Creation: The Life-Tree Igdrasil. The modern '*Machine*' of the Universe.' (21.) — The Norse Creed, as recorded, the summation of several successive systems: Originally the shape given to the national thought by their first 'Man of Genius.' Odin: He has no history or date; yet was no mere adjective, but a man of flesh and blood. How deified. The World of Nature, to every man a Fantasy of Himself. (29.) — Odin the inventor of Runes, of Letters and Poetry. His reception as a Hero: the pattern Norse-Man; a God: His shadow over the whole History of his People. (38.) — The essence of Norse Paganism not so much Morality, as a sincere recognition of Nature: Sincerity better than Gracefulness. The Allegories, the after-creations of the Faith. Main practical Belief: Hall of Odin: Valkyrs: Destiny: Necessity of Valour. Its worth: Their Sea-Kings, Woodcutter Kings, our spiritual Progenitors. The growth of Odinism. (42.) — The strong simplicity of Norse lore quite unrecognized by Gray. Thor's veritable Norse rage: Balder, the white Sungod. How the old Norse heart loves the Thunder-god, and sports with him. Huge Brobdingnag genius, needing only to be tamed-down, into Shakspeares, Goethes. Truth in the Norse Songs: This World a show. Thor's invasion of Jötunheim. The Ragnarök, or Twilight of the Gods: The Old must die, that the New and Better may be born. Thor's last appearance. The Norse Creed a Consecration of Valour. It and the whole Past a possession of the Present. (47.)

LECTURE II

THE HERO AS PROPHET. MAHOMET: ISLAM

The Hero no longer regarded as a God, but as one god-inspired. All Heroes primarily of the same stuff; differing according to their reception. The welcome of its Heroes, the truest test of an epoch. Odin: Burns. (p. 58.) — Mahomet a true Prophet; not a scheming Impostor. A Great Man, and therefore first of all a sincere man: No man to be judged merely by his faults. David the Hebrew King. Of all acts for man *repentance* the most divine: The deadliest sin, a supercilious consciousness of none. (60.) — Arabia described. The Arabs always a gifted people; of wild strong feelings, and of iron restraint over these. Their Religiosity: Their Star-worship: Their Prophets and inspired men; from Job downwards. Their Holy Places. Mecca, its site, history and government. (65.) — Mahomet. His youth: His fond Grandfather. Had no book-learning: Travels to the Syrian Fairs; and first comes in contact with the Christian Religion. An altogether solid, brotherly, genuine man: A good laugh, and a good flash of anger in him withal. (71.) — Marries Kadijah. Begins his Prophet-career at forty years of age. *Allah Akbar;* God is great: *Islam;* we must *submit* to God. Do we not all live in Islam? Mahomet, 'the Prophet of God.' (74.) — The good Kadijah believes in him: Mahomet's gratitude. His slow progress: Among forty of his kindred, young Ali alone

joined him. His good Uncle expostulates with him: Mahomet,
bursting into tears, persists in his mission. The Hegira. Propagating by the sword: First get your sword: A thing will propagate itself as it can. Nature a just umpire. Mahomet's Creed
unspeakably better than the wooden idolatries and jangling
Syrian Sects extirpated by it. (79.) — The Koran, the universal
standard of Mahometan life: An imperfectly, badly written,
but genuine book: Enthusiastic extempore preaching, amid the
hot haste of wrestling with flesh-and-blood and spiritual enemies.
Its direct poetic insight. The World, Man, human Compassion;
all wholly miraculous to Mahomet. (88.) — His religion did not
succeed by ' being easy:' None can. The sensual part of it not of
Mahomet's making. He himself, frugal; patched his own clothes;
proved a hero in rough actual trial of twenty-three years.
Traits of his generosity and resignation. His total freedom from
cant. (96.) — His moral precepts not always of the superfinest
sort; yet is there always a tendency to good in them. His Heaven
and Hell sensual, yet not altogether so. Infinite Nature of Duty.
The evil of sensuality, in the *slavery* to pleasant things, not in
the enjoyment of them. Mahometanism a religion heartily *believed*. To the Arab Nation it was as a birth from darkness into
light: Arabia first became alive by means of it. (101.)

LECTURE III

THE HERO AS POET. DANTE ; SHAKSPEARE

The Hero as Divinity or Prophet, inconsistent with the modern progress of science: The Hero Poet, a figure common to all
ages. All Heroes at bottom the same; the different *sphere* con-
stituting the grand distinction: Examples. Varieties of aptitude. (p. 107.) — Poet and Prophet meet in *Vates:* Their Gospel
the same, for the Beautiful and the Good are one. All men
somewhat of poets; and the highest Poets far from perfect.
Prose, and Poetry or *musical Thought.* Song a kind of inarticulate unfathomable speech: All deep things are Song. The Hero
as Divinity, as Prophet, and then only as Poet, no indication that
our estimate of the Great Man is diminishing : The Poet seems
to be losing caste, but it is rather that our notions of God are
rising higher. (110.) — Shakspeare and Dante, Saints of Poetry

Dante: His history, in his Book and Portrait. His scholastic education, and its fruit of subtlety. His miseries: Love of Beatrice: His marriage not happy. A banished man: Will never return, if to plead guilty be the condition. His wanderings: '*Come è duro calle*.' At the Court of Della Scala. The great soul of Dante, homeless on earth, made its home more and more in Eternity. His mystic, unfathomable Song. Death: Buried at Ravenna. (116.) — His Divina Commedia a Song: Go *deep* enough, there is music everywhere. The sincerest of Poems: It has all been as if molten, in the hottest furnace of his soul. Its Intensity, and Pictorial power. The three parts make-up the true Unseen World of the Middle Ages: How the Christian Dante felt Good and Evil to be the two polar elements of this Creation. Paganism and Christianism. (125.) — Ten silent centuries found a voice in Dante. The thing that is uttered from the inmost parts of a man's soul differs altogether from what is uttered by the outer. The 'uses' of Dante: We will not estimate the Sun by the quantity of gas it saves us. Mahomet and Dante contrasted. Let a man *do* his work; the *fruit* of it is the care of Another than he. (139.) — As Dante embodies musically the Inner Life of the Middle Ages, so does Shakspeare embody the Outer Life which grew therefrom. The strange outbudding of English Existence which we call 'Elizabethan Era.' Shakspeare the chief of all Poets: His calm, all-seeing Intellect: His marvellous Portrait-painting. (143.) — The Poet's first gift, as it is all men's, that he have intellect enough, — that he be able to *see*. Intellect the summary of all human gifts: Human intellect and vulpine intellect contrasted. Shakspeare's instinctive unconscious greatness: His works a part of Nature, and partaking of her inexhaustible depth. Shakspeare greater than Dante; in that he not only sorrowed, but triumphed over his sorrows. His mirthfulness and genuine overflowing love of laughter. His Historical Plays, a kind of National Epic. The Battle of Agincourt: A noble Patriotism, far other than the 'indifference' sometimes ascribed to him. His works, like so many windows, through which we see glimpses of the world that is in him. (148.) — Dante the melodious Priest of Middle-Age Catholicism: Out of this Shakspeare too there rises a kind of Universal Psalm, not unfit to make itself heard among still more sacred Psalms. Shakspeare an 'unconscious Prophet;' and therein greater and truer

than Mahomet. This poor Warwickshire Peasant worth more to
us than a regiment of highest Dignitaries : Indian Empire, or
Shakspeare, — which ? An English King, whom no time or
chance can dethrone: A rallying-sign and bond of brotherhood
for all Saxondom: Wheresoever English men and women are,
they will say to one another, 'Yes, this Shakspeare is *ours!*'
(156.)

LECTURE IV

THE HERO AS PRIEST. LUTHER; REFORMATION: KNOX; PURITANISM

The Priest a kind of Prophet; but more familiar, as the daily
enlightener of daily life. A true Reformer he who appeals to
Heaven's invisible justice against Earth's visible force. The
finished Poet often a symptom that his epoch itself has reached
perfection, and finished. Alas, the battling Reformer, too, is at
times a needful and inevitable phenomenon : Offences *do* accumulate, till they become insupportable. Forms of Belief, modes of
life must perish; yet the Good of the Past survives, an everlasting
possession for us all. (p. 162.) — Idols, or visible recognised
Symbols, common to all Religions: Hateful only when insincere:
The property of every Hero, that he come back to sincerity, to
reality: Protestantism and 'private judgment.' No living communion possible among men who believe only in hearsays. The
Hero-Teacher, who delivers men out of darkness into light. Not
abolition of Hero-worship does Protestantism mean; but rather
a whole World of Heroes, of *sincere,* believing men. (169.) —
Luther; his obscure, seemingly-insignificant birth. His youth
schooled in adversity and stern reality. Becomes a Monk. His
religious despair: Discovers a Latin Bible: No wonder he should
venerate the Bible. He visits Rome. Meets the Pope's fire by
fire. At the Diet of Worms: The greatest moment in the
modern History of men. (179.) — The Wars that followed are
not to be charged to the Reformation. The Old Religion once
true: The cry of 'No Popery' foolish enough in these days.
Protestantism not dead: German Literature and the French Revolution rather considerable signs of life ! (190.) — How Luther
held the sovereignty of the Reformation and kept Peace while
he lived. His written Works: Their rugged homely strength:

His dialect became the language of all writing. No mortal heart to be called *braver*, ever lived in that Teutonic Kindred, whose character is valour: Yet a most gentle heart withal, full of pity and love, as the truly valiant heart ever is: Traits of character from his Table-Talk : His daughter's Deathbed: The miraculous in Nature. His love of Music. His Portrait. (193.) — Puritanism the only phasis of Protestantism that ripened into a living faith: Defective enough, but genuine. Its fruit in the world. The sailing of the Mayflower from Delft Haven the beginning ol American Saxondom. In the history of Scotland properly but one epoch of world-interest, — the Reformation by Knox: A ' nation of heroes;' a *believing* nation. The Puritanism of Scotland became that of England, of New England. (200.) — Knox ' guilty' of being the bravest of all Scotchmen: Did not seek the post of Prophet. At the siege of St. Andrew's Castle. Emphatically a sincere man. A Galley-slave on the River Loire. An Old-Hebrew Prophet, in the guise of an Edinburgh Minister of the Sixteenth Century. (205.) — Knox and Queen Mary: ' Who are you, that presume to school the nobles and sovereign of this realm ?' ' Madam, a subject born within the same.' His intolerance — of falsehoods and knaveries. Not a mean acrid man; else he had never been virtual President and Sovereign of Scotland. His unexpected vein of drollery: A cheery social man; practical, cautious, hopeful, patient. His ' devout imagination' of a Theocracy, or Government of God. Hildebrand wished a Theocracy; Cromwell wished it, fought for it: Mahomet attained it. In one form or other, it is the one thing to be struggled for. (209.)

LECTURE V

THE HERO AS MAN OF LETTERS. JOHNSON, ROUSSEAU, BURNS

The Hero as Man of Letters altogether a product of these new ages: A Heroic Soul in very strange guise. Literary Men; genuine and spurious. Fichte's ' Divine Idea of the World:' His notion of the True Man of Letters. Goethe, the Pattern Literary Hero. (p. 215.) — The disorganised condition of Literature, the summary of all other modern disorganisations. The Writer of a true Book our true modern Preacher. Miraculous influence of Books: The Hebrew Bible. Books are now our actual University, our Church, our Parliament. With Books, Democracy is inevitable. *Thought* the true thaumaturgic influence, by which man works all things whatsoever. (221.) — Organisation of the 'Literary Guild:' Needful discipline; 'priceless lessons' of Poverty. The Literary Priesthood, and its importance to society. Chinese Literary Governors. Fallen into strange times; and strange things need to be speculated upon. (230.) — An age of Scepticism: The very possibility of Heroism formally abnegated. Benthamism an *eyeless* Heroism. Scepticism, Spiritual Paralysis, Insincerity: Heroes gone-out; Quacks come-in. Our brave Chatham himself lived the strangest mimetic life all along. Violent remedial revulsions: Chartisms, French Revolutions: The Age of Scepticism passing away. Let each Man look to the mending of his own Life. (236.) — Johnson one of our Great English Souls. His miserable Youth and Hypochondria: Stubborn Self-help. His loyal submission to what is really higher than himself. How he stood by the old Formulas : Not less original for that. Formulas; their Use and Abuse. Johnson's unconscious sincerity. His Twofold Gospel, a kind of Moral Prudence and clear Hatred of Cant. His writings sincere and full of substance. Architectural nobleness of his Dictionary. Boswell, with all his faults, a true hero-worshipper of a true Hero. (246.) — Rousseau a morbid, excitable, spasmodic man; intense rather than strong. Had not the invaluable 'talent of Silence.' His Face, expressive of his character. His Egoism: Hungry for the praises of men. His books: Passionate appeals, which did once more struggle towards Reality: A Prophet to his Time; as he could, and as the Time could. Rosepink, and artificial bedizenment. Fretted, exasperated, till the heart of him went mad: He could be cooped, starving, into garrets; laughed at as a maniac; but he could not be hindered from setting the world on fire. (256.) — Burns a genuine Hero, in a withered, unbelieving, secondhand Century. The largest soul of all the British lands, came among us in the shape of a hard-handed Scottish Peasant. His heroic Father and Mother, and their sore struggle through life. His rough untutored dialect: Affectionate joyousness. His writings a poor fragment of him. His conversational gifts: High duchesses and low ostlers alike fascinated by him. (261.) — Resemblance between Burns and Mira-

beau. Official Superiors : The greatest 'thinking faculty' in
this land superciliously dispensed with. Hero-worship under
strange conditions. The notablest phasis of Burns's history his
visit to Edinburgh. For one man who can stand prosperity, there
are a hundred that will stand adversity. Literary Lionism.
(265.)

LECTURE VI

THE HERO AS KING. CROMWELL, NAPOLEON : MODERN
REVOLUTIONISM

The King the most important of Great Men ; the summary of
all the various figures of Heroism. To enthrone the Ablest Man,
the true business of all Social procedure : The Ideal of Constitutions. Tolerable and intolerable approximations. Divine
Rights and Diabolic Wrongs. (p. 272.) — The world's sad predicament ; that of having its Able-Man to *seek*, and not knowing
in what manner to proceed about it. The era of Modern Revolu-
tionism dates from Luther. The French Revolution no mere
act of General Insanity : Truth clad in hell-fire ; the Trump of
Doom to Plausibilities and empty Routine. The cry of 'Liberty
and Equality' at bottom the repudiation of sham Heroes. Hero-
worship exists forever and everywhere : from divine adoration
down to the common courtesies of man and man : The soul of
Order, to which all things, Revolutions included, work. Some
Cromwell or Napoleon the necessary finish of a Sansculottism.
The manner in which Kings were made, and Kingship itself first
took rise. (277.) — Puritanism a section of the universal war of
Belief against Make-believe. Laud a weak ill-starred Pedant ;
in his spasmodic vehemence heeding no voice of prudence, no
cry of pity. Universal necessity for true Forms : How to distinguish between True and False. The nakedest Reality preferable
to any empty Semblance, however dignified. (283.) — The work
of the Puritans. The Sceptical Eighteenth century, and its constitutional estimate of Cromwell and his associates. No wish to
disparage such characters as Hampden, Eliot, Pym ; a most constitutional, unblamable, dignified set of men. The rugged outcast
Cromwell, the man of them all in whom one still finds human
stuff. The One thing worth revolting for. (287.) — Cromwell's
'hypocrisy,' an impossible theory. His pious Life as a Farmer

until forty years of age. His public successes honest successes of a brave man. His participation in the King's death no ground of condemnation. His eye for facts no hypocrite's gift. His Iron-sides the embodiment of this insight of his. (293.) — Know the men that may be trusted: Alas, this is yet, in these days, very far from us. Cromwell's hypochondria : His reputed confusion of speech: His habit of prayer. His speeches unpremeditated and full of meaning. His *reticences;* called ' lying ' and ' dissimulation: ' Not one falsehood proved against him. (300.) — Foolish charge of ' ambition.' The great Empire of Silence: Noble silent men, scattered here and there, each in his department; silently think-ing, silently hoping, silently working. Two kinds of ambition; one wholly blamable, the other laudable, inevitable : How it actually was with Cromwell. (306.) — Hume's Fanatic-Hypocrite theory. How indispensable everywhere a *King* is, in all movements of men. Cromwell, as King of Puritanism, of England. Constitu-tional palaver: Dismissal of the Rump Parliament. Cromwell's Parliaments and Protectorship: Parliaments having failed, there remained nothing for him but the way of Despotism. His closing days: His poor old Mother. It was not to men's judg-ments that he appealed; nor have men judged him very well. (315.) — The French Revolution, the ' third act ' of Protestant-ism. Napoleon, infected with the quackeries of his age : Had a kind of sincerity, — an instinct towards the *practical.* His *faith,* —' the Tools to him that can handle them,' — the whole truth of Democracy. His heart-hatred of Anarchy. Finally, his quack-eries got the upper hand: He would found a ' Dynasty: ' Be-lieved wholly in the dupeability of Men. This Napoleonism was *unjust,* a falsehood, and could not last. (328.)

ADDITIONAL NOTES, COMMENTS, AND SUGGESTIONS FOR STUDY

LECTURE I

PAGE 1

Heroes, Hero-worship: to understand fully what C. means by these words is an important part of the student's business with the book. The simplest definition is given in the first sentence. In reading, make notes of all the passages in the book which contribute material toward a final full definition. The subject may have been suggested to C. by a passage in Hume, of whose works C. was a close student : — " The same principles naturally deify mortals superior in power, courage, or understanding, and produce hero-worship." **Universal History**: other points of view for the study of history ? their merits or shortcomings ?

PAGE 3

Note the *positive* definition of religion; emphasize "practically " and " mysterious."

PAGE 6

The comment on the truth of " Grand Lamaism " is the first of many passages in the book which, taken together, set forth C.'s theory of government.

PAGE 10

Not only to understand, but to feel and "practically lay to heart " the meaning of this page and the next two is to be in sympathy with C. in one of his most characteristic and fundamental teachings about life. Compare pp. 217, 218, and add. note. Read in this connection his "stupendous Section " on "Natural Supernaturalism," *S. R.*[1] III, viii; see also I, viii.

PAGE 11

' There . . . rot ? ' C. often, as here, quotes or adapts from his own writings: " The withered leaf is not dead and lost; there are Forces in it and around it, though working in inverse order ; else how could it *rot ?* " *S. R.* I, xi. **if such . . . possible**: full meaning of this clause ?

PAGE 13

With the first paragraph compare Tennyson's *The Higher Pantheism*, beginning: —

[1] *Sartor Resartus.*

> "The sun, the moon, the stars, the seas, the hills and the plains, —
> Are not these, O Soul, the Vision of Him who reigns?"

And also his

> "Flower in the crannied wall,
> I pluck you out of the crannies,
> Hold you here, root and all, in my hand,
> Little flower — but *if* I could understand
> What you are, root and all, and all in all,
> I should know what God and man is."

'a window . . . itself:' "Rightly viewed no meanest object is insignificant; all objects are as windows, through which the philosophic eye looks into Infinitude itself." *S. R.* I, xi. **The mystery . . . "I":** "There come seasons, meditative, sweet, yet awful hours, when in wonder and fear you ask yourself that unanswerable question: Who am *I;* the thing that can say "I" . . . the sight reaches forth into the void Deep, and you are alone with the Universe, and silently commune with it as one mysterious *Presence* with another . . . Sure enough, I am; and lately was not: but Whence? How? Whereto? The answer lies around, written in all colours and motions, uttered in all tones of jubilee and wail, in thousand-figured, thousand-voiced, harmonious Nature: but where is the cunning eye and ear to whom that God-written Apocalypse will yield articulate meaning?" *S. R.* I, viii.

PAGE 15

deepest root: not "earliest." **greatest of all Heroes:** note C.'s expression of reverence here and elsewhere. Compare "Look on our divinest Symbol: on Jesus of Nazareth, and his Life, and his Biography, and what followed therefrom. Higher has the human thought not yet reached: . . . whose significance will ever demand to be anew inquired into, and anew made manifest." *S. R.* III, iii.

PAGE 16

Society . . . Worship of Heroes: state fully to yourself, with concrete illustration, the meaning of this sentence. The thought recurs constantly in the following pages.

PAGE 21

In that strange island: a striking example of C.'s vivid word-painting. To feel by contrast the peculiar quality of Carlyle, read the finely detailed descriptions in Tennyson's *Lancelot and Elaine.* For other examples of C.'s descriptive work see near the beginnings of chaps. vi and ix of *S. R.* II.

PAGE 24

split **in the glance:** what phenomenon does this really have reference to?

PAGE 25

Wish: take note of the rest of this paragraph. C. recurs to the thought frequently. **Higher considerations:** the doctrine of "The Everlasting Yea" in *S. R.* II, ix.

PAGE 29

What he says : the thought of pp. 17, 18 from a different point of view.

PAGE 31

Councils . . . Dantes, Luthers : this pluralizing of proper names is a favorite device with C. for achieving greater vividness and concreteness of expression.

Page 34

How the man : the paragraph is worth dwelling upon, both for its thought and for its style with the fine burst of poetical enthusiasm at the end.

PAGE 37

The world . . . 'Image of his own Dream:' consider, for concrete example, how different an impression of any common object one gets through a microscope from that which he receives from looking with his unaided eye; or how different would be the impressions of an autumn landscape seen by an artist and by a color-blind man at the same moment: and then consider how little we can know of what the world really is, as compared with the knowledge possible to a being of infinitely powerful and infinitely delicate senses. Compare *S. R.* I, viii: "So that this so solid-seeming world, after all, were but an air-image, our ME the only reality: and Nature, with its thousandfold production and destruction, but the reflex of our own inward Force, the 'phantasy of our Dream;' or what the Earth-Spirit in *Faust* names it, *the living visible Garment of God.*" See, also, below, add. note to p. 217, "Transcendental philosophy."

PAGE 44

true to this hour: compare pp. 41 and 57.

PAGE 45

No Homer: compare Horace, Odes IV, ix, "Many mighty men lived before Agamemnon; but they all are overwhelmed in the long night, unwept and unknown, for want of a sacred bard."

PAGE 47

Gray's fragments: Prof. Kittredge (Phelps's *Selections from Gray* [Ginn & Co.], xli–l) points out that Gray's enthusiasm for Scandinavian study was not accompanied with any real scholarly knowledge of the original sources. A few stanzas from *The Fatal Sisters* follow (the Valkyrs sing): —

"Glitt'ring lances are the loom,
Where the dusky warp we strain,
Weaving many a Soldier's doom,
Orkney's woe, and Randver's bane.

"See the griesly texture grow,
('T is of human entrails made,)
And the weights, that play below,
Each a gasping Warriour's head.

. . . .

"Ere the ruddy sun be set,
Pikes must shiver, javelins sing,
Blade with clattering buckler meet,
Hauberk crash, and helmet ring.

. . . . . .

"Sisters, hence with spurs of speed :
Each her thundering faulchion wield;
Each bestride her sable steed.
Hurry, hurry to the field."

Pope ... Homer: see Matthew Arnold's *On Translating Homer*.

PAGE 49

Thor ... Thialfi: compare *King Lear*, II, iv, 68, 69, "We'll set thee to school to an ant, to teach thee there's no laboring i' the winter."

PAGE 50

Hamlet: see notes on sources of the plot in any good edition of *Hamlet*.

PAGE 51

this world ... but a show: compare p. 37.

PAGE 54

law of mutation: compare the expression of this thought in the "Messianic Prophecies" of the Old Testament, in the description of the Judgment in Matt. xxv; in 1 Cor. xv; and in the last book of the New Testament.

PAGE 55

the *last* mythus of ... Thor: note how fittingly this story closes C.'s appeal for the recognition and appreciation of the best elements of "old Norse thought." See above, note to p. 44.

The day after this lecture was delivered C. wrote to his mother: "First lecture over. I thought I should get something like the tenth part of my meaning unfolded to the good people, and I could not feel that I had got much more. However, they seemed content; sate silent, listening as if it had been gospel. I strive not to *heed* my own notion of the thing, *to keep down the conceit and ambition of me*, for that is it. I was not in good tune. I had awoke at 4½."

LECTURE II

PAGE 59

For at bottom ... one stuff: a fundamental principle of C.'s Hero-doctrine; amplified statement of it on pp. 108, 109; also on p. 162.

PAGE 60

hundred-and-eighty millions: now increased by upwards of thirteen-and-a-half millions more. (*Encycl. of Missions.*)

PAGE 62

sincerity ... the first characteristic: this being C.'s "primary definition of a Great Man," it is of the utmost importance to note carefully all the passages that throw light on what Carlyle means by "sincerity." See the very important comments on this point on p. 217.

PAGE 63

'inspiration ... understanding:' Job xxxii, 8: But there is a spirit in man: and the inspiration, etc. Other Bible verses laid under tribute by C. in the remaining pages of this one lecture are given all together here (notice, in reading, the places where they appear) by way of emphasizing an important characteristic of C.'s style, resulting from his home training: Acts xiii, 22: I have found David the son of Jesse, a man after mine own heart, which shall fulfil all my will. Jer. x, 23: O Lord, I know that the way of man is not in himself: it is not in man that walketh to direct his steps. Job xxxix, 19: Hast thou given the horse strength? hast thou clothed his neck with thunder? xli, 29: Darts are counted as stubble: he laugheth at the shaking of a spear. (Said of the leviathan, not the horse as C. remembers it.) 1 Kings xix, 11, 12: And a great and strong wind rent the mountains . . . but the Lord was not in the wind: and after the wind an earthquake; but the Lord was not in the earthquake: And after the earthquake a fire; but the Lord was not in the fire: and after the fire a still small voice. Gal. i, 15, 16: But when it pleased God . . . To reveal his Son in me . . . immediately I conferred not with flesh and blood. Job xiii, 15: Though he slay me, yet will I trust in him. Job i, 20, 21: Then Job arose, and rent his mantle. . . . And said, Naked came I out of my mother's womb, and naked shall I return thither: the Lord gave, and the Lord hath taken away; blessed be the name of the Lord. See also p. 68, n. 3.

PAGE 70

most important Event: compare above, note to p. 15.

PAGE 76

A Hero . . . looks through the shows of things: another definition of the sincere man.

PAGE 77

transitory garment: try to state just what C. means by this.

PAGE 78

highest wisdom . . . to submit to Necessity: compare this with C.'s comment on the Norse "Destiny inexorable" (pp. 43, 44), and note its bearing on the idea of the god Wish (p. 25).

PAGE 84

first get your sword: meaning?

PAGE 85

Nature . . . umpire . . . can do no wrong: this doctrine, that in the long run might and right are the same, has been a rock of offense to many readers; the abuses of the principle are of course obvious. The idea reappears constantly in *Heroes* and in C.'s other books; it is worth while to stop and consider just exactly what he means by it.

PAGE 95

material world . . . Nothing: compare p. 51, and add.
note to p. 217.

PAGE 97

Not happiness: " There is in man a HIGHER than Love of
Happiness: he can do without Happiness and instead thereof
find Blessedness. . . . Love not Pleasure; love God; This
is the EVERLASTING YEA." *S. R.* II, ix.

PAGE 98

last words: Muir (*Life of M.*) describes the scene: " 'Lord,
grant me pardon; and join me to the companionship on
high.' Then at intervals : ' Eternity in Paradise ! ' ' Pardon ! '
' The blessed companionship on high ! ' He stretched himself gently. Then all was still. His head grew heavy on
the bosom of Ayesha. The prophet of Arabia was no
more."

PAGE 103

the Infinite Nature of Duty: compare *S. R.* II, vii :
" Thus, in spite of all Motive-grinders, and Mechanical Profit-and-Loss Philosophies with the sick ophthalmia and hal-
lucination they had brought on, was the Infinite nature of
Duty still dimly present to me."

PAGES 103, 104

What is the chief end . . . not Mahomet: there were
few, if any, things under the sun for which C. entertained
so energetic a hatred as for the utilitarian " Profit-and-Loss "
philosophy. He had already delivered himself on this subject in *S. R.* III, iii : " Man is by birth somewhat of an owl.
Perhaps, too, of all the owleries that ever possessed him, the
most owlish, if we consider it, is that of your actually exist-
ing Motive-Millwrights . . . to fancy himself a dead Iron-
Balance for weighing Pains and Pleasures on, was reserved
for this his latter era. There stands he, his Universe one
huge Manger, filled with hay and thistles to be weighed
against each other; and looks long-eared enough. . . . And
now the genius of Mechanism smothers him worse than any
nightmare did ; till the Soul is nigh choked out of him, and
only a kind of Digestive, Mechanic life remains."

" Perhaps the most energetic expression of his ideal of
disinterested duty is the onslaught on Benthamism in ' Hero
Worship,' which, as Carlyle pronounced the word ' beggarlier,' brought Mill to his feet with an emphatic No ! " —
Richard Garnett's *Thomas Carlyle*, p. 171. See also earlier
in the present lecture, p. 78, and later, pp. 239, 240.

The day after the lecture Carlyle wrote to his mother:
" I gave them to know that the poor Arab had points about
him which it were good for all of them to imitate; that

probably *they* were more of quacks than he; that, in short, it was altogether a new kind of thing they were hearing to-day."

LECTURE III

PAGE 109

there are aptitudes: note the qualification of the statement of the previous paragraph, "that the Hero can be Poet," etc.

PAGE 110

all Appearance . . . the *vesture:* the various brief expositions of C.'s transcendental philosophy scattered through *Heroes* are worth careful attention.

PAGE 112

We are all poets: compare C.'s *Essay on Burns* (R. L. S. No. 105), pp. 28, 29 : "The feelings, the gifts that exist in the Poet, are those that exist, with more or less development, in every human soul: the imagination which shudders at the Hell of Dante, is the same faculty, weaker in degree, which called that picture into being. How does the Poet speak to men, with power, but by being still more a man than they?"

PAGE 115

notions of God . . . *higher:* "An honest God's the noblest work of man," says the parodist.

PAGE 117

Portrait: this description and that of the portrait of Luther are striking examples of C.'s graphic power. They are also characteristic of his love of the concrete as an aid to making real his ideas. He had a screen in his library on which he posted portraits of the various heroes, ancient and modern, that he could get pictures of. Holman Hunt reports an interesting conversation in which, in the course of very unfavorable comment on Hunt's picture, *The Light of the World*, Carlyle told him : "I am only a poor man, but I can say in serious truth that I'd thankfully give one third of all the little store of money saved for my wife and old age, for a veritable contemporary representation of Jesus Christ, showing Him as He walked about, while he was trying with his ever invincible soul to break down the obtuse stupidity of the cormorant-minded, bloated gang who were doing, in desperate contention, their utmost to make the world go devilward with themselves." *Pre-Raphaelitism and the Pre-Raphaelite Brotherhood*, I, 355 ff. The portrait of Dante, reproduced in the present volume opposite p. 118, was discovered July 21, 1840, more than two months after the delivery of this lecture, on a wall in the Palace of the Podestà in Florence. It had been covered over with plaster for about **two** centuries and was almost lost even to memory. The story of its discovery is told by Professor Norton in a Note on the Portraits of Dante (reprinted in Dinsmore's *Aids to the Study of Dante,* pp. 149-154). In spite of the denials of some critics it seems practically certain that this is the portrait by Giotto, tradition of which had long existed. It represents, of course, the young Dante of the *Vita Nuova,* not the stern exile described by Carlyle. In the course of the Note above-mentioned Professor Norton describes the Dante death-mask: "The face is one of the most pathetic upon which human eyes ever looked. . . . Strength is the most striking attribute of the countenance. . . . The look is grave and stern almost to grimness ; there is a scornful lift of the eyebrow, and a contraction of the forehead as from painful thought ; but obscured under this look, yet not lost, are the marks of tenderness, refinement and self-mastery, which in combination with the more obvious characteristics, give to the countenance of the dead poet an ineffable dignity and melancholy." Two views of the death-mask are given by Dinsmore, pp. 156, 158. See also Lowell's *On a Portrait of Dante, by Giotto.*

PAGE 124

made me lean : why, then, did he write it ? See p. 311, last half.

PAGE 126

terza rima: "I, the writer, heard Dante say that never a rhyme had led him to say other than he would, but that many a time and oft he had made words say in his rhymes what they were not wont to express for other poets." *L'ottimo Commento,* Longfellow's *Inferno: Illustrations.*

PAGE 127

people of Verona: see *Dante at Verona,* in *Collected Works of Dante Gabriel Rossetti,* I. (London, 1897.) He narrates also the "like to like" story.

PAGE 133

so Dante discerned: so also did Shakespeare, and expressed it supremely in *King Lear.*

PAGE 138

incompatibility absolute and infinite: compare p. 103.

PAGE 140

the one sole secret: compare p. 90.

PAGE 142

empire of *Silence:* meaning ?

PAGE 146

best judgment . . . of Europe : "The first page of Shakespeare that I read," said Goethe, "made me his for life;

and when I had finished a single play I stood like one born
blind, on whom a miraculous hand bestows sight in a moment."

PAGE 151

**without morality . . . could not know anything at
all:** it is of the first importance to understand the sense in
which C. uses the words morality and intellect. The former
does not mean perfection, freedom from defect. "What *we*
call pure or impure, is not with [Nature] the final question.
Not how much chaff is in you ; but whether you have any
wheat." See the whole paragraph : "On the whole, we make
too much of faults," p. 64 ; and "We will not assert that
Cromwell was an immaculate man," p. 316. Note too that
intellect does not mean cleverness, knack, or skill in doing
— even conspicuously well — anything. "The seeing eye!
It is this that discloses the inner harmony of things ; what
Nature meant . . ." By way of illustration of the sentence
under discussion, try to enumerate the moral qualities which
the scholar, the scientist, the explorer, must possess that he
may come to know anything worth telling to the world.

PAGE 153

Sonnets: "With this key Shakspeare unlocked his heart."
— Wordsworth. "The less Shakspeare he." — Browning.
For the autobiographical significance of the Sonnets see
Sidney Lee, *A Life of William Shakespeare*, chaps. vii, viii,
and x. **sat like a bird on the bough ; and sang forth:**
see Milton, *On Shakspeare :* —

> "For whilst, to the shame of slow-endeavouring Art,
> Thy easy numbers flow,"

and *L'Allegro :* —

> "Or sweetest Shakspeare, Fancy's child,
> Warble his native wood notes wild."

PAGE 156

No man works save under conditions: suggest passages or characteristics of the plays that give evidence of
the truth of this statement as applied to Shakespeare.

PAGE 161

he cannot yet speak: modern Russian literature was just
getting on its feet as Carlyle was establishing himself in
London. The first of the modern poets, Pushkin, died in
1838, at the age of thirty-nine (see translations by N. H.
Dole in *Poet Lore*, 1889–1891); and Lermontov, his greatest
successor, died in 1841, at the age of twenty-seven. Such
work as that of Tolstoi, Turgenev, and "K. R." suggests
that it is hardly appropriate any longer to call Russia "a
great dumb monster."

LECTURE IV

PAGE 166

as handled: note the modifying phrase, and "the fact itself seems certain enough." See C.'s handling of the idea in *S. R.* III, vii ("Organic Filaments").

PAGE 168

what a melancholy notion: compare pp. 41, 44, and 57.

PAGE 172

Sincere-Cant: just the meaning? It is the property of every Hero: another definition of sincerity.

PAGE 174

Dante had not put-out his eyes: Dante's "Liberty of private judgment" enabled him to place several popes in Hell, and to predict the arrival there later of the one then reigning.

PAGE 178

If Hero mean: the closing sentences of this paragraph comprise a summary of the ethical appeal of the book.

PAGE 191

The cry of 'No Popery:' provoked by the Oxford, or Tractarian, Movement, also called the Anglo-Catholic Revival, then at its height, for the defense of the English Church against spiritual lethargy, and political and ecclesiastical liberalism. The year after the *Lectures on Heroes*, Newman, then an Anglican clergyman, afterwards a cardinal of the Roman Catholic Church, of whom Carlyle said that he had "the brains of a good-sized rabbit," wrote the famous *Tract No. 90*, contending that the articles of the English Church were not essentially at variance with the doctrines of Rome.

PAGES 192, 193

Popery can build . . . welcome to do so . . . Let it last as long as it can: with the thought of this paragraph compare pp. 84, 85, and 169, "Are not all true men," etc. Tolerance, even the rather patronizing variety here exhibited, was not C.'s usual attitude on this subject. See also pp. 194 and 210 ; and *P. and P.*[1] II, xv, end.

PAGE 194

A rugged honesty, etc.: this character sketch of Luther would not do ill for C. himself.

PAGE 197

Islam is all: various reminders of Mahomet in this lecture recall to us C.'s definition of the priest as "the Prophet shorn of his more awful splendour."

PAGE 204

too true what we said, That many men: was this just what C. said? See p. 168.

[1] *Past and Present.*

Page 206
    obscure . . . age of forty: compare Mahomet and Crom-
    well, pp. 74 and 296.
Page 207
    'burst into tears :' compare Mahomet, p. 82.
Page 211
    a kind of . . . Presidency and Sovereignty: this is
    true in a sense of all of C.'s heroes: compare p. 20 and else-
    where, concerning the "indestructibility of Hero-worship.'
    a true eye for the ridiculous : a point that C. would not
    miss.
Page 214
    Let them introduce : another " might and right " passage.

LECTURE V
Page 215
    Johnson, Rousseau, Burns : it would have been interest-
    ing to hear the remarks of these three men, assembled to-
    gether and confronted with one another as types of the
    Hero-Man-of-Letters. " Necessity makes strange bed-fel-
    lows." " The common point of resemblance is in their being
    sincere men : defined sincerity as the earnest living belief
    in what you profess to believe in." C. Fox's *Journals*,[1] p. 96.
    endeavouring to speak-forth : notice that this definition
    does not include Dante or Chaucer or Shakespeare. Milton
    could n't have " found subsistence " for long on the paltry
    sum paid him for *Paradise Lost*. Dick Steele (*Tatler*, 1709–
    1711) was one of the earliest authors that won any success
    in an attempt to eke out an insufficient income by the help
    of the printing-press.
Page 217
    inspired . . . 'originality,' 'sincerity,' 'genius:' what
    other terms has C. used in these lectures for the same
    quality ? Read, mark, learn, and inwardly digest the rest of
    this paragraph. C.'s Hero, it seems, must, like C. himself,
    hold the Transcendental Philosophy expounded in the next
    paragraph. Compare p. 51. Transcendental : "Ascending
    beyond the senses." "To a Transcendentalist, Matter has
    an existence, but only as a Phenomenon: were *we* not there,
    neither would it be there ; it is a mere Relation, or rather
    the result of a Relation between our living Souls and the
    great First Cause ; and depends for its apparent qualities
    on *our* bodily and mental organs ; having itself *no* intrinsic
    qualities ; being, in the common sense of that word, No-

---

[1] *Memories of Old Friends . . . from the Journals and Letters of Caroline Fox*,
London, 1882.

thing. The tree is green and hard, not of its own natural virtue, but simply because my eye and my hand are fashioned so as to discern such and such appearances under such and such conditions. . . . Bring a sentient Being with eyes a little different, with fingers ten times harder than mine and to him that Thing which I call Tree shall be yellow and soft, as truly as to me it is green and hard. Form his Nervous-structure in all points the *reverse* of mine, and this same Tree . . . shall simply have *all* properties exactly the reverse of those I attribute to it. There is, in fact, says Fichte, no Tree there; but only a Manifestation of Power from something which is *not I*. The same is true of material Nature at large . . . all are Impressions produced on *me* by something *different from me*. . . . Time and Space themselves are not external but internal entities: they have no outward existence; there is no Time and Space *out* of the mind." C.'s *Essay on Novalis.*

PAGE 218

a perpetual Priesthood: the comparison reminds one of the discussion of *Vates*, pp. 110 ff. One might go farther, and point out that the god Odin as handled by C. is the "camera-obscura image" of his ideal king. Compare pp. 275, 276, and add. note.

PAGE 220

Our chosen specimen . . . Goethe: "And knowest thou no Prophet, even in the vesture, environment, and dialect of this age? None to whom the God-like had revealed itself . . . in whose inspired melody, even in these rag-gathering and rag-burning days, Man's Life again begins, were it but afar off, to be divine? Knowest thou none such? I know him, and name him—Goethe." *S. R.* III, vii. **such is the general state of knowledge. . . . Speak as I might**: granted that such was the state of knowledge also about Odin or Mahomet, the very fullness of Carlyle's knowledge and hero-worship of Goethe made the task of interpreting him to his hearers seem more difficult than in the case of the others. C. evidently felt that Goethe's practical philosophy of life was very unlike that of the average of an English audience: see Goethe's saying "which has staggered several," p. 112. Though C. had written abundantly of Goethe he could hardly take for granted his hearers' familiarity with the *Goethe* Essays as he could their acquaintance with his *Burns.*

PAGE 221

fashioning a path: how is this truer as said of the literary man than in the case of the lawyer, minister, or physician? "Carlyle would even have his fraternity organised like the

members of other professions, though he could ill chalk out
the plan." C. Fox's *Journals*, p. 96.

PAGE 223

In Books lies the *soul:* read the rest of this paragraph
aloud, exaggerating the stresses, or, better, mark the ac-
cented and unaccented syllables; and note how truly rhyth-
mical, without being regularly metrical, it is. Compare
pp. 114 and 125.

PAGE 227

Byron : C.'s dislike for Byron appears in his writings under
various forms. He adopts Southey's name, "The Satanic
School," for the school of Byron in poetry. "A dandy of
sorrows and acquainted with grief" is C.'s formula for Byron in his *Journal*. " Art thou nothing other than a Vulture,
then, that fliest through the Universe seeking after somewhat to eat; and shrieking dolefully because carrion enough
is not given thee? Close thy *Byron;* open thy *Goethe*."
S. R. II, ix. " He [C.] thinks that we, on the whole, do our
Hero-worship worse than any Nation in this world ever did
it before : that the Burns an Exciseman, the Byron a Literary Lion, are intrinsically, all things considered, a baser and
falser phenomenon than the Odin a God, the Mahomet a
Prophet of God." *P. and P.* I, vi.

PAGES 230, 231

If you asked me . . . I should beg to say : C. has been
found fault with abundantly for more successfully diagnos-
ing the world's ailments than suggesting remedies. An answer to this criticism is suggested on pp. 233, 234: " For as
soon as men get to discern," etc. and "Light is the one thing
wanted," etc. **no evil to be poor :** C. certainly could
speak with authority on this subject. International copyright
laws have removed one of the aids to literary poverty of
C.'s time. If the next paragraph be sound doctrine, one can
only pity the modern Man (or more accurately Woman) of
Letters as author of the month's " Best Seller."

PAGE 236

Parliament : C.'s opinion of the British House of Commons
is concretely expressed in *S. R.* I, v, end : " Man is a Tool-
using Animal . . . he collects, apparently by lot, six-hun-
dred and fifty-eight miscellaneous individuals, and says to
them, *Make this nation toil for us, bleed for us, hunger and
sorrow and sin for us ;* and they do it."

PAGE 239

a more beggarly one : see p. 104, and add. note.

PAGE 241

not even a devil: " And now we are deprived of the hope
of a future life, Hell being a myth." — Freshman theme on

The Decay of Faith. **Belief I define to be** : in connection with this paragraph and the two following, re-read pp. 166, 167.

PAGE 245

gleam of Time between two Eternities : "Thus, like some wild-flaming, wild-thundering train of Heaven's Artillery, does this mysterious MANKIND thunder and flame, in long-drawn, quick-succeeding grandeur, through the unknown Deep. Thus, like a God-created, fire-breathing Spirit-host, we emerge from the Inane. . . . O Heaven, whither? Sense knows not; Faith knows not; only that it is through Mystery to Mystery, from God and to God. ' We are such stuff . . . '" *S. R.* III, viii, end.

PAGE 248

stalking mournful : there is abundant material for a quite different, but equally true, picture of Johnson. He was much of a humorist and fun-lover : one of his Oxford tutors described him as " gay and frolicksome."

PAGE 249

The essence of *originality:* compare p. 176.

PAGE 253

' **in a world where much is to be done** :' the phrase occurs in one of Johnson's prayers, "Against inquisitive and perplexing thoughts," which illustrates his conservatism : . . . " enable me to drive from me all such unquiet and perplexing thoughts as may mislead or hinder me in the practice of those duties which Thou hast required. . . . And while it shall please Thee to continue me in this world, where much is to be done, and little to be known, teach me by Thy Holy Spirit, to withdraw my mind from unprofitable and dangerous enquiries, from difficulties vainly curious, and doubts impossible to be solved." . . . Boswell's *Johnson* (year 1784). ' **Clear your mind of Cant** :' compare p. 99. One definition of cant given by Johnson in his *Dictionary* is: "A whining pretension to goodness in formal and affected terms." Boswell reports, May 15, 1783, the following remarks of Johnson: "My dear friend, clear your *mind* of cant. You may *talk* as other people do : you may say to a man, 'Sir, I am your most humble servant.' You are *not* his most humble servant. . . . You tell a man, 'I am sorry you had such bad weather the last day of your journey, and were so much wet.' You don't care six-pence whether he is wet or dry. You may *talk* in this manner; it is a mode of talking in Society: but don't think foolishly." **a measured grandiloquence**: Boswell (year 1773) reports Goldsmith's saying to Johnson : "If you were to make little fishes talk, they would talk like WHALES." Macaulay says that John-

son's sentences were "done out of English into John-
sonese." Johnson himself observes (*Idler*, No. 70), "He
that thinks with more extent than another will want words
of larger meaning." He remarked of a dramatic burlesque
(*The Rehearsal*): "It has not wit enough to keep it sweet;"
then after a pause: "It has not vitality enough to preserve
it from putrefaction." Perhaps the best example of his
"size of phraseology" is the famous *network* definition in the
Dictionary : "Anything reticulated or decussated, at equal
distances, with interstices between the intersections." For
one of the best examples of prose style extant, read Johnson's famous letter to Lord Chesterfield, Feb. 7, 1755, concerning the dedication of the *Dictionary*.

PAGE 254

**his Dictionary, one might have traced there . . . a
genuine man**: the mark of Johnson's personality as well
as his learning is here and there discoverable: "*Lexico-
grapher*. Writer of dictionaries; harmless drudge that
busies himself in tracing the original, and detailing the significance of words." His dislike of all things Scotch pro-
vokes the following definition: "*Oats*. A grain which in
England is generally given to horses, but in Scotland supports the people." **Bozzy**: after Macaulay's assertion that
Boswell's success was an accidental consequence of his super-
lative asininity, and Carlyle's that it was a greatness inev-
itably thrust upon him by his hero-worship, Mr. Birrell's
suggestion (*In the Name of the Bodleian: The Johnsonian
Legend*), that Bozzy really knew what he was (artistically)
about, is worth pondering.

PAGE 257

Egoism; . . . the source . . . of all faults: compare the
god Wish, p. 25 and elsewhere.

PAGE 259

His Books: "The Confessions are the only writings of his
which I have read with any interest; there you see the man
such as he really was, though I can't say that it is a duty to
lay open the Bluebeard chambers of the heart." Report of
the lecture in C. Fox's *Journals*, p. 97.

PAGE 261

Hero . . . Robert Burns : the whole of C.'s short *Essay
on Burns* ought to be read in connection with the following
pages. Notice at how many points C. was at one with Burns
in the circumstances of early life, and therefore supremely
qualified to understand him. "Burns was the last of our
heroes, and here our Scotch Patriot was in his element.
Most graphically did he sketch some passages in the poet's
life." C. Fox's *Journals*, p. 98.

PAGE 262

Father ... *silent* Hero: compare C.'s own case.

PAGE 264

His writings ... only a poor fragment: compare pp. 155, 156.

PAGE 271

But —! —: not many writers would venture just such an ending. The spoken lecture had a more conventional close: "He then told us he had more than occupied our time, and rushed down-stairs." C. Fox's *Journals*, p. 98.

LECTURE VI

PAGE 273

Ideals ... never ... completely embodied: "For, alas, the Ideal always has to grow in the Real, and to seek out its bed and board there, often in a very sorry way. No beautifulest Poet is a Bird-of-Paradise, living on perfumes; sleeping in the æther with outspread wings. The Heroic, *independent* of bed and board, is found in Drury Lane Theatre only; to avoid disappointments, let us bear this in mind." *P. and P.* II, iv.

PAGE 276

a Divine Right or else a Diabolic Wrong: this sentence rightly understood contains the essence of C.'s thought on hero-worship. In its special application to Kings, compare *S. R.* III, vii: "He carries with him an authority from God, or man will never give it him. Can I choose my own King? I can choose my own King Popinjay, and play what farce or tragedy I may with him: but he who is to be my Ruler, whose will is to be higher than my will, was chosen for me in Heaven. Neither except in such Obedience to the Heaven-chosen is Freedom so much as conceivable." "Every ruler has a divine right to govern, in so far as he represents God, but in no other." C. Fox's *Journals*, p. 100. Compare also *P. and P.* I, vi: "Yes, friends: Hero-kings, and a whole world not unheroic, — there lies the port and happy haven, towards which, through all these stormtost seas, French Revolutions, Chartisms, Manchester Insurrections, that make the heart sick in these bad days, the Supreme Powers are driving us. On the whole, blessed be the Supreme Powers, stern as they are! Towards that haven will we, O friends: let all true men, with what of faculty there is in them, bend valiantly, incessantly, with thousand-fold endeavour, thither, thither! There, or else in the Ocean-abysses, it is very clear to me we shall arrive."

PAGE 277

the *beginning* ... Luther: see p. 173.

PAGE 284

whose whole world is forms: "I labored nothing," said Laud, "more than that the external worship of God . . . might be preserved, and that with as much decency and uniformity as might be, — being still of opinion that unity cannot long continue in the church when uniformity is shut out at the church doors."

PAGE 285

Forms which *grow*: see pp. 170, 250; also *S. R.* III, ii ("Church Clothes").

PAGE 286

the essence of all Churches: compare Ruskin, *Sesame:* "For there is a true church wherever one hand meets another helpfully, and that is the only holy or Mother Church which ever was or ever shall be."

PAGE 293

Cromwell's falsity . . . incredible: note the similarities between C.'s vindication of Cromwell and his vindication of Mahomet.

PAGE 308

Great men are not ambitious in that sense: but compare Milton: —

> "Fame is the spur that the clear spirit doth raise
> (That last infirmity of noble mind)
> To scorn delights, and live laborious days."
>
> *Lycidas*, 70–72.

PAGE 311

To unfold your *self*, to work: "Hence, too, the folly of that impossible Precept, *Know thyself;* till it be translated into this partially possible one, *Know what thou canst work at.*" *S. R.* II, vii. "Produce! Produce! Were it but the pitifullest infinitesimal fraction of a Product, produce it in God's name! 'T is the utmost thou hast in thee: out with it, then." II, ix.

PAGE 316

Cromwell's last words: "Truly God is good; indeed He is ; He will not " — Then his speech failed him, but as I apprehended, it was, " He will not leave me." This saying, " God is good " he frequently used all along ; and would speak it with much cheerfulness, and fervour of spirit, in the midst of his pains. — Again he said: " I would be willing to live to be farther serviceable to God and His People: but my work is done. Yet God will be with His People." Carlyle's *Cromwell*.

PAGE 321

Milton . . . could applaud:

> "Cromwell, our chief of men, who through a cloud
> Not of war only, but detractions rude,
> Guided by faith and matchless fortitude,
> To peace and truth thy glorious way hast ploughed,

> . . . .
> And Dunbar field, resounds thy praises loud,
> And Worcester's laureate wreath : yet much remains
> To conquer still; Peace hath her victories
> No less renowned than War.
>
> Sonnet, *To the Lord General Cromwell.*

PAGE 327

His complaint . . . of the heavy burden: "I would
have been glad," said Cromwell, "to have lived under my
woodside, to have kept a flock of sheep, rather than undertake such a government as this."

PAGE 328

rash . . . to pronounce him . . . honest man: various
rather mild attempts were made from the beginning of the
eighteenth century to vindicate the character of Cromwell,
but the people at large remained partially or not at all convinced. Carlyle was already making plans and gathering
material for his *Cromwell,* which appeared a few years
later, and still stands as the authoritative exposition of
Cromwell's character. He wrote to Emerson a few months
later: "I am now over head and ears in *Cromwellian* Books;
studying, for perhaps the fourth time in my life, to see if it
be possible to get any credible face-to-face acquaintance with
our English Puritan period ; . . . Nevertheless courage ! I
have got, within the last twelve months, actually, as it were,
to *see* that this Cromwell was one of the greatest souls ever
born of the English kin; a great amorphous semi-articulate
Baresark; very interesting to me." "After many other most
effective touches in this sketch, which compelled you to side
with Carlyle as to Cromwell's self-devotion and magnanim-
ity, he gave the finishing-stroke with an air of most innocent
wonderment — ' And yet I believe I am the first to say that
Cromwell was an honest man ! ' " C. Fox's *Journals,* p. 101.
The day after this lecture C. wrote to his mother: "I contrived to tell them something about poor Cromwell, and I
think to convince them that he was a great and true man,
the valiant soldier in England of what John Knox had
preached in Scotland."

PAGE 330

blamable ambition: see p. 311. **A man in no case has
liberty to tell lies :** it is worth while noting C.'s opinion
on this point, when the contrary view is so often defended.

PAGE 338

"He then told us that the subject which he had endeavoured
to unfold in three weeks was more calculated for a six
months' story ; he had, however, been much interested in
going through it with us, even in the naked way he had
done, thanked us for our attention and sympathy, wished us
a cordial farewell, and vanished." C. Fox's *Journals,* p. 102.

BIBLIOGRAPHY FOR OUTSIDE READING

Lect. I. Morley's *English Writers*, I, 264–275, and II, 335–365, including translation of *Völuspa;* Mallet's *Northern Antiquities* (Bohn Libr.) esp. 79 ff. and 402–456; R. B. Anderson's *Norse Mythology;* S. Laing's Translation of *Heimskringla* (New Ed., Anderson, 1889); Grimm's *Teutonic Mythology;* G. Vigfusson's *Prolegomena* to Ed. of *Sturlunga Saga;* Mabie's *Norse Stories Retold from the Eddas;* *Corpus Poeticum Boreale.*

Lect. II. Lives of Mahomet by Muir, Sprenger, and Syed Ameer Ali; Bosworth Smith's *Mohammed and Mohammedanism;* W. Irving's *Mohammed and his Successors;* Gibbon's *The Decline and Fall of the Roman Empire*, chap. 1; Wherry's *A Comprehensive Commentary on the Qurán*, with Sale's Translation ; Rodwell's Translation (attempting to arrange chapters in chronological order); Nöldeke's *The Koran*, in *Sketches from Eastern History;* Burckhardt's *Travels in Arabia.*

Lect. III. C. A. Dinsmore's *Aids to the Study of Dante ;* M. F. Rossetti's *A Shadow of Dante;* Davidson's Scartazzini's *Handbook to Dante;* Symonds's *A Study of Dante;* Lowell's *Dante* (Essay); Norton's and Rossetti's Translations of *La Vita Nuova;* Norton's literal prose Translation of *The Divine Comedy;* Longfellow's, Dean Plumptre's, and Cary's verse Translations. Sidney Lee's *Life of Shakespeare* is the best authority on that subject.

Lect. IV. Lives of Luther by Michelet (translated), J. Köstlin (translated), J. A. Froude, and H. E. Jacobs; Luther's Ninety-five Theses are given in Larned's *History for Ready Reference*, IV, pp. 2446 ff.; Luther's *Table-Talk* (translated); Ranke's, D'Aubigné's, and Fischer's Histories of the Reformation ; Seebohm's *The Protestant Revolution.* Lives of Knox by McCrie, and Hume Brown; Knox's *History of the Reformation in Scotland;* Carlyle's *The Portraits of John Knox.*

Lect. V. B. Hill's *Boswell's Life of Johnson;* Macaulay's *Johnson* (written for *Encycl. Brit.*) ; Macaulay's and Carlyle's Essays reviewing Croker's *Boswell's Johnson.* John Morley's *Rousseau;* Lincoln's *Rousseau and the French Revolution;* Davidson's *Rousseau and Education according to Nature;* Lowell's *Rousseau* (Essay). Lives of Burns by Lockhart,

Blackie, Shairp; R. L. Stevenson's "Burns" in *Familiar Studies of Men and Books*.

Lect. VI. Carlyle's *Oliver Cromwell's Letters and Speeches;* Lives of Cromwell by S. R. Gardiner and Theodore Roosevelt; Essays on Cromwell in Goldwin Smith's *Three English Statesmen,* and Forster's *Biographical Essays;* Chapters on "Puritan England" in J. R. Green's *Short History of the English People.* Lives of Napoleon by W. M. Sloane, and J. H. Rose; *Memoirs* of Bourrienne, and Las Casas.

SUGGESTIONS FOR TEACHING

The objects of studying *Heroes* may be resolved into three main points: (1) knowledge of the characters and influence, and, to a varying extent, the lives, of certain of the greatest men in history, — this was the purpose of the lectures as avowed by Carlyle himself at the beginning of the course; (2) acquaintance with the teachings, literary style, and character of one of the most forceful and interesting personalities in the nineteenth century, as revealed through one of his most popular books; (3) increase of that general culture of the moral as well as of intellectual faculties which " cometh not with observation " so much as from unconscious absorption of the best in the best books and the best men. Carlyle's relentless earnestness and insistence on the side of truth and high endeavor, and his enormous range of reading in literature and history make *Heroes* one of the richest of books for the furtherance of this purpose. The editorial material of the volume has been prepared with these aims in view; but in what manner, by what illustration or discussion the class-room exercises may be made to contribute most to the student's profit must of course be left in each case to the teacher's own device. A suggestive — far from exhaustive — list of topics for consideration in class, or for written recitation or examination, is given below: an eight to ten minute written test on the day's lesson, followed by general, informal discussion with the class is an excellent (with large classes often the only possible) way of making the most of the recitation hour.

The book gains in significance with every bit of acquaintance with the widely varied style and subjects of Carlyle's other writings, — particularly *Sartor Resartus*, which (or at least selected chapters from which) the student may be most profitably encouraged to read and helped to understand. The Editor has found the assignment of a few lessons in Prof. Bliss Perry's *Selections from Carlyle* in the Little Masterpieces Series very helpful in bringing before the student other aspects of Carlyle as teacher, historian, and literary artist, or in enforcing those presented in *Heroes*. If the time allotted to the study of the book is short, it will be found better on the whole to study I, III, and V thoroughly in detail, and II, possibly VI, and if quite necessary IV, more hastily.

Lecture I. Definition of religion; of worship; of hero-worship. Distinction between Paganism, Christianism, and Scepticism. The divineness of Nature. Description of Iceland; its importance to the student of Norse religion and literature. The tree Igdrasil. The career of the man Odin. The gods and jötuns of the Norse religion; its morals. Anecdotes about Thor. Reasons why C. chose the Norse religion for his illustration in preference to any other.

Lecture II. Description of Arabia and Arab character ; the *Book of Job*. Mahomet's life, 570–622. His personal characteristics. The chief truths of Mahomet's religion and how he learned them. Its chief defects. Mahomet and miracles. The *Koran*. The Mahometan idea of the future life; the truth of it. With what arguments does C. refute the "impostor theory ? "

Lecture III. "The distinction and identity of Poet and Prophet." Present arguments to defend and to refute the assertion "that the Hero can be Poet, Prophet, King, Priest, or what you will," etc. C.'s views on poetry. The life of Dante. The characteristics of his personality and his work; illustrate from his *Divine Comedy*. Enumerate the points of resemblance between the religions of the Norsemen, Mahomet, and Dante. The morality of Shakespeare. "It is the Poet's first gift, as it is all men's, that he have intellect enough." "Shakspeare's Art is not Artifice." Shakespeare's laughter. Shakespeare as historian. Shakespeare unconsciously a prophet. The political value of Shakespeare to the English race. Comparison of Dante and Shakespeare.

Lecture IV. The relation of the religious beliefs of past, present, and future; "originality" in religion. Idolatry characteristic of all religions. The three acts of Protestantism. The life of Luther previous to the Diet of Worms. His trial at Worms. His prose style. Resemblances between Luther and Mahomet; Luther and Dante. Knox's services to Scotland. Knox's ideal of government; C.'s comment.

Lecture V. Definition of the genuine man of letters ; its applicability to Carlyle. The functions of books in the modern world. Enumerate the obstacles against which Johnson had to contend. Johnson's gospel. Rousseau's heroism; his mission. Resemblances between Burns and Carlyle. Burns's "Lionism."

Lecture VI. The divine right of Kings. The significance and achievement of Puritanism. Arguments presented by Carlyle in vindication of Cromwell. Cromwell and his Parliaments. Napoleon's "kind of sincerity ; " his "faith," his "quackeries."

General. Define " Hero." The value of hero-worship. Hero-worship the test of any age. C.'s ideas on government. Belief and action. Scepticism; its consequences. The French Revolution. Profit-and-loss philosophy. Silence. The world of external nature as treated of in *Heroes*. Discuss, and illustrate by specific passages, the characteristic qualities of C.'s style in *Heroes*. What has the study of *Heroes and Hero-Worship* been worth to *you*?

CARLYLE'S INDEX